"Essential reading for academics and practitioners who care about evidence-based democratic innovation and forging lasting change."
**Mark Evans, Director Democracy 2025**

"Despite the faltering of electoral democracy, Matt Ryan's carefully researched book shows how and why innovations like participatory budgeting are enabling the democratic project to deepen and progress. An essential contribution to the rapidly developing field of democratic innovation."
**Mark E. Warren, University of British Columbia**

# WHY CITIZEN PARTICIPATION SUCCEEDS OR FAILS

## A Comparative Analysis of Participatory Budgeting

Matt Ryan

BRISTOL
UNIVERSITY
PRESS

First published in Great Britain in 2021 by

Bristol University Press
University of Bristol
1-9 Old Park Hill
Bristol
BS2 8BB
UK
t: +44 (0)117 954 5940
e: bup-info@bristol.ac.uk

Details of international sales and distribution partners are available at bristoluniversitypress.co.uk



British Library Cataloguing in Publication Data
A catalogue record for this book is available from the British Library

ISBN 978-1-5292-0992-1 hardcover
ISBN 978-1-5292-0994-5 ePub
ISBN 978-1-5292-0993-8 ePdf



Cover design by blu inc
Front cover image: Brain light – alamy.com
Bristol University Press uses environmentally responsible print partners.
Printed and bound in Great Britain by CPI Group (UK) Ltd, Croydon, CR0 4YY

FSC
www.fsc.org
MIX
Paper from responsible sources
FSC® C013604

# Contents

# List of Figures and Tables

## Figures



## Tables

# List of Abbreviations

| | |
|---|---|
| PB | Participatory budgeting |
| PT | Partido dos Trabalhadores |
| CSO | Civil society organization |
| DI/PDI | Democratic innovation(s)/participatory democratic innovation(s) |
| HDI | Human Development Index |
| IGO | Intergovernmental organization |
| INUS | Insufficient Necessary part of an Unnecessary but Sufficient factor |
| N | Number |
| NDC | New Deal for Communities |
| NGO | Non-governmental organization |
| QCA | Qualitative comparative analysis |
| fsQCA | Fuzzy-set qualitative comparative analysis |
| SUIN | Sufficient but Unnecessary part of an Insufficient but Necessary factor |
| TQCA | Temporal qualitative comparative analysis |
| UAMPA | Porto Alegre Union of Neighbourhood Associations |

# Acknowledgements

It has taken a long time to get here, and naturally there have been many people who have helped out along the way. I have met numerous excellent colleagues and made some great friends, from staff and students in Southampton to colleagues I have collaborated with on different related projects, to networks and associations of intellectuals and not-so-intellectuals in the UK and elsewhere. All have contributed in immeasurable ways to helping me get here. If I named them all it would take too long and I would forget people I should not, but I will let them know again how they helped me, and thank them when I see them in person.

I would like to thank the School of Social Sciences at the University of Southampton for funding many of the contributions to this body of research, and more recently allowing research leave that enabled me to produce the final book. I would also like to thank colleagues at the University of Canberra in Australia for hosting me in 2018 where I made some headway with this project. From 2020 I was helped by the support of UK Research and Innovation (UKRI) funding (grant Ref MR/S032711/1).

I owe special thanks to the many academic support staff that help provide a fruitful working environment in Southampton. I feel lucky to have spent many years working as academic staff in the Department of Politics and International Relations and the Faculty of Social Sciences with a bunch of colleagues who create a really stimulating academic environment. All the colleagues I have worked with gave me valuable insights and often handy advice on research, writing and coping, when it was needed. Maybe they thought they were just doing their job, but each of them seemed to go beyond the call, whether providing advice, opportunities or reassurance to support and smoothen my development as a young researcher when I was juggling a bunch of commitments in an unfamiliar environment.

I have had to put down and pick up this project at long intervals, and some people have helped especially in making sure it got there.

This book would certainly never have happened at all without Graham Smith and David Owen's encouragement, and would possibly never have ended without Gerry Stoker and Will Jennings keeping on at me to finish it. Mercifully I eventually grew clever enough to try doing what they all told me at some point. My publishers at Bristol University Press, particularly Stephen Wenham, Caroline Astley and Catriona Allon, were very considerate with their advice and their patience. I am very grateful to the anonymous reviewers who made several important suggestions in a collegiate manner, which helped me improve the presentation. The book was completed at a time of significant upheaval, both in my own personal life and during a global pandemic. The constants throughout were Nele, Colm, Ben, Ellen, Mam and Dad. Their support and patience is essential.

All errors and omissions in the book are, of course, my responsibility alone.

# Preface

There are other books about democracy and participation in politics. I want to take a moment to explain why I wrote this book.

There is no personal motivation quite like injustice. The feeling of being wronged, treated unfairly or seeing others treated in such a way often stirs in us anger and an admirable determination to stand up to defend ourselves and others. As individuals faced with small-scale injustices, many of us are pretty good at fighting our corner. We march up to counters to give our two cents. We stay 'on hold' over the phone with excruciating labyrinths of interactive voice response ('dial 1 then 3 if you'd like to, later press 2') to defend our rights. We spend years taking legal action against neighbours over ownership of some hedgerow (so I've heard anyway). Even though the efficacy of those actions may be guaranteed by a collectively enforced constitutional order, and threat of competition in relatively free markets, both market and court remedies for injustices work on a logic of relatively independent decisions that can add up to wider change. Yet many of us seem to feel that on the greatest issues we face together as both local and global societies, things are *hopelessly* unjust. Collective injustices like the unequal distribution of morbidity, violence, insecurity and systematic discrimination seem so ingrained and wicked that when we are faced with overcoming them, the familiar individual motivation to fight wrong is sucked away into a collective ennui and inertia. While many people recognize suffering, everyone has a slightly different take on its remedies, or is just worn out by the whole thing. Wider change requires more strategic decision-making and more consciously collective kinds of social action. We might admit that we do need politics, but individuals who want to effect political change often don't know where to start.

I have been convinced that when we feel lost in the complexities of how best to do politics, the ideal of democracy gives us something to come back to. Democracy promises so much precisely because it has provided a coherent set of ideas for dealing with collective injustices as they arise. We all necessarily have different experiences; we see the world differently and we will disagree. Rather than let disagreement control us, democracy offers a means to collectively control that disagreement, to harness collective knowledge to solve the less tractable, interlinked and larger-scale injustices.

The world is now full of what we recognize as democratic states, and yet the growth in democratic regimes still does not seem to deliver on its promise of collective control and flourishing for many people living in democracies. It is common for collective decisions to be considered 'undemocratic' by both individuals and groups. They feel decisions prioritize the interests of others, or perhaps worse still, that their own needs are being ignored completely. Part of the problem is expectations – a functioning democracy is often characterized by nobody getting what they initially wanted. If some identifiable group is always winning and others always losing, then you are not living in a functioning democracy. If you get your way all the time, that may seem good in the short run, but you can bet someone else is losing, resenting it, and that, in the long run, is going to cause you problems. In a democracy people should not expect to get everything they want. The conundrum for democratic support is that democracy, as Gerry Stoker puts it, seems 'designed to disappoint' (2017: 10), because it is a vessel for compromises rather than immediate personal gain.

To those who yearn for dramatic and transformational societal change to redress injustices, and to those who fear any radical change could cause greater injustice, such a politics of compromise can seem a little underwhelming. Rather than leading to ingenious collective problem-solving, the practice of politics, with its 'slow, powerful drilling through hard boards with a mixture of passion and sense of proportion' as Weber (2004: 93)[1] described it, often seems to bring much frustration and collective whining (which, I'll admit, provides some comradely solace at times). At its best, however, democracy offers not just awkward bargaining and slow compromise, but also harnesses the altruism and ingenuity of collaboration that makes humanity worth celebrating. An ongoing commitment to compromise can be both transformational and reassuring.

I had often been a critic of the way politics is done, a whiner maybe, but my introduction to the field of democratic innovations was life-changing, because it opened me up to a world of people

[1] This famous passage is often translated as 'boring through the hard boards', which, despite its delicious alliteration, provides some confusion for those who come across it for the first time out of context.

who were not just whining, but working together to do something about the problems of democracy as practised. Some of their schemes surprised a sceptic like me because they really seemed to get people to contribute positively and often inventively to collective problem-solving. Democratic innovations at their best reinvent democracy by reimagining and implementing new ways of doing politics without reverting away from the fundamental ideas that distinguish democracies from other forms of rule.

Political scholars since Gallie have tended to hold to his contention that democracy is an 'essentially contested concept'. Rival accounts of the essence of democracy are not only inevitable, but provide essential critical value for the betterment of one's own interpretation (1955: 193). Gallie was partly motivated to justify the benevolence of the survival of rival accounts of important concepts because he recognized that the alternative was often tyranny. Those unsatisfied by their inability to quickly persuade others to the perceived righteousness of their preferred version of democracy might damn rivals as heretics, with violent and tragic consequences. Taking that cautionary approach, I appreciate why people are now talking again more with resignation than hope about democracy, and imagining what might replace it. Salient cautionary tales about the end of democracy tend to focus more on how the institutions that delivered what we understood to be democracy in one context can later fail to consistently deliver what we understand to be democracy in another (see, for example, Levitsky and Ziblatt, 2018; Runciman, 2018).

To me, what is important about democracy is that it assumes that *everybody* has something worthwhile to contribute. I do not think it would be good for any of us if we dropped that assumption. An affirmation that everyone has both the potential and the right to pull together to solve collective problems is good enough as a principle for collective self-government.

We should be designing political institutions around that principle. Rather than move on to search for a new type of governing regime to replace representative democracy, I think it may still provide a pretty good option available to us that just needs some reinvention and rehabilitation. I study democratic innovations and compare the evidence because I want to know what rehabilitative measures are most likely to bring democracy to fuller health. While holding to democratic principles, I would not want to curtail the imaginations of those who feel another world is possible. As Graham Smith used to say with infectious enthusiasm when he first taught me about many of these institutional innovations, the most amazing thing, given their often-elaborate designs, is that some people somewhere actually thought this up in their head and then went out and made it happen. The institutional reforms studied by scholars of democratic innovations are problem-oriented and inventive, but are not kneejerk reactionary politics, nor merely the ephemeral wacky whiteboard thinking of boffins at an away day. They are the result of hours of labour and the ingenuity of many optimists, activists and servants of the civic. For those democratic soldiers I have the utmost admiration, and I only hope that the work presented in this book will help them and those who come after them hasten in the democratic practices and political solutions we require and that they deserve.

*January 2021*

# PART I

When and how do ordinary citizens gain substantial control over important collective decisions affecting their lives? This book provides new answers to this question by systematically accumulating evidence in novel ways. From calls for 'no taxation without representation' to 'defunding the police', questions regarding the authority to make and implement public spending decisions have played an important role in the imagination and practice of democracy. It is perhaps no surprise, then, that the idea and practice of participatory budgeting (PB), expanding the 'power of the purse', has garnered such interest. PB has been widely implemented by committed reformers in politics, bureaucracies and civil society, and has been studied by a number of committed scholars. The research I present here offers critical insights into when and how PB programmes succeed and fail in increasing democracy by allowing citizens greater influence over collective decisions. The work is based on bringing together the work of other scholars as well as providing a more systematic investigation of existing claims about PB using advanced comparative methods. Rather than search for further 'unique' examples of public policy innovations in the field, I bring together existing research that, in the end, provides unique insights that can only be found through such a procedure.

I show that popular claims that there are several single necessary conditions for citizens to gain such control over collective decisions have been imprudent. Successes (and, for that matter, failure) can be demonstrated where conditions that have been touted as necessary are both present and absent. Nevertheless, a political leadership committed to participation is almost always required for sustained citizen control of political decisions over the longer term. The meaningful involvement of citizens in collective governance often requires a combination of will and capacity to implement programmes from political leaders, but there is evidence that these good outcomes only occur where those willing leaders can rely on strong support and competence from administrative staff, or alternatively, where participatory leaders have strong fiscal independence. Perhaps controversially, the evidence for the importance of civil society conditions, which have played a strong role in theories of successful citizen participation, is mixed. Whether civil society is relevant to explanations of successful participation depends on the level of uncertainty that researchers are willing to accept in their theories, and reveals issues of conceptualization of civil society roles in participatory programmes. The evidence is less certain, but where politicians and bureaucratic staff are committed to supporting programmes, the resource capital provided by dynamic, demanding and autonomously mobilized civil society organizations (CSOs) may serve to overcome fiscal constraints. The story of PB, then, is not simply one of benign and enlightened leaders, nor simply one of power conceding nothing without a demand.

There are several possible scenarios in which participation can deepen or negate democracy, but it is certainly not a case of 'anything goes'. The absence of political leadership is almost always sufficient for disappointing participatory programmes, but where willing and capable bureaucrats are absent, combined with constraints on spending and a demobilized and placid civil society, no amount of political leadership can avoid disappointing results that are characterized by often anti-democratic politics.

The book is split into three parts. Part I explains why participatory democracy has become a key focus for politics, as PB has become the most widely adopted democratic innovation since its emergence in the late 1980s. I explain how the study of PB has developed as the concept has travelled, and elaborate on the insights from a maturing field of research. I demonstrate that a large number of high-quality and in-depth studies of PB have been produced, but their overall lessons remained unclear, until now. In Part II, I explain where our current understandings of participatory democracy are at and where they fall short, detailing the important considerations we need to take account of if we are to improve the sophistication of our accumulated knowledge. I demonstrate the value and novelty of the relatively rare medium-N analysis of 30 cases to provide insights by retaining the advantages of breadth and depth using systematic, qualitative comparative analysis (QCA). In Part III I present evidence using QCA to systematically review existing material on PB to answer three questions: what conditions are necessary and sufficient for citizen control of PB and negation of citizen control of PB? What is left unanswered by the data we have accumulated? In light of the findings, how should we now understand the value of democratic innovation and its implications for theories of democracy?

In the final chapter of the book I turn to outline the implications of comparing democratic innovations for democratic reform. I widen the scope of the argument to insist that a better comparative method in social sciences is crucial to a better policy science of evidence-based practice. Policymaking in an era of networked governance sometimes suffers both from increased pressures and opportunities to innovate. This 'innovation' requires vigilance among political scientists and policy learners interested in classifying phenomena, providing explanations and understanding what should be done to buttress democracy. Where we are attracted to understand cases because of the seemingly unique stories they tell, it raises the question of how we can build on in-depth knowledge to provide systematic evidence for our theories. The book therefore also seeks to address practically the important issues raised when political reforms are recognized for their exceptional characteristics and policy analysts wish to move beyond the lessons of one or two strong exemplars.

# 1

# Understanding Participation as a Response to Democratic Deficits

Governing mass societies is a complicated enterprise. As populations have grown, and become more interdependent, maintaining the democratic legitimacy of collective decisions has become ever more challenging. Increases in external constraints, especially financial, on representative government's capacities to govern both nationally and locally are well documented in the vast literature on globalization. Authoritarians and populists have capitalized on the inconsistencies in delivery of democratic goods by existing institutions. Citizens of traditional democracies increasingly react with a mixture of anger and despair when they feel the blunt consequences of decisions that seemingly were made without their obvious consent and often without much regard for their collective benefit or cost. Perhaps the most glaring example of this in modern times is manifest in the continuing fallout of the global financial collapse of 2007–08, now exacerbated by 2020–21's pandemic.

Liberal democracy in the 20th century provided citizens with the opportunity to choose rulers and to hold them to account as well as to form interest groups and pressure rulers to respond between elections. These equalities and freedoms when practised in large numbers were the great bulwark that democracy promised against decisions that would not work in the interests of the citizenry. Increasingly, those institutions do not appear to suffice, producing outcomes that large swathes of citizens recognize as neither democratic nor just. While support for the principles of democracy has risen worldwide, participation in the traditional institutions of government in democratic states (elections and political parties) has fluctuated and generally declined since at least the 1970s (Mair, 2013; Stoker, 2017). In response to this crisis of legitimacy, some democratic rulers have actively begun to invite citizens to take a more direct and ongoing role in political decision-making.

It is important to emphasize that this phenomenon of government actively seeking sustained and often substantial citizen input into its work is historically rare. For a whole host of reasons, people who have power, especially political power, do not normally voluntarily give it over to others. Notwithstanding the long history of direct democratic practices, particularly where town meetings or referenda are part and parcel of political culture, Mark Warren has identified an increasing worldwide trend towards 'governance-driven democratization' (2009). Democratic government has moved further away from the simplified ideal of responding to externally generated public demands such as campaigns, protests or writing to MPs. In response to crises of legitimacy, democratic rulers have actively begun to invite interest groups and citizens to take a more direct and ongoing role in political decision-making in domains that were previously the preserve of specialist administrators. Although they may take some inspiration from as far back as ancient Athens, many of these initiatives introduce a novel take on the appropriate architecture for democratic government. They are what Smith calls 'democratic innovations' – 'institutions that have been specifically designed to increase and deepen citizen participation in the political decision-making process' (Smith, 2009: 2).

This phenomenon of governance-driven democratic innovation has gathered pace since at least the early 1970s. A variety of processes, differently named, have claimed to help bridge the gap between governors and the governed. In some lauded cases these innovations have led to genuine changes in power relations. In others they have not. Some cases have mixed results. As scholars of power relations, political scientists ought to be both excited and sceptical about this phenomenon. The variance in cases presents the kind of puzzle that might justify the existence and maybe, if we can help solve it, even the wages of political scientists.

So how can scholars understand what is happening to explain changes in power relations? Especially in an emerging field, each individual research study must deal with the enduring analytical problem of many potential explanatory variables and few cases. Often, the primary remedy to this dilemma is to increase the number of observations as much as possible (Lijphart, 1971: 686; King et al, 1994). This tactic in the circumstances of PB research raises some significant but not insurmountable problems. In the build-up of rich case study literature and the development of several causal explanations for the outcomes of a democratic innovation like PB, an opportunity now arises. There is the potential for moderate generalizations in a larger systematic cross-case comparison of processes that have been institutionalized to differing degrees in different parts of the world. Casework and existing smaller comparisons suggest that causation is likely to be complex. Wampler, for example, suggests, 'successful PB cases depend on a series of factors converging to support the delegation of authority' (2007a: 159). Moreover, Peruzzotti has claimed that, 'democratic innovation is more likely to take place in a relatively grey area, where neither all of the significant variables promote change nor do all of them conspire against it' (2009: 58). Yet, at this juncture, a meaningful comparison of PBs based on conventional inferential statistical analysis is difficult to conceive. Despite the number of named PB processes now running into the tens of thousands, if explanations depend on complex conjunctions of factors and the goal is explaining how citizens gain meaningful control of decision-making, we do not appear to have the right kinds of data on enough cases on which to use correlational methods. Where those methods have been used, it has been mostly to predict health-related outcomes (Campbell et al, 2018). They do not (at least at the time of writing in 2020) appear useful for helping us filter signal from noise[1] in cross-regional studies of PB's democratic outcomes.

This book presents a new approach in applying QCA to provide a stronger assessment that clarifies and synthesizes the necessary and sufficient conditions for democratic deepening in cases of participatory policymaking. The QCA approach allows for an interplay between induction and deduction, united with a theoretical framework that is sufficiently anchored but comfortable with floating to identify novel theoretical contributions. I present a procedure that uses systematic Boolean logic when constructing research design in a way that has not been tried to such an extent before in the field of participatory innovation, to derive useful typologies and general explanations of how ordinary citizens gain control of political decisions.

## Democracy and participation

Vast swathes of the world's population see democracy as desirable (at least as far as a common understanding of the concept can be assumed)

---

1 A commonly used phrase in statistical analysis especially when dealing with high volumes of different data, which refers to overcoming data that is 'noisy' because it stops you identifying the 'signal' – i.e. the data that actually reveals what is going on in the world.

(Stoker, 2017: 24). Ideology, social movements, economic growth and revolution have variously been responsible for shifting vast populations from subjects of leviathan rulers to sovereign citizens of democratic states. Yet, despite the many definite historical accounts of progressive instances, the sense remains that this is an ongoing, contingent and precarious venture. Any teleological understanding of a democratic project has been challenged in contemporary times. The expansion of civil liberties, political and social rights were crucial to advancing the democratic project in previous eras (Marshall, 1950). However, while this expansion continues in some areas, increasing retrenchment of liberties and decreasing participation in formal politics in other democracies reveals a fragmentation of democratic progress that can be seen to be at best, in the responsive phase of a dialectical progression, or worse still, the precursor to permanent decline (O'Tuama, 2009: 142; Stoker, 2017).

In significant contexts 'democracy' can be taken to mean everything from an abstract ideal type of governance where sovereignty is located with the people as a whole, to a formula of institutional arrangements that denotes a type of political regime, to a placeholder for a perpetual struggle with imbalances of power. Schumpeter famously defined democracy in very minimal terms as an institutional method by which elites compete for votes to rule over relatively uneducated masses (1942 [1995]: 269). For long periods during the 20th century, political theorists and those working within the emerging discipline of empirical political science accepted this wisdom. Nevertheless, since the 1960s, developments in empirical social science have shown that participation by citizens in the governing of their collective affairs beyond voting for representatives is possible and, very often, desirable (Dahl, 1961; Mansbridge, 1983; Bryan, 2004). Pateman (1970) has documented a long and rich history of more participatory democratic theory, which normative assertions that 'too much' democracy is undesirable do not withstand. With these empirical and theoretical accounts, democracy is imbued with far more potential. Yet, visions of what political equality could or should look like, and how it would be achieved, continue to be debated. And it remains an empirical question (with some competing evidence) as to whether, 'another world is possible' (see Michels, 1911 [2001]; Hibbing and Theiss-Morse, 2002; Santos, 2005; Pateman, 2012).

What is often missing from these debates about desirable and potential limits of participation in democracies, and the realization of democratic goods, is systematic analysis of a wider range of cases. We continue to produce more nuanced knowledge on specific processes and their context, yet few scholars have examined the contextual and structural features of political systems that could provide a better understanding of success and failure in empowered democratic innovation. If we want to change the world for the better, we need information on the context in which democratic devices are most likely to succeed or fail. Adoption of democratic innovations often takes place against a backdrop of perceived democratic failures. In advance of introducing PB and reviewing in depth the most recent scholarship on that celebrated innovation, it is worth providing an overview of the background in which democratic failures that necessitate reform have been identified.

## Malaise and innovation

'It may work in theory, but does it work in practice?' is not an unfamiliar refrain for supporters of democracy to contend with. For those who wish to deepen democracy, there is a tension between grand republican ideas of citizens 'forced to be free' and 'acting in concert', as Rousseau and Arendt might have suggested, and the praxis of engaging those who are otherwise decided for in many difficult collective decisions.

Even for those who retain faith in existing democratic institutions there is much evidence of a 'democratic malaise'. Levels of traditional political participation have fallen, in terms of both party membership and turnout at elections (Stoker, 2017: 11, 33). In the UK alone, membership of the main political parties has fallen from over 5 per cent of the electorate in 1964 to a low of just 0.8 per cent in 2013 and 1.1 per cent in 2018 (Audickas et al, 2019: 5). While some may point to the increase in opposition party membership in the UK following the 2015 general election, its small scale despite the unprecedented salience of Westminster politics in those intervening years serves to reinforce the overall trajectory of decline. The trend across Western Europe is 'incontrovertible: party membership is in decline to such an extent that the dues-paying party member is in danger of becoming a dying breed' (Andeweg and Farrell, 2017: 77). While the longevity of cadre parties and the continuing establishment of those significant issue-based parties across the ideological spectrum show that the party is not quite over, mass mobilization and large-scale political engagement via political parties appears a thing of the past (Delwit, 2012).

The decline in voting is less terminal but still an important indicator of developments in the health of the traditional institutions of democracy. In the UK, evidence from the Hansard Society's yearly Audit of Political Engagement showed the share of respondents who said they would be certain to vote in an immediate general election falling from 51 to 41 per cent between 2004 and 2013. In the same period, respondents who claimed to be either 'very' or 'fairly' interested in politics reduced from 50 to 42 per cent. Yet these numbers have seen an uptick to 61 and 53 per cent respectively in 2019.[2] Actual turnout in the recent tumultuous elections between 2015 and 2019 in the UK has generally stabilized from a low of 59 per cent in 2001. However, we should caution against taking too much solace in plateaus. It is worth remembering that turnout figures in the 60–70 per cent range often mean that a minority of those affected by government decisions are voting, given registration barriers and voting restrictions on certain subgroups such as the young and migrants. An even smaller minority group is expressing a strong preference for the government, no matter the system of vote allocation. Hansard's Audit shows that this is certainly not the Britain of citizens imbued with a strong belief in their political efficacy that Almond and Verba (1963) encountered in their influential comparative study of 1963. The number of respondents to the Hansard survey strongly disagreeing that political involvement could change the way the UK is run hit a 15-year high in 2018. The British case is used here as an illustration, but there is plenty of evidence that the trend is replicated across the world (Dalton, 2004; Norris, 2011; Mair, 2013; Stoker, 2017). Across old and new democracies from the 1960s onwards, the number of citizens who have completely checked out of engaging with politics on a regular basis has increased slowly, but sizeably.

Not even the most radical participatory democrat would look to turn citizens of democracies into obsessed political anoraks. Some people have better things to do with their time. The trouble is that we are approaching a tipping point where disengagement begins to undermine the legitimacy of democracy. Anti-politics, alienation and support for populist interventions is reaching a worrying prevalence (Stoker, 2017). It is perhaps most interesting that in these same surveys, respondents who believed the system of government did not work well and could be improved 'a lot' or 'a great deal' rose from 60 per cent to 72 per cent. There appears a strengthening majority view that the institutions of government do not produce the democracy citizens would recognize.

In 1996, Arend Lijphart reminded the American Political Science Association in his presidential address of what he labelled democracy's remaining 'unresolved dilemma' – participation in these traditional

[2] The Hansard Society's annual reports, which began in 2004, are available at: www.hansardsociety.org.uk/projects/audit-of-political-engagement

institutional mechanisms of decision-making remains 'systematically biased against less well-to-do-citizens' (1997: 1). It is likely that the growing trends in anti-politics since the mid-1990s see these groups even further marginalized. The explanation for the relationship between inequality and disengagement remains a puzzle. While aggrieved citizens ought to be most likely to want to express their dissatisfaction in a system of equal voting, their circumstances may serve to reduce their feelings of political efficacy to the point at which the grievance no longer motivates a positive response (Harrison, 2020).

Are the institutions themselves the root cause of this cycle of malaise? Lijphart advocated compulsory voting as a response, and I have sympathy with his ideas. Compulsory voting does force unheard political voices 'into the room', which, in theory, should produce responsiveness to those voices, but there is no clear evidence that compulsory voting provides a magic bullet for the problem where it exists. In lieu of, or as well as, providing a compulsion to vote in major elections, can we design new institutions to complement the traditional ones? Perhaps new designs can overcome failings, expose better the viable paths to complementary reform of existing institutions, or reproduce some of the democratic goods that no longer seem to be provided?

Towards the end of the 20th century, forthright critiques of existing democratic decision-making systems came from a broad church of participatory and deliberative democratic theorists (for example, Pateman, 1970; Gutmann and Thompson, 1996; Bohman, 1997; Young, 2000). At the superficial level at least, these criticisms share a common problematization of existing liberal representative democracy. They challenge the analytical focus on traditional forms of participation, such as voting, because those kinds of political participation do not engender significant and long-term engagement (Pateman, 1970), and only aggregate what some characterize as relatively uninformed preferences (Bohman, 1997). From this broad mix of tensions and critiques emerges a growing interest in democratic innovations that recast the relationship between political elites and citizens. Interest turns to the design of institutions that engage the disengaged and give political efficacy to those who have never known it in representative democracies. What does this look like?

## Reform: when theories of democratic legitimacy meet the history of governing societies

While changes in the role governments play in governing has had an impact on accountability to citizens, citizens have, in turn, grown more educated and more critical (Beck, 1992; Inglehart, 1997; Stoker, 2017). Faced with a series of legitimacy crises, governors have been driven to respond. What is most interesting about the trend that has followed is that rulers have actively begun to create more direct roles for citizens in political decision-making.

Although the trend in governance-driven democratization has accelerated more recently, we can trace it at least as far back as the 1960s and to the US context. Against the backdrop of civil rights struggles, a new wave of citizen consultations were implemented in a putative effort to tackle some of the pervasive social and political inequalities in US municipalities, many focusing on the contentious issue of housing. They soon drew criticism. But salient criticism of those efforts at democratic reconstruction came not from traditional elitists anxious of engaging 'the great unwashed'; rather, it was founded on a scepticism that pointed to the dangers of superficial increases in participation, and therefore called for full citizen control of decisions (Arnstein, 1969). Arnstein's contention was that much of what passed for citizen consultation was an empty ritual aimed at consolidating elite rule. Consultations of this type can at worst be a mollifying 'incumbent democracy' that tranquilizes the genuine critical collective socialization that lies at the heart of ingenuity in free societies (Blaug, 2002). For Blaug, this engineering of participation by government must be met with a degree of scepticism as it may fundamentally be interpreted as a Bismarckian bid to protect the 'representative core' of the system. Yet, it is in response to some of these criticisms of derogatorily branded 'manipulatory' institutions that a new breed of institutions can be said to have emerged, 'institutions that have been specifically designed to increase and deepen citizen participation in the political decision-making process' (Smith, 2009: 2). Françoise Montambeault draws a useful distinction between autonomy from the state and autonomy within (2016: 35). While societies ought to value external critique of the state, they will want to work interdependently with the state apparatus to harness its power. We must remain sceptical and vigilant to processes and programmes that either set out to or otherwise end up co-opting citizens rather than engaging them on their merits. However, we should not deny the possibility, in fact the necessity, for governance-driven democratization to prosper.

The relationship between design and observation of these democratic innovations, and the critical democratic theory highlighted, is less straightforward than it may seem. Dalton (2004) has spoken of 'an unhelpful gap' in the literature between democratic theory and practice. Although the aforementioned critiques surely have had some influence on invention, the emerging field of academic study surrounding democratic innovations is more often characterized by a handful of determined democratic theorists catching up with practice than by experimentalists trialling their own grand designs (with some notable exceptions that attempt both, for example, James Fishkin's Deliberative Opinion Polls®). In an influential article, Fung recognized that 'political theorists and scientists would do well to learn from the emerging practice of mini-publics that are "creating instances of more perfect public spheres"' (2003: 338). Does what seems to work in practice work in theory, and how can empirical political science improve and refine democratic theories and vice versa?

## Participatory budgeting

In the period from the 1600s to the 1800s 'No taxation without representation' emerged to become an enduring slogan for democratic revolutionaries, securing support for an idea and a movement that gathered momentum and changed forever how we understand legitimate governance. Yet, as regime change and universal suffrage extended out across the world in the 20th century, concerns about the persistence of injustices and inequalities in democracies have remained in focus. The declining membership of political parties and the re-emergence of populist leaders has signalled alarm for some of the most iconic democratic regimes (Mair, 2013; Levitsky and Ziblatt, 2018). In contrast, the continued emergence of participatory *democratic innovations* (DIs, or PDIs; see Smith, 2009: 1) – suggests a reformed and elevated democracy may be just beyond the horizon. PB fits into this wider historical picture, by bringing together the value of accountability for public spending with the move to more citizens participating more directly in governance.

Among these democratic innovations of the last number of years, the one that has excited governors, civil society activists and academics more than any other is participatory budgeting. Perhaps not since the acceleration of the cooperative movement in the last century has a participatory innovation seen such rapid diffusion. PB has been taken up in waves by a wide number of governments, as well as other public and semi-private decision-making bodies in Latin America, Europe, North America, Asia and Africa, and even in non-democratic states (Sintomer et al, 2008, 2010, 2013, 2016; Cabannes and Lipietz, 2018; Dias, 2018). PB had a long affinity with the World Social Forum and was promoted internationally throughout its networks of committed activists who recognized its potential to democratize spending decisions (Porto de Oliveira, 2017). It has been lauded by the World Bank as a model of 'good governance' and actively promoted by a small unit within the Bank (Goldfrank, 2012). It has also been promoted and supported by the United Nations (UN) through its HABITAT programme, by national governments from Peru (McNulty, 2011) to Portugal (Dias et al, 2018), and significant regional governments from Lazio in Italy (Sintomer et al, 2016: 76) to Scotland in the UK (Escobar et al, 2018). A recently published scoping review for the *Handbook of Democratic Innovations and Governance* by Stephen Elstub and Oliver Escobar (2019: 2) shows not only that DIs have rapidly become a significant field of scholarship, but that among studies of DIs, PB receives by far the most attention. Although PB has begun to wane in some areas (Spada, 2010), it continues to diffuse so rapidly that the total number of cases is still growing. In many places it has reached what Fedozzi et al call, with reference to Brazil, 'a time of maturity that has gone beyond experimentalism' (2018: 105). PB is almost certainly the most diffused democratic innovation since the 1990s, and we now have a good vantage point to assess it. So what is this idea, innovation or institutional design that so captivates?

PB can be defined at a minimum 'as the involvement of citizens in the budgetary decisions of a public body and labelled as such by the actors' (Talpin, 2011: 32). However, most definitions would establish a higher set of requirements to distinguish PB from the budget consultations that have traditionally been carried out with select groups of citizens or society representatives, such as incorporated stakeholders including business groups and trade unions.

There are dangers in definitions that are too prescriptive of levels of participation. Not everyone can or will want to participate in politics all the time – and that is almost certainly a mercy rather than a concern. Moreover, as PB has travelled, it has borrowed from different democratic traditions employing different selection mechanisms for participation. Nevertheless, Ganuza and Baiocchi are keen to point out that the origins of PB in open participation as opposed to strictly association-based advocacy had profound consequences in shaping PB as a vehicle for open governance over more protected forms of corporative-style bargaining (2019: 78). Yves Sintomer and colleagues, who have done more than most to try to bring some order to a concept that has diffused rapidly around the globe, provide the following six minimal criteria for PB:

> [The process] … allows the participation of non-elected citizens in the conception and/or allocation of public finances and …. The financial and/or budgetary dimension must be discussed; participatory budgeting deals with scarce resources.
>
> The municipal level must be involved or a (decentralised) district with an elected body and some power over administration (the neighbourhood level is not enough).
>
> It must be a repeated process (one meeting or one referendum on financial issues are not examples of participatory budgeting).
>
> The process must include some form of public deliberation within the framework of specific meetings/forums (the opening up of administrative meetings or traditional representative instances to "ordinary" citizens is not participatory budgeting).
>
> Some accountability with regard to output is required. (Sintomer et al, 2008: 168; 2013: 3; 2016: 20)

The challenges in pinning down a definition of PB as the concept travels and the institutional innovation diffuses are returned to later in the book. The comparative approach I take offers a good overview of what is at stake in more open or restrictive conceptions of PB. My primary goal, nonetheless, is to identify the conditions within PB that explain citizen control of collective decisions.

Understanding the mix of conditions that explain success and failure in achieving meaningful citizen control of decisions across different circumstances is an important objective. PB has been lauded by academics, activists, intergovernmental organizations (IGOs), non-governmental organizations (NGOs) and many other governing bodies and agencies worldwide. Governments and the governed seem to think it is a good idea. Where PB has been successful it has given succour to democracy, re-engaging the disengaged and improving capacities and political skills through participation. As well as engaging people in performing democracy, PB has been shown to contribute to substantive outcomes including redistributing public funds to those most in need, counteracting clientelism and encouraging effective governance. However, where PB fails it risks increasing disengagement, strengthening clientelist or malevolent elite rule and increasing anti-democratic attitudes by diminishing any hope that ordinary people can make valuable contributions to collective decision-making.

It is not surprising, then, that there has been growing academic interest in PB. Scholars from a range of disciplinary backgrounds have sought to understand its potential and to analyse its successes and failures. Despite this, Goldfrank summarized the state of the art after some 20 years of scholarship as follows:

> With some exceptions, scholars have either provided long lists of potentially relevant variables or attempted to extract lessons from one or more successful cases, making general conclusions difficult … recent research offers some clues as to why [PB] experiments are increasingly successful, yet a compelling framework that integrates actors, preconditions, and institutional design remains elusive. (2011: 24–5)

Some years later, systematic comparisons of many cross-national, cross-regional cases remain elusive (Wampler et al, 2018: 19, 50). Most of the scholarly work on PB has taken the form of single case studies or small-N comparisons of a handful of cases. There are several reasons scholars may not have been disposed to do more. For one thing, the rapid diffusion and adaptation of PB can make it appear a somewhat moving target, disincentivizing those who prefer to work with more neatly defined populations. To move beyond the impasse will require a degree of methodological innovation. Nevertheless, previous work does provide the research community with two invaluable assets: (1) much skilfully generated data describing cases of PB processes and their associated conditions; and (2) several competing hypotheses on the necessary and sufficient conditions for success and failure in participatory governance.

The large field of study dedicated to understanding democratic innovation that has emerged over many years is now (over)loaded with good case studies and small-N comparisons (where N stands for number of cases in a study). PB research often relies on ethnographic methodologies. This has led to a call for more systematic cross-case comparisons involving more cases (Smith, 2009; Ryan, 2018, 2019). In order to convince those with the power to do so to redesign, we need good evidence of what works, where, and how. Democratic practitioners will want to put into effect the conditions identified with success and avoid those identified with failure. The research presented in this book attempts to harness the lessons of the first studies of PB. My work stands on the shoulders of those case researchers, but I accumulate their work systematically to allow a more robust explanation drawing on more data across more cases.

## Why compare?

PB is not only of interest in this book because it can provide clear evidence of what works and when for those motivated by concerns for more participatory governance. Studying an emerging phenomenon like PB also provides the opportunity to ask important questions as to how comparative social science should seek to make sense of seemingly new, innovative and emerging forms of policy.

The era of governance-driven policymaking, where networks of actors must more often engage in competition for funding or other resources, has increased both the pressures and opportunities to innovate. This gold rush in institutional innovation requires some vigilance among political scientists interested in classifying phenomena and providing causal explanations of classes of phenomena. Social scientists are often attracted to understand cases because of the seemingly unique stories they tell. Nevertheless, if our focus is drawn to unique cases of participatory governance, it raises the question as to how we can build on an in-depth knowledge of a handful of cases to provide systematic evidence for causal theories (Ryan, 2019). This book therefore seeks to address practically the important issues raised when political reforms are recognized for their exceptional characteristics and political scientists wish to move beyond the lessons of one or two strong exemplars.

The research presented here is among the first to apply a QCA approach to the field of participatory governance. I bring together an approach and set of methodological tools at the cutting edge of case-based comparative politics with a field of study that is also growing exponentially. The result is new insight for those interested in the study of political participation and democracy as well as those interested in comparative research in the social sciences more generally. I assess the merits of QCA as an approach for cultivating insights into an emerging field of research. Each tool in the social science toolbox has different strengths and weaknesses in performing tasks. Scholars of innovation tend to work with concepts that are perhaps less easy to formalize because one of their defining characteristics is a departure from established norms. I learned that approaching PB research at this stage of its development provided advantages in understanding conceptual and methodological trade-offs that might benefit other subfields at similar stages of development.

Much like more established forms of modelling, QCA is a method that can provide parsimonious summaries of complex relationships that may signal relationships of cause and effect across large numbers of cases. Unlike more established statistical modelling techniques, QCA is designed to expose set-theoretic relationships (for example, relationships of necessity and sufficiency) among variables (Schneider and Wagemann, 2012). Researchers using QCA focus on research questions or hypotheses framed in terms of 'If X, then Y' rather than 'The more of X, the more of Y' (Thiem et al, 2016).

Any decision about research strategies requires the weighing of several factors relevant to the availability and structure of data. Early proponents of QCA would claim that the method can very commendably harmonize theory, qualitative data and quantitative data (Ragin, 2000), and this it is a particularly apt approach when a researcher is faced with a medium-N population of cases (Berg-Schlosser and Cronqvist, 2005). What those observers had in mind are opportunities for research where there exist more than a handful of cases and less than enough cases to avail of powerful statistical techniques for analysing correlations to identify probabilities when controlling for confounding factors. Ragin makes the intriguing observation that studies of more than a handful and less than a lorry-load of cases are unusual in social sciences (2000: 25). Despite its exponential growth in use among social scientists as well as other disciplines prior to my acquaintance with the method (see Thiem and Dusa, 2013; see also Rihoux et al, 2013), QCA's methodological scholarship has matured as I undertook this research. More recent methodological debates on QCA have argued quite convincingly that it is the underlying set-theoretic and propositional logic, rather than numbers of cases studied, that distinguishes it as a method (Thiem et al, 2016). Nevertheless, I was attracted to both the puzzle of how to cumulate systematic evidence beyond a handful of cases holistically as well as correctly test for necessity and sufficiency relationships that are relevant to PB scholarship. I return to what I learned about both of those issues regularly. I recognized in approaching the puzzle of what led to citizen control of PB processes that we had at our disposal rich data on a medium-N of cases (cumulating existing studies), and numerous competing causal claims, the majority of which, as I will explain, are set-theoretic rather than correlational. The PB phenomenon seemed fertile ground for QCA research. The QCA method is still maturing. This book shows how developments in comparative method apply to an emerging population of cases in PB, and provides an assessment of the effectiveness of the QCA approach in providing interesting insights in such a scenario.

## Beyond techniques for policymaking and social science: wider significance

There are a number of important debates beyond municipal-level democracy and comparative social science to which evidence from a more systematic comparison of PB speaks. All relate to the proper place (if there is any) for political participation and the extent of a role for the 'ordinary citizen' in the governance of modern societies. 'Ordinary citizens' are most often taken to be citizens who do not take an established part in state decision-making as elected representatives or public administrators. The common use of scare quotes around the term indicates the distinction between ordinary and otherwise is not always easy to make. Its sense is often evoked in popular opposition to a 'political class' – those who have systemic influence and interaction with formal decision-making including politicians, senior civil servants, media and interest groups – what is, for example, sometimes known in the UK as the 'Westminster bubble'. It is easy for the same individual to identify with ordinary and not-so-ordinary depending on circumstances – populists are one example. Nevertheless, it remains a useful heuristic to identify those who have less or more constant access to formal democratic decision-making.

A first wider debate this research aims to contribute to is that which sets a standard for the need for democratic innovation at all. The question centres on whether participatory innovation can be a useful contributor to representative democracy and effective public administration. For some, democracy is justified by its ends and is 'not an end in itself', as only an elite few can make good decisions that truly benefit the collective (Schumpeter, 1942 [1995]: 242). Minimal safeguards in the form of regular(ish) elections can ensure competition among elites and negate reactionary mob rule. Democracy is simply a 'method' of cycling among elites and avoiding absolute tyranny. The problem with this account is that the method is not working, and we still desire the end. So the first debate is whether democratic innovations provide a solution, or do they open the door to folly or mob rule?

Opposing supporters of elite rule, others argue that opportunities for participation, even in between elections, can often be beneficial. If we assume that the standard for democratic decisions is that they approach as much as possible the benefit of all, well-designed opportunities to gather information from citizens and to allow them to respond to one another could improve rather than reduce the quality of collective decisions. Although scholars take the concept of 'deliberation' in a variety of directions, this is its most recurring contribution to democratic theory. Deliberative democrats are keen that a wider spectrum of discourses and experiences are brought to bear on a problem. They are interested in the solutions that come from the communicative rationality of bringing together and reconciling diverse perspectives. We may believe that there are good reasons for restricting elements of decision-making to experts and elected representatives (for example, on grounds of competence, or because the entire nation is an 'unworkable committee', as Schumpeter aptly puts it; 1942 [1995]: 261). However, it may be that we would like to provide decision-makers with complimentary institutions that harness what we might call 'proximal expertise'.[3] By proximal expertise I mean the innate expertise of the citizen who knows best how decisions currently and potentially affect them and others close to them. Schumpeter, in fact, is keen to recognize this expertise in his influential writings, although he sees no reason for why or how that kind of expertise should be brought to bear on matters of higher politics. There is a vibrant debate about the conceptualization of expertise in policymaking, but we have enough evidence now to show that firm restrictions on what counts as expertise can be as dangerous as denials of the value of established experts. Representation is often an inadequate route to including proximal expertise in decisions. One intriguing finding from the first PB in Porto Alegre was that citizens' expressed priorities for expenditure on public works differed from what their representatives thought their priorities were (Abers, 2000; Baiocchi, 2005; Santos, 2005).

If it can be shown that, at least some of the time, democratic innovations that are tried in traditional settings but in different contexts are recognized as effective modes of governing with positive outcomes for citizens, then it suggests that those who see elections and parties as the only effective institutions for democratic governance need to think again. Financial decisions are often considered the 'black box' of government, a realm of decision-making restricted on grounds of necessary competence to technocrats and seasoned professional politicians skilled in bargaining. For Carole Pateman, PB, as practised in Porto Alegre, provides an example of 'how central components of participatory democracy can be institutionalized successfully in what is conventionally seen as an expert, technical area' (2012: 10). And 'ordinary citizens' with little formal education have shown capacities to increase their budget literacy through participation in PB (Abers, 2000). An extension to the first debate, then, which speaks to a higher standard for democratic innovations, accepts that we may need democratic innovation, but asks what the conditions for successful democratic innovation and adoption of innovations might be. Ideal PB enables

[3] There is a good discussion of the different theoretical traditions that favour citizens' knowledge in participatory process in Sintomer et al (2016: 178–80).

increased popular control over elements of budgets by institutionalizing citizens' participation in making spending decisions. The question the research presented here can answer that speaks to these wider debates is under what conditions might a more transformative and sustained citizen control of decision-making in political participation occur (and under what conditions is it negated)?

The next debate to which we might want to speak is whether participatory designs can be enablers for change at a more systemic level. There is much debate among deliberative democrats about the conditions for a 'deliberative system' (Mansbridge et al, 2012), and what role different institutions might play in that system. Gret and Sintomer, for instance, argue that participants in successful PB can act as a type of 'social vanguard', providing a positive example that can organically grow to involve those across the spectrum interested in reconnecting with democracy (2005: 92–6). For democratic innovations to have a systemic or cultural effect is a higher standard still, and one for which we may only be able to produce indicative evidence at this juncture. But by highlighting the conditions associated with successful outcomes across cases, I can pinpoint the cases and types of cases that speak to such outcomes. I am also better able to identify the puzzles that remain. This evidence may require closer scrutiny and fresh examination via other appropriate methodological tools such as combinations of process-tracing and network analysis to understand more systemic effects.

A final important debate revolves around what the appropriate methodological tools are for comparative political scientists wishing to cumulate rich, in-depth qualitative pieces of research that combine both common and disparate elements. Some of QCA's ambitions lie in providing at least modest solutions to the challenge of combining the essential knowledge of micro-processes that tell the rich stories of interesting cases with analysis that builds on this knowledge by providing robust systematic cross-case comparison. Yet only a few QCA studies have set out explicitly to cumulate existing and diverse qualitative pieces, and almost none have attempted to look at emerging subfields using fuzzy-set qualitative comparative analysis (fsQCA). The tendency has been to focus on established concepts – comparing welfare states, wars or political parties. My work therefore also looks to speak to wider debates about what value developments in set-theoretic analysis can add for comparative politics, and provide a test of the use of QCA where interesting questions are not easily answered using traditional methods of inquiry.

## Understanding democratic deepening

As innovative programmes of participatory politics have emerged and diffused over time, interested scholars have turned to fieldwork, and, in the first instance, to the construction of detailed case studies of types of innovation. Examples can be drawn across very different institutional designs, from popular assemblies such as town meetings (Mansbridge, 1983), community policing beat meetings and school boards (Fung, 2004), to participatory budgets (Abers, 2000; Baiocchi, 2005), and randomly selected citizens' assemblies (Davies et al, 2006; Warren and Pearse, 2008). These authors have broadly concerned themselves with recognizing interesting innovations that, on the face of it, warrant investigation because of their perceived or acknowledged exceptional potential for increasing democratic legitimacy – what case study researchers might call information-oriented selection of extreme cases (Flyvbjerg, 2006).

Beyond and because of this pioneering work, a more systematic comparative turn in the process of understanding these phenomena became possible. Following Fung's agenda (2003), I identify what it is that allows some cases of adoption of innovation to deliver democratic goods in the form of citizen control (and what negates such an outcome). Finally, I return to consider what the evidence of attempted participatory governance teaches us about both our theories of democracy and its practical advancement – what the value of democratic innovation is. It is these questions and the potential of new methods to provide new and important answers to them that lie at the heart of the book.

In the following two chapters, I provide an overview of the emergence of PB as a phenomenon as well as an object of academic scholarship. I show how social science has developed its inquiries of PB, explaining why systematic cumulation and comparison is not always prevalent, and why it should be in order to produce a scientific approach to understanding PB and other instances of participatory governance. I show how the best studies of PB have moved us in the direction of better understanding PB's potential, and reinforce the necessity of comparative research to overcome myopic responses to the problems facing democracy.

2

# Participatory Budgeting: How Do We Understand Exceptional Democracy?

## The scholarship of participatory budgeting

> Today, dozens of regular forums and councils discuss nearly every area of local decisionmaking. Seminars, conferences, and community meetings in which state officials and citizens discuss and decide together on issues ranging from street lighting to economic development policy are an everyday occurrence. Civic groups outside the state-sponsored participatory structure – ranging from innumerable neighbourhood associations to a powerful Urban Reform Movement – have bloomed in the context of political opportunity. (Abers, 2000: 217)

So wrote Rebecca Abers in the first book-length scholarly account of PB in Porto Alegre to be published in the English language: *Inventing Local Democracy* (2000). This summary is striking and inspiring because few people would recognize such a description as normal in their experience of municipal governance. It offers, perhaps, a real example of what might otherwise be seen as radical and sometimes utopian theories (Fung and Wright, 2003). More than 20 years on, a distinct yet diverse body of work has emerged analysing the various effects of PB in Porto Alegre, the diffusion of this innovation across the world, and lately, the different outcomes in different cases of its implementation. But given that attempts to do politics differently are not uncommon (Smith, 2005), why did this phenomenon that began in this city capture the imagination of so many? What is it, and what is unique about it? And why are broader comparative analyses so rare?

Chapter 1 showed that there are low-bar definitions of PB that are inclusive of any and all participation in public budgeting, where someone or some group decide to call what is being done 'participatory budgeting'. PB has had its dalliances with fashion in public policy in different contexts, and the labelling of processes can be an issue of some contention for onlookers and participants alike. Calling a process PB says little about levels of citizen control. PB is a renowned democratic innovation because in its ideal type it promises a tangible increase in democratic legitimacy, and subsequently, a more equitable redistribution of goods. Ideal PB enables increased popular control over elements of budgets by institutionalizing citizens' participation in making spending decisions. It exemplifies a successful materialization of participatory political theory into institutional design by encouraging open and diverse participation, allowing 'ordinary citizens' to create, shape and renew institutions and rule-structures themselves. Much of the design of PB has common tenets with Athenian democratic practices and principles in realizing democratic goods (Smith, 2009). In ideal PB this exceptional scale of deep, public participation is combined with structured deliberation and design-rules that limit the threat of co-option and capture by powerful vested interests, resisting the evolution of new elites.

PB is a relatively young phenomenon, its inception now generally traced to the late 1980s in the Brazilian municipality of Porto Alegre, although similar participatory experiments had been undertaken in other Brazilian cities around the same time (Gilman, 2016: 25). Defining PB, even in one city, is no easy task. Take Porto Alegre: a concise definition would need to negotiate the emphases that different observers place on different aspects of the case. Like many things, the procedures and the success of PB in Porto Alegre were the product of a mixture of design, hard work and accident. Even so, it remains the template on which the Workers' Party (Partido dos Trabalhadores, or PT) later introduced PB in several Brazilian municipalities and some federal states. Governing parties from across the political spectrum then introduced PB in various Brazilian municipalities, as well as in other states. The programme's historical roots are indelibly linked to the PT, yet its instigation, promotion and facilitation has continued in the participatory policies of many parties. The programme's success also owes a debt to Brazilian cultures of organized participation that preceded democratization, flourished after for some time, and despite recent retrenchment, continues to have strong foundations in large parts of that society. Yet, unlike almost all other ideas of the same generation that show similar democratic potential, this innovation has become institutionalized in many diverse locations, and has diffused rapidly across municipal, national and cultural borders. Diffusion has come through numerous channels with many significant IGOs and NGOs advocating for PB in various forms. The experiences and results of its adaptation to other decision-making venues have been highly differentiated (Sintomer et al, 2008, 2010, 2013, 2016; Dias, 2018).

Wampler (2007b) summarizes the key components of PB based on the original Brazilian model as concisely as possible. He notes that the 'guiding tenets' are: a municipality divided into regions; the provision of budget information by the government and the facilitation of regular meetings at various stages of the budget cycle for deliberation and election of delegates; a 'quality of life' index based on technical criteria used to redistribute resources based on need; a 'bus caravan of priorities' in which elected delegates visit all project sites; a municipal council made up of two councillors per region; a right to veto the budget for the municipal legislature; and regional committees elected to monitor the implementation of projects (2007b: 26). Avritzer, more abstractly, yet more concisely, emphasizes four characteristics: the delegation of sovereignty to regional assemblies; the combination of direct and representative participation; self-regulation; and the 'inversion' of priorities by technical criteria to favour redistribution (2006: 623–4). Other features that could be added to definitions might include outreach to disadvantaged groups by government in promoting participation and reorganization of bureaucracies to prioritize and implement projects, to name just a few.

There is some consensus, then, on where PB has come from and what it is. Although the Porto Alegre model may be the inspiration for programmes, PB has necessarily been implemented in different ways in different contexts. Years of working with policymakers have taught me that it is not uncommon after explaining the ins and outs of complicated processes to hear them reply, 'Yes, but we are already doing that here.' Often these policymakers are deceiving the listener, and often they are also deceiving themselves, but quite often, too, they are on or close to the mark. Very similar participatory processes have grown in different local and national contexts that perhaps differ only in name or in the presence or absence of some key components. Sometimes researchers who build their careers on finding differences too quickly deny the possibility of similarities, as much as researchers who focus on finding similarities gloss over important differences too quickly.

We are biased as analysts, but our training ought to allow us to reduce that bias. Although PB has changed and adapted, and sometimes been adopted in different ways, that variance presents researchers aiming to explain a phenomenon with an important resource. George and Bennett put it well: 'when explanations for the outcome of individual cases vary, the results can be cumulated and contribute to the development of a rich differentiated theory about that phenomenon' (2005: 216). This sounds a simple statement, but it is surprising how little cumulation takes place and how difficult it can be. It is within the study of PB that the most interesting examples of comparative work on democratic innovations have emerged. In order to contribute to a rich and differentiated theory, I now trace the developments in PB scholarship on which I later build.

## Starting from a single case: Porto Alegre, Brazil

Our understanding of a class of phenomena called democratic innovations and/or PB, and therefore of what cases make up that class, evolves over time. That again may seem obvious, but it is important for those interested in cumulation and interpretation of earlier work to keep in mind that earlier studies of a phenomenon can only have intuitions, but never firm knowledge, about what their cases will look like to those classifying them much later (Ryan, 2019). The natural starting point for any significant phenomenon that appears to observers quite new or different in comparison to known phenomena is, to begin with, an ethnographic study. Abers described her approach to an in-depth study of the Porto Alegre case as follows:

> On the first trip I discovered that Porto Alegre was the only PT administration at the time around which there was widespread consensus that participatory policy had been successful at mobilizing people and at actually giving participants real deliberative power. This consensus led me to choose that city as an "exemplary" case of a successful participatory policy. (2000: 230)

Baiocchi saw the contribution of his empirical research on Porto Alegre to theory development in similar terms:

> … the case study of a relevant or unique case can allow for theoretical innovation because of its attention to process and anomaly … as an instance of state–civil society relations,

> [Porto Alegre] forces us to *rethink theory*. (2005: 165; original emphasis)

Their selection-logic is sound, and shows the need for awareness of background theory, other cases and conditions is an important part of any good case study. Lazy criticism of case study researchers tends to elide this inalienable feature of the case study process.

These first observers identified Porto Alegre as an extreme or unique case of 'participatory policy' or 'state–civil society relations'. The extensive observations and interviews carried out by both Baiocchi and Abers rely on multi-method approaches to data collection with a focus on the advantages of ethnography in exposing in detail the conditions underlying unusual phenomena. They provide good insights into the relationship between politics, administrative reform and civil society activism. Gret and Sintomer (2005) take a slightly more top-down, theory-led case study approach, focusing on how the innovative practices developed in Porto Alegre relate to a wide range of broader political, social and critical theories. Still, this allows them to make important observations about the theoretical relationship between direct and representative democracy in the light of the case; for example, they consider how lot and referenda favoured by many theorists of democratic reform are less familiar as devices for guaranteeing democratic equality in Porto Alegre (2005: 133). These three book-length studies represent the first academic treatments of PB in Porto Alegre to appear in the English language (one translated from French). They are complemented by detailed articles based on their own first-hand research by Santos (2005)[1] and Goldfrank (2003).

The extensive theory-informed descriptive data are important because, to put it in Baiocchi's own words, they 'sought to contribute to the already extensive discussion of democratic theory through an actual examination of instances of popular participation in government decision making' (2005: 142). This greater emphasis on empirics in participatory democracy becomes increasingly common in research that started to appear in the 21st century. Those *actual examinations* of cases of democratic innovation were, at least until the 2010s, all too rare. There are some notable early exceptions – examples include Bryan (2004) and Mansbridge (1983) on town meetings, Davies et al's investigation of NICE's Citizen's Council (2006), Warren and

[1] An earlier version of that research was also published in *Politics & Society* (1998), 26(4), 461–510.

Pearse's edited collection examining the Citizens' Assembly in British Columbia that took place in 2006 (2008), and Fishkin's (1996) and Dienel's (1989) accounts of their own designs – Deliberative Opinion Polls® and Planning Cells respectively.

These numerous in-depth case studies are invaluable. Methodologists sometimes argue that multiple case studies of a single case can provide something close to replication, with the advantages of corroboration and triangulation. The dispersion and reach of in-depth knowledge on the Porto Alegre case also provides a useful yardstick for calibrating comparisons of other cases among several disparate researchers. The different theoretical lenses used to interpret the empirical data in the case study also highlight the possibilities of alternate adaptations and combinations of democratic devices with PB and within PB, something that is later picked up on by Smith (2009: 190). I continue to argue that case studies and the accumulation of case studies can provide advantages for creativity and novel interpretation as well as testing the evidence for prevailing, bounded assumptions. I return to a discussion of sequencing democratic innovations and devices in the concluding parts of the book. With greater collaboration and consolidation of the field, and improved networks, technologies and methodologies for research, larger-N studies of democratic innovations have become possible. Many challenges in establishing validity when using samples remain when working with this rapidly evolving caseload (see Gastil et al, 2017; Spada and Ryan, 2017; Ryan, 2019), and a discussion of the development of PB scholarship in line with the emergence of new cases and research strategies will highlight some of the trade-offs. The story starts with understanding how Porto Alegre compares to what went before and after.

## What made Porto Alegre exceptional?

Porto Alegre is a sprawling metropolis perched on a large lagoon at the southern end of Brazil, and could be described as a relatively unremarkable city at a superficial level. It is a relatively well-off city by the standards of middle-income countries, and has been so by Brazilian standards. It certainly boasts excellent restaurants – you will probably see some chimarrão drinking, and further befitting of Brazilian culture, it has produced one world footballer of the year. Its politics is lively, and frequently unavoidable in a quite literal sense, with politics often taking place out in the streets through a dense, organized and loud civil society. But for those interested in deeper forms of political participation and alternative forms of democracy, Porto Alegre has, or had for a time at least,[2] taken on a real symbolic quality as a place where ideas for change found practical success.

Porto Alegre stands out even among the Southern Brazilian cities with longer histories of activism, and some of Brazil's culture and practices of participatory decision-making in politics long predate formal democratization at the federal level (Pogrebinschi and Samuels, 2014; Lüchmann and Borba, 2018: 90). PB-like practices were emerging in some other cities around the same time (Wampler, 2007a). Nevertheless, Porto Alegre, partly due to the vivid successes of its programme, and partly through the strength of its role in international diffusion in both established and novel fora such as the World Social Forum, came to be understood as the archetypal process.

Ethnography is not often suited to parsimonious accounts that rigidly distinguish and index variables for systematic comparison. Describing rich complexity to evoke novel and often-creative insight is its strength. The attention to detail of the early accounts highlights numerous conditions and processes that have ostensibly made the key contributions to the exceptional outcomes in this case. How did these field researchers interpret this Porto Alegre exception?

Both Baiocchi and Abers focus on a change in state–civil society relations as a key condition of interest (in writing up at least, if they may have begun with a more grounded approach). This interest speaks to theories that focus on the necessity of organized, combative civil society organization for holding government to account in functioning democratic polities. Baiocchi suggests that under specific conditions, combative civil society can be bolstered and perhaps even incarnated by state action (2005: 145). For Baiocchi, what was interesting about the Porto Alegre experiment was that for the first time demands from civil society were decoupled from political allegiance (2005: 138). For PB to succeed, it was of the utmost importance that the PT administration helped create an institutional space where both social movements and unorganized citizens could participate on an equal footing (2005: 150; see also Ganuza and Baiocchi, 2012, 2019). Although the party, in this case the PT, may have had an instrumental goal of creating strong grassroots support, it gambled on achieving this through a long-term commitment to participatory ideology and institutionalizing the

[2] After becoming successively more fragile following the removal of PT from the executive in 2004, with the arrival of Porto Alegre's latest new mayor, Nelson Marchezan Júnior in 2017, PB was eventually suspended amid escalating financial and political crises in Brazil (see Nuñez, 2018). Porto Alegre now has an online citizen consultation process that draws some inspiration from PB.

devolution of power. This involved significant commitment to change in the face of potential political barriers. The government took on a complete reorganization of the planning bureaucracy and increased the municipal tax-take (Santos, 2005: 328). There are also vivid accounts of the very uncertain beginnings and many failures and troubles that greeted the PT's participatory agenda in the early years (see Goldfrank, 2003). Strong resolve in rejecting pressure to resort to old ways of doing political business were required (Baiocchi and Ganuza, 2016). Perhaps the most important lesson for us from these studies of Porto Alegre is that of the commitment needed for the institutionalization of participatory innovations.

Abers explains that over time the introduction of PB in Porto Alegre resulted in a virtuous cycle whereby increased mobilization and the reduction of inequalities gradually augmented one another, benefiting from a political commitment to support meaningful participation and execute priorities decided on and written into the participatory budget (2000: 218). Mobilization of groups that had not previously been organized is of central importance in her account. Abers also submits that these groups flourished and were not co-opted. Her work provides a degree of empirical evidence to refute the considerable scepticism in the literature towards forms of top-down mobilization. In Porto Alegre the government acted as an 'external agent' in the same way as NGOs have traditionally done to mobilize movements. What is more, by implementing participants' decisions, mobilization was increased almost exponentially in the first few years via these 'demonstration effects' (2000: 138). As Goldfrank explains, 'participants could point out to their neighbours and friends the very projects that they had prioritised the year before … compared with 1990, participation in the 1991 budget assemblies more than tripled' (2003: 39).

It is important to remember that the gains in Porto Alegre were not just seen in greater inputs to the political system. Participation was an important part of an effective administration. Many scholars of democratic innovations have preoccupied themselves with the internal workings of deliberative fora. They pay lip service to the need for evaluation of effects in implementation rather than performing analysis (Pogrebinschi and Ryan, 2018). In Porto Alegre, Goldfrank reports that of those involved in the participatory budget he interviewed, 'all could name various public works projects that they and their neighbours had demanded' (2011: 232). PB wasn't just about people feeling good that they had talked about a difficult issue, learned a bit about it and then gone home (the latter is unfortunately the case with many but far from all mini-publics). PB in Porto Alegre meant streets being paved to open access to transportation and the economic possibilities going with it; sanitation and health increasing by placing open sewage into pipes – meaning a twelvefold increase in sewage treatment in a short number of years; legalizing squatters' claims to land to improve housing; and building schools, hospitals and clinics (Goldfrank, 2011: 232–3). Importantly, PB in Porto Alegre (and in some other places, as we shall see) shows that following through with the hard slog of democratic participation can have transformative consequences.

Porto Alegre possessed a distinctively vibrant civil society during the last years of the military dictatorship (Santos, 2005: 313). When PB struggled in its first two years, the willingness and capacity of civil society activists to defend the process but challenge the execution of it at the expense of the mayoral administration's public reputation was a key factor in stimulating the structural changes described previously (Goldfrank, 2003: 35–7). What is of interest here is the role played by an autonomous umbrella group representing civil society across neighbourhoods in the city. The Porto Alegre Union of Neighbourhood Associations (UAMPA) is where the idea and impetus for community control over municipal finances can be first recognized (Avritzer, 2005: 386; Ganuza and Baiocchi, 2012: 3). Both Baiocchi and Abers stress that UAMPA later declined and was, in effect, replaced by PB. Rather than mobilize existing PT sympathizers, PB in Porto Alegre mobilized PT sympathy by providing for new groups (Wampler, 2007a: 125). We get a sense from these accounts that PB really was transforming how politics was done, and how the state interacted with citizens in the city. Baiocchi's comparison of districts within Porto Alegre's PB structure allows him to conclude that 'pre-existing civic networks were not found necessary to ensure the routinization of the process, and in fact, very strong associations proved a stumbling block', for example, in the Norte region (2005: 138). Nevertheless, urban associations still became the primary sources of information on matters to do with PB (Gret and Sintomer, 2005: 84). These discussions of Porto Alegre have orientated the investigations of interested observers of other PB successes and failures. Later comparativists have taken up and identified the history of organized combative civil society activism, for example, as pertinent to successes in their accounts (see, for example, Wampler, 2008).

A further important contribution to the successful appeal of the Porto Alegre case comes in the development of rules that encouraged participants to put themselves in others' shoes. Rules matter in shaping how and what we decide, and, as Smith and Wales succinctly put it, 'preferences are not exogenous to institutional setting' (2000: 52; see also Fung and Wright, 2003). In Porto Alegre the rules successfully balanced different logics. For example, the rules combined majoritarian democracy in voting for delegates, but with a rotation of offices. They offered prioritization according to expressed needs, but with distribution according to technical knowledge of measured need in weighing funding allocations. The rules also offered separation of roles and powers at various levels of decision-making – for example, separating those who set agendas from those who implement and monitor decisions (Gret and Sintomer, 2005: 44–52). The act of creating democratic rules for themselves can have a functional overspill that allows participants to take ownership of, and advance, even more innovative solutions to democratic dilemmas. Abers shows that in the districts that she observed, citizens eventually took ownership of developing rules themselves that fostered and institutionalized solidarity and democratic norm formation (2000: 179). The separation of rule-making from the application of those rules emulated some original liberal democratic practices that have, lamentably, been lost in modern legislatures, and Nuñez (2018) explains that it was the breakdown of these delicate balances that led to the demise of PB in Porto Alegre.

The appeal of institutional redesign in PB in Porto Alegre is not limited to those obsessed only with how a process might achieve a relatively narrow conception of deliberative empowerment of participants. For instance, Santos (2005) remarks on five different observable changes, including changes to bureaucratic organization; methods of distribution; representative accountability; autonomy of participatory institutions; and accommodating competing legitimacies of inclusion and representative expertise. Many observers have been attracted to PB in the first instance because it achieves distributional justice (more so than democracy per se). That aim was certainly embedded from the beginning in PT objectives and in the PB rules (Santos, 2005: 325). The relationship between democracy and equality of outcome is a complex one and (although I simplify) leftist sympathizers were traditionally associated with schools of thought that see the equal outcomes preceding democracy and not the other way around. While a detailed discussion of democracy and justice is beyond the scope of this book, the important point about PB in Porto Alegre is that although rules for yearly spending decisions obliged distribution towards poorer regions, these rules were formed and re-formed through public deliberation across various levels of PB (see Santos, 2005: 325–9; Abers, 2000: 180).

Nevertheless, there are important caveats that point to the need for further work on measurements and comparison of empirical observations. It is interesting that Marquetti et al (2012) report that during the period from 1990 to 2000 in Porto Alegre some measures show relative inequality rising, despite an improvement in absolute conditions of the poor (2012: 79). As they point out, it is likely that this is as a result of a number of external factors, but it puts the overall redistributive potential of strong local economic democracy in perspective. Deliberation in Porto Alegre was never ideal, and was accompanied by other forms of political arbitration (Baiocchi, 2005: 78). Individual participation itself took on some familiar patterns associated with rational-actor models of politics:

> ... often people who organised in the effort to resolve immediate needs demobilised once the needs were fulfilled. It took many years for the regional budget forums to initiate serious discussions of broader-based issues such as economic development and city planning, and only a small number of regional budget participants went on to join broader policymaking groups such as the thematic forums. (Abers, 2000: 221)

Although the prerogatives of deliberative theorists may be to narrow the conception of democracy to one that draws its legitimacy from ideal publicity and justification, for many, deliberation is a necessary but not sufficient condition for democracy (Pateman, 2012: 8). PB would never achieve all the necessary goods for ideal conceptions of democracy, or be transformational for all participants. Nevertheless, when compared to the inertia and clientelism all too pervasive in modern societies, it seems to provide some image of what the 'school of democracy' theorists (Pateman, Dewey, 2012) might have had in mind. It is not a 'rosy picture', but it is an improved alternative (see Smith, 2009; Ryan and Smith, 2014).

Before moving on from Porto Alegre, it is important to note that PB became more brittle after the PT lost control of the executive in 2004, and the new administration downgraded its priority and PB was suspended in 2017. There are many lessons in the second half of the Porto Alegre story. Although the persistence of any party in government for a decade or more in a democracy raises its own questions, the PT's defeat owed at least some of its explanation to a process that ignored the significant overhead costs incurred in the expansion of departments and infrastructure in the 1990s (Sintomer et al, 2016: 15). Suspension of the PB itself in 2017 came after significant loss of political will, economic centralization in Brazil following financial and political crises, and a consequent rising inability for the already diminished PB to deliver projects (Nuñez, 2018: 521). We must seek to explain what leads to the absence of deepened democracy as well as what creates it, and I turn to that question in the next chapter.

Nuñez provides some instructive recommendations for sustaining participatory practices based on elements of Porto Alegre's elaborate PB design that worked against itself in the long run. As he explains, there was no mechanism for dealing democratically with excessive unmet demands that built up over time. Financial transparency decreased because formal oversight was not effectively institutionalized in the good years (2018: 525–7). Moreover, he highlights two pathologies that have yet to be taken seriously enough by proponents and theorists of many democratic innovations in my experience – first, an under-appreciation for capacity-building, recognizing the differential needs of participants with different capacities, and second, a lack of mechanisms to avoid inevitable oligarchy in any long-term process. Both were relevant in the demise of neighbourhood meetings and removal of term limits for delegates in the process. There was a process of internal and incremental regulatory change that Nuñez characterizes as 'participatory democratic suicide' (2018: 530). I will come back to discuss these issues, and what can be done to avoid the capture of incrementalism, by identifying the combinations of conditions that are associated with the absence of deepened democracy, and ultimately, recommending their avoidance.

The book-length narratives to which I refer here provide a far greater description of events in this case than it would be right for me to reproduce. Both Santos (2005) and Smith (2009) provide clear and full explanations of the entire PB process in Porto Alegre. I could have included even more articles and essays on Porto Alegre, as some have laterally appeared as a result of translations, but a review of the literature would become saturated at this point. My aim is to get across a sense that trained, first-hand observers have done the hard work to communicate a story about how exceptional outcomes relevant to desires for a deepened democracy occurred in Porto Alegre around the turn of the 21st century. They did this by carefully identifying the conditions that appear non-trivial in relation to explaining those exceptional outcomes from those that appear irrelevant or trivial. Their work also provides a clear narrative for us to follow, explaining the quality or degrees of difference in these conditions with respect to accepted or previous norms.

At this point in the necessarily stylized story of the evolution of PB scholarship, all we have is one exceptional case. The worth of the case studies discussed in this chapter should not be valued solely for their potential contribution to developing more general theories or as a stepping-stone to large-N research. In and of themselves they are inherently valuable because they draw together coherent sets of observations that activate numerous relevant theories. Our attempts to move towards larger-N research over a more systematic range of variables or more circumscribed range of theories can only create a supplementary rather than a comparatively better form of knowledge. Secondary analysis introduces some sources of error while correcting others – a trade-off that seems to be better understood by small-N than large-N researchers, in my experience. We must inevitably move up the ladder of abstraction without stretching concepts (Sartori, 1970), and lose some of the detail and understanding of process that can only be garnered by direct observation and intensive treatment of a single case. Nevertheless 'each case is only a case, and it is difficult to build any theoretical generalizations from the individual cases' (Peters, 2013: 167). This is especially true when it is not made clear what the case is a case of – or at least, when the focus is primarily on how a case *departs* from a class of cases. In what follows I will discuss new ways of increasing the number of cases we can coherently engage with in one sitting, with the aim of harnessing rather than replacing case-based knowledge. Ethnographies can open doors for several research endeavours.

## How comparison follows from a single case

The foundation of scientific research is comparison. Scholarly work that appears superficially to be a study of a single case almost always involves systematic comparisons of elements within the case as well as implicit or explicit comparison with other known cases. Both Abers and Baiocchi have a comparative element to their study at the city-district level – Abers chose to focus her investigation in the Glória and Extremo do Sul district, with Baiocchi similarly comparing three districts. Both utilize a most-different case selection strategy comparing districts with varying degrees of clientelistic practices. Their selection of districts for comparison means that they can explain more systematically outcomes that depend on whether civil society was in a more positive or negative frame of health from the outset of PB. Also, as I have outlined, they chose to study PB in Porto Alegre in a context of useful background knowledge of other cases. Abers, for instance, suggests the failure of similar early efforts at PB in Brasília were probably down to the PT neglecting to make participation a central element of their political strategy – thus the beginnings of inductive musings on some general theories are evident here. Comparison is the method at the heart of both theory generation and testing the scope and proper application of theories. As John Stuart Mill more eloquently put it, 'as the general conception is itself obtained by a comparison of particular phenomena, so, when obtained, the mode in which we apply it to other phenomena is again by comparison' (1950: 298).

There is no getting away from the appearance of exceptionality that motivates and attracts interest in Porto Alegre. Baiocchi, at one point, describes it as 'the Mecca of the Left' (2005: 157). Its conditions are relatively extreme. Further, even if we can find similar cases in other cities nationally, many accounts are quick to emphasize the unique circumstances within Brazil. Authors highlight, for instance, an extraordinarily patrimonial political culture where votes are exchanged for the most basic of material promises; the effect of rapid urbanization as unprecedented swathes of rural poor moved to cities, leading to large unplanned settlements (favelas); and a new set of political institutions and opportunities in the wake of the democratic transition with the opening up of the political opportunity structure following the demise of the military regime (see Santos, 2005: 208–9; Abers, 2000: 26–8; Pont, 2004: 115; Gret and Sintomer, 2005: 14–15). In many ways Porto Alegre is an archetype for subsequent cases of democratic innovation within and without Brazil, and we will have more to say about the methodological implications for comparison.

Nevertheless, perceived exceptionalism is as good a reason as any around which to organize comparison. The rich descriptions of exceptionalism earlier in the chapter have often led to arguments that other cases cannot 'meaningfully' be compared with cases like Porto Alegre or cases in Brazil because conditions are extreme. Many will be used to the scholarly caution of comparing apples with oranges or pears or with other sorts of fruit. Yet too often nowadays the caution is erroneously seen as a justification for not comparing things that do not appear relatively similar. The caution actually exists to ensure the comparativist is sensitive to issues of conceptualization and measurement when they compare and make inference, but the comparison itself is necessary to understand the issues. We need to regularly compare apples with apples, pears, oranges, parliaments, and all sorts, so we know what's what. The important point is that 'if the study is conducted outside a comparative framework, it is easy for the researcher to make a number of assumptions about the exceptionalism of the case' (Peters, 2013: 4). Without a relatively comprehensive comparative framework the exceptionalism and its degree in Porto Alegre is more assumed than analysed and understood. Too often 'comparability' is used as an excuse. It is used either to justify asking inanely boring research questions to cover many similar observations while offering careful controls but results of no practical use, or for avoiding any increase in observations and consoling oneself with the comfort of assumption. Systematic cumulation of existing studies, even where different kinds of data extraction have been employed, despite imperfections, is preferable (or at least a necessary complement) to other kinds of research strategies.

The news of the Porto Alegre case certainly inspired others to think about how it related to alternative institutional innovations, knowledge of which, as we saw, began to spread. Notable among them were those interested in real-world applications of democratic theory, for example, Fung (2003), Fung and Wright (2003) and Smith (2009). Their work looks at very innovative, but very different, institutional designs, and they draw parallels across different democratic institutions, showing that there are multiple practical ways to realize the democratic goods heralded by abstract theories. The cases that Fung and Smith discuss in their work tend to be of this variety – ground-breaking innovations in participatory institution-building that embody diverse theoretical principles of democracy. Theirs is effectively a most-different systems design following closely the logic of Mill's method of agreement. Using the initial organizing principle of divergence from a less democratic norm as a common outcome, they select several different cases that achieve novel democratic deepening and try and draw some similarities across the cases while documenting many differences.

That work is essential reading and foundational to the subfield that has emerged to study PDIs, but is not without its problems. If the first cases brought to attention are all those with exceptional outcomes, we might expect that a typical case should not be so exceptional. If we are too focused on exceptionalism, we cannot be sure of what the typical case looks like and how it differs from our exceptional ones. We would expect that, much like in Galton's original understanding of the statistical problem, the child of the exceptional parent (say, the Porto Alegre archetype) would regress towards the mean. As Spada and Ryan point out,

> … the problem here is that we don't have a good sense of a population and we don't know what the mean might look like. If we took a sample of participatory processes over time, we would probably expect that the results in Porto Alegre were atypical. (Spada and Ryan, 2017: 774)

> … without sampling carefully to uncover evidence for causality we do not know that the factors identified as crucial to explaining the cases' successes in these early accounts, if removed, would be recognised to some extent as artefacts of the order in which they were encountered …. This does not take away from … pioneering work but it warns us to continue down the road of research cumulation before getting too excited. (Ryan, 2019: 562)

Perhaps more quickly than analysts could publish their (mostly positive) reviews of Porto Alegre's experiences, PB was diffusing and being taken up by other governments at an encouraging rate. This was thanks in no small part to committed activists in various fora and networks (Porto de Oliveira, 2017). Their efforts were boosted by Porto Alegre's relationship with the World Social Forum, and in another way by endorsements from the World Bank and the UN (Goldfrank, 2012). Many writers speak of waves of diffusion as PB spread first across Brazil, then Latin America, later to Europe and North America and further east, even to non-democracies (Cabannes, 2004; Sintomer et al, 2013). Developments then saw an increasing uptake in the US. PB diffusion is often characterized by adaptation of the model to local conditions, with individual actors playing a strong influential role. One of Röcke's unique contributions to the literature is to show the multi-level character of PB diffusion through different channels and actors who then adapt PB to both local conditions and national 'frames' of political participation in implementation (2014). This is food for thought for those interested in scoping a population of worldwide participatory budgets for comparison and generalizations. There have been notable attempts to track, index or generalize the 'who, what, why, and where' of diffusion of PB around the world (see, variously, Cabannes, 2004; Sintomer et al, 2005, 2008, 2010, 2012, 2013, 2016; Shah, 2007; Herzberg, 2011; Goldfrank, 2012; Dias, 2014, 2018; Röcke, 2014; Baiocchi and Ganuza, 2016; Porto de Oliveira, 2017; Cabannes and Lipietz, 2018). Building on that work, the primary aim of this book is to establish what effects important differences in implementation and context have had on the empowerment of citizens, and what causal inference we can engage in using advanced tools for logical induction and deduction.

Despite some heated debate (and dogma), I think it is safe to say that social scientists are made aware in the course of their training of some of the limitations in drawing general conclusions from a single case study. More interestingly, I think, social scientists should also be sensitive to the availability bias 'which anchors their understanding of what kinds of cases are possible to what kinds of cases they are aware of at any point in time' (Ryan, 2019: 562). Our perceptions are bound and shaped by the order in which information is received (for example, which cases we hear of first and then later), and there is a collective path dependency if a single case is held to be archetypal. Despite all best intentions and training in scientific methods, there are many mixed incentives that can guide case selection:

> Scholarly reputations are made by claiming a case is unique or at least unusual, and that makes cumulation difficult. Claims of uniqueness, however, are sometimes overstated, and if cases are examined together then there is the capacity to create some generalisations out of apparently disparate cases … even with all the potential problems, cumulation of case materials is preferable to no cumulation …. (Peters, 2013: 170)

The key lesson of science is that the information that reaches you in your life is biased, and the scholarly mission is to reduce that bias through a set of techniques and protocols. In social science it can be argued that we need more vigilance, and a wider complement of perspectives, knowledge and techniques because the truth (if there is *one*) is more difficult to ascertain as experimental conditions are rare or impossible. As Keith Dowding puts it, 'Social science is not rocket science. It's much harder than that' (2016: 249). As PB moved beyond the Porto Alegre 'exception', how have PB scholars dealt with this mission up to now?

3

# From Exceptions to Cases of a Participatory Budgeting Phenomenon

In the development of our understanding of PB as a successful democratic innovation, first steps towards examining multiple cases came in the form of early comparisons of carefully selected cases of PB. While studies of individual cases in Brazil and beyond continue to dominate the literature, cross-case comparative analysis began to contribute to our knowledge. Valuable work now led by Paolo Spada (2017), building on initial data collections from Ana Clara Torres Ribeiro and Grazia de Grazia (2003), and Leonardo Avritzer and Brian Wampler (2005), has collected a census of PB in Brazil. Data begins in 1989, with a new wave of data collection in swing as I write. It shows that if survival of PB is a good indicator of its success, then the data is sobering – on average half the processes are discontinued within four years of inception (Spada and Ryan, 2017: 772). But that is getting ahead of the story. PB has now accumulated several good in-depth small-N case comparisons.

William Nylen (2003b) was early to identify the need for research to attend to 'failed' cases. He provides an in-depth account and compares two cases in the state of Minas Gerais – Betim and João Monlevade – where the PT was voted out of office following a clear opposition mandate to remove all traces of such participatory programmes (2003b: 96). Nylen contrasts the overt mobilization of *petistas* (affiliates or supporters of PT) at the expense of working with existing neighbourhood associations in João Monlevade's first short-lived PT administration, with subsequent conscious efforts to avoid partisan mobilization in Betim's PB.

Although the PT survived an extra term in Betim, the result – an end to PT rule and to participatory programmes in the face of fierce political competition – was not averted. In both cases Nylen reports that a strong and sometimes violent opposition were able to recast PB as partisan and inefficient regardless of the PT's efforts. Despite the variance in effort, the result was the same. Based on Mill's principle of agreement we can discard these active efforts to avoid partisanship by a ruling party instigating PB as a sufficient condition for enduring change. An all too often ignored strength of these simple comparative techniques in the empirical social sciences is the potential to discount factors that might be theorized to be relevant to an explanation. The PT in Betim may have thought they were learning lessons from João Monlevade, but a less partisan approach to PB when implemented in a relatively similar context was not enough to help them. The question of how to develop open participation in the face of entrenched partisanship crops up again and again in reviewing the cases of PB, and it is one for which there appears to be no simple answer.

The selection of these cases also exploits the logic of the method of difference, in that these are 'failed' cases where the bequest of deepened democratic consciousness that evolved in Porto Alegre was not observed. Extreme forms of clientelism returned.[1] So Nylen also goes some way to providing cumulative evidence for what quality of a potentially important explanatory variable is required for empowered democracy. Regardless of how it is achieved, successful non-partisan mobilization would appear to be a necessary condition for PB flourishing and deeper democratization on the evidence of these three cases. We can combine Nylen's finding with evidence of weak opposition highlighted in the description that Benjamin Goldfrank gives of PB's inception in Porto Alegre (now cumulating knowledge from diverse case studies) to hypothesize that the weak opposition is the context that enables non-partisan mobilization. Thus, we might surmise that when weak opposition is combined with a PT-initiated PB programme, partisan PB that is susceptible to a lack of buy-in from those outside the PT is avoided.

Yet we might know that PB still had good outcomes in the face of strong opposition in some cases – Goldfrank offers the example of the Limatambo district in the Cusco region of the Peruvian Andes (2011: 259–60). On the evidence of all these cases taken together, a weak opposition is an INUS condition (that is an Insufficient

1 Later work by Baiocchi et al (2011) suggests João Monlevade did achieve a more empowered democracy, but only after the PT returned in 1997.

but Necessary part of a combination of conditions which is itself Unnecessary but Sufficient) (see Mackie, 1988 : 62), for deepened participatory democracy. We are cumulating and developing cross-case insights, but they are adding up to a mouthful! This is a small insight into the logical thinking of case-based comparative methods. But it is usually too difficult to transfer these comparisons beyond a small number of cases as it becomes too difficult to consider all potential combinations of causal factors in one researcher's head. QCA offers some tools to overcome that problem, as I will show in the chapters that follow.

## How variance in design as well as context explains outcomes – comparison within Brazil

Several contributors have offered comparisons that show that explanatory conditions for empowered democracy in PB are rarely a matter of black and white. As with Nylen, Marcelo K. Silva (2003) compares two Brazilian cases – this time on the outskirts of Porto Alegre in the state of Rio Grande do Sul – Alvorada and Gravataí. His focus is on the effect of PB on civil society and his key question is whether a policy innovation from a nearby metropolis works in a similar way in cities with different 'associative environments' (2003: 114). He describes a complex patchwork of both positive and negative and changing relationships between associations and PB in both cases, with engagement from different groups ebbing and flowing. Despite dense networks of neighbourhood associations, those were often characterized by clientelist politics and internal disputes. The support for popular participation characterized by some accounts of the CSOs in Porto Alegre was absent or opposed to a certain degree in some of the CSOs in these cases. Silva provides the salutary lesson that we should not assume that CSOs will necessarily see themselves as carriers of radical democratic norms. The important contribution here is to illustrate that the character of civil society in a municipality cannot easily be dichotomized as supportive or unsupportive of participation in an absolute sense. CSO support for participation is not indeterminate, but it ranges in value where organizations can be both supportive and not supportive to various degrees. That is, cases of PB have fuzzy membership in the set of civil society support for participation.

Another excellent contributor to the development of comparative analysis of democratic innovation is Leonardo Avritzer (2005). Avritzer has described PB in Porto Alegre in conjunction with the process in

Belo Horizonte. He can show that PB rules can be effectively adapted to new settings, and 'invention' is often conditioned by pre-existing arrangements and cultures of participation and politics (2005: 391). Then, by contrasting trends using individual-level data for the number of participants in Porto Alegre and Belo Horizonte, he expands our understanding of incentives for participation by observing citizen behaviour in response to change. When a new administration was elected in the Belo Horizonte case, participation waned, before waxing again the following year when it had been demonstrated that this new administration was still committed to implementing PB.

Avritzer's work also leads the way in comparing different designs. In earlier work (2002) he compares two participatory publics: PB in Porto Alegre with another participatory innovation in Mexico. This is one of many examples of comparisons across types of democratic innovation. While I focus in this book on comparing PB, my comparison can be seen as a test case for comparisons of greater number of cases within and across types of democratic innovation, and I return to the implications for doing so. In a later work as part of a wider comparison of participatory institutions including health councils and participatory planning (2009), Avritzer compares three participatory budgets – adding the case of São Paulo to Porto Alegre and Belo Horizonte. Of interest here for scholars of democratic innovations is a critique of what he calls Fung and Wright's 'static model' of institutional design for deepening participatory democracy (2009: 63–4). Avritzer points out the methodological disadvantages in early research that considered only the most successful cases. The lack of failed cases is often a function of the stage of phenomenological development where the understanding of what a case is a case of, and hence what constitutes an exceptional or average case, is not self-evident to a scattered, nascent research community. Avritzer does not choose exceptional or failed cases, however, but cases whose redistributive and deliberative outcomes are successful to a matter of degree. He shows that redistributive and deliberative successes in Sao Paulo, an 'almost unsuccessful case' (2009: 115), were tempered by a context in which the potential for a powerful opposing coalition to form was greater than in the other cases, leading the administration to provide alternative avenues for public politics that weakened PB (2009: 113). Where PB has become successful it has often become *the* venue for inclusive democratic policymaking above other competing mechanisms.

Avritzer's critique also rounds on cultural factors. What Fung and Wright overlook is 'the presence of other variables, such as clientelism or party interest. Those more specific variables may hinder local participation, even when broad enabling conditions are present' (2009: 63). His warning that cultural variance means that participatory design cannot be a drag-and-drop solution is a sage one. We should expect results to vary with similar designs and democratic deepening to be achieved with different ones. I will also argue in the penultimate section of this chapter that attention to the importance of cultural idiosyncrasies in causal explanation can be as dangerous as it is advantageous.

Avritzer highlights a more fundamental aspect of comparative logic often overlooked by some preferred methods in social science: the relative presence or absence of a single condition in any logically possible conjunction of design and context can fundamentally alter the effect of all other variables on an outcome. His comparison leads him to strongly avow that it is dynamic 'interaction between civil and political society' (2009: 64), where voluntary associations develop participatory mechanisms *and* political actors choose to embed participation in their way of governing that clearly explains successful participatory design. In other words, as is almost always the case in social science, explanations have identifiable but key contingencies, and causation is conjunctural.

Each possible combination of presence or absence of relevant causal conditions – participatory leadership, strength of civil society, relative wealth etc – represents a logicallly unique combination of conditions. Any number of substantive empirical cases may display the same values of presence or absence of conditions at some level of abstraction. For example, we may find Belo Horizonte and Porto Alegre have similar levels of all variables of interest – participatory leadership, strength of civil society, and so on. Also, in social scientific inquiries there are almost always logically possible combinations of conditions for which we have no empirical examples. These are sometimes known as logical remainders, or, more often, counterfactuals. They indicate what we do not know but may need to find out about, or at least make transparent our assumptions about what we think would happen were such conditions to combine. Our agenda as researchers is to iteratively theorize and study the world to fill in these gaps. The comparisons of two or three cases I discussed develop the literature and make important discoveries about what works in PB, hinting at the relevance and irrelevance of potential causal factors. Still, we cannot rely on unconnected small-N comparative designs alone to develop better theories. It is very difficult, if not impossible, for even well-designed comparisons of two to three cases to allow enough variation across key factors. This is even more obvious if we accept that the degree of presence of one causal factor may alter the effect of another. So, small-N comparisons should also be cumulated where possible.

## More cases, larger-N comparisons

A significant and welcome recent development has seen large-N comparisons of cases of Brazilian PB. Avritzer and Wampler (2005) use descriptive statistics to illustrate the diffusion of PB through Brazil, paying attention to the ideological hue of parties, relative wealth and development, and the size and location of municipalities adopting programmes. They show that there was a general trend to PB adoption by governments further to the ideological right and in less wealthy municipalities over time. They also provide some figures for the number of CSOs across cities implementing PB in the state of Minas Gerais.

In Brazil also, Touchton and Wampler compare larger municipalities where PB was adopted with those where it was not. They find associations between PB adoption and increases in municipal healthcare and sanitation spending, with estimated effects becoming greater over time (2014: 1456). They also find evidence that adopting PB increases the number of CSOs and reduces infant mortality. They provide a nice comparison to try to separate the effects of PT control of the executive from those of PB adoption. While greatest estimated gains are seen in municipalities where PT governments adopted PB, they show that in two out of three cases (healthcare spending and infant mortality) estimates are more attractive for non-PT-led cases of PB than in PT-led municipalities where PB was not adopted. This finding is important because it provides evidence that successful outcomes of governance change associated with PB are not entirely party dependant. Sónia Gonçalves' parallel investigation allows for general corroboration of the findings on living standards between the two studies. Her analysis finds that spending on healthcare and sanitation has an increased effect on reductions in infant and child mortality where PB is adopted, independent of political party and state (2014: 104).

Spada uses sophisticated econometric modelling techniques to compare the effect of introducing PB on city finances and separately on the re-election of the incumbent political party to the mayoral administration (2010). He is one of the first to give a good indication of the effect of implementing PB over time and whether there are lags in its effects. He can show that there is no clear evidence for claims for an improvement in municipal finances in the medium to long term across Brazilian municipalities adopting PB. His second model is equally salutary in that it reorients us towards the realpolitik and potential gains at play for parties adopting and discontinuing participatory policies. There is a general trend towards short-term gains for both these actions (with some differences based on size of municipality and ideological hue of party). His work was another serious advancement and perhaps representative of a wave of research that came after the initial positive evaluations to show more mixed outcomes from PB.

Large-N variable-oriented analysis of PB is still relatively nascent in Brazil and elsewhere. I should also clarify that I am principally concerned here with studies where the unit of analysis is the political community in which PB takes place. There are good examples of PB surveys that analyse individual PB participants sometimes across cases (see Wampler and Avritzer, 2004; Ganuza and Francés, 2012), but my analytical focus is not at the individual level. The findings of individual-level surveys can contribute to higher-level comparison by helping to provide evidence to aid measurement of higher-level conditions.

The advantage of large-N analysis is that it allows us, by way of some abstraction in stepping back from the complexity of the case, to ascertain which claims have more general application. Greater accumulation of findings can force us to go back to the cases and think again about which elements of explanations might be more or less relevant in the light of information provided by other cases. For example, reports based on observations of early cases excitedly hypothesized that both electoral and financial reward would accrue for municipalities with PB programmes. Large-N analysis showed a lack of clear evidence for a significant relationship between PB and electoral and financial gain, or that the effect was at best short-lived (Spada, 2010). Nevertheless large-N analysis cannot be a substitute for accounts that establish how combinations of factors manifest within cases and therefore what kinds of abstractions are reasonable. Perhaps the effect of electoral and financial gains is rare but is sustained in specific types of cases, and we can explain the confusion that way. Later reflections on generalizations that jumped the gun may allow those with knowledge of the cases to clarify, for instance, that tax reform and recoupment was an aid to, rather than an outcome of, early PB successes (Baiocchi and Ganuza, 2016; Ganuza and Baiocchi, 2019).

## What prospects for a middle way?

Brian Wampler's comparison of eight participatory budgets in Brazil was the first to show the significant possibilities for moving beyond two or three cases while retaining the virtues of holistic case-based complexity in explanations (2007a). He provides a detailed narrative of processes within cases, but also systematically selects cases to help in understanding what conditions are necessary and sufficient for a high quality of citizen-led decision-making across cases. Wampler's comparative design again moves beyond best-case examples to include variations in outcome and explanatory conditions. He looks at different design features and capacities and incentives for those who wield power in government and contest power in civil society. In his chapters describing each case, he highlights CSO activity, mayoral support, mayor–legislative relations, the financial basis for implementation of the programme and the 'rules of the game' as influential in determining the depth of democracy coming out of PB processes. In analysing effects, he awards priority to the influence of CSO activity, mayoral support and the rules of the game. He concludes that 'to produce a strong PB programme, it is necessary to have high levels of mayoral support, a civil society that can engage in both cooperation and contestation, and rules that delegate specific types of direct authority to citizens' (2007a: 35).

In a more simplified account towards the end of that book he places emphasis on two explanatory conditions and suggests that mayoral support interacts with CSOs' willingness to use contentious politics to give four very different types of outcomes across which his cases are split. Where there are high qualities of both mayoral support and civil society capacities, as in Porto Alegre and Ipatinga, participatory democracy is institutionalized, whereas when both are absent, participation is emasculated, as in Rio Claro and Blumenau (2007a: 258). Other cases with relatively mixed civil society support differed in type by their mayoral support. In short, Wampler searches for an appropriate parsimony, while taking the likely complexity of causality seriously, and provides the reader with transparency in outlining those decisions. In the following chapters I accumulate research to see if these conclusions hold when we include a wider range of cases in the sample, and outline again transparently the interpretive decisions necessary in doing so. I also show how measurement and coding decisions affect conclusions.

A further sophisticated approach to medium-N comparison comes from Baiocchi, Heller and Silva (2011). They recognize from the outset that the case for participatory democracy, despite much spilt ink, still rests on 'rather fragmented and thin empirical grounds' (2011: 1). While the study design again relies on some rich and demonstrably well-executed fieldwork, the case selection logic applied also adds merit to the study. The researchers apply a matched-pair approach to the selection of cases to increase relevant control and isolate conditions of interest. Their outcome of interest is centred on the changes in civil society and its interactions with the state where PB is implemented. Most comparisons discussed up to now have focused on a population of cases where a participatory innovation has already been introduced, basing the case selection decision on variation in outcomes and key causal conditions. Baiocchi et al's design allows them to also ascertain the differences between cases where PB is introduced and similar cases where it was not, controlling for scale, geography and civil society support for the PT.

Baiocchi et al are also able to give us some insight into the variation in democratic mobilization of civil society across their four cases where PB is implemented, renewing discussion of a common theme that variation in the capacity of civil society to act autonomously and contentiously results in different forms of participatory democracies. They find co-optation is more a danger where weak civil society can be observed in combination with an organized top-down process, but also that different kinds of participatory democracy can emerge depending on how governments choose to mobilize or bypass CSOs. These findings bring some nuance to those mentioned earlier. A weak or strong civil society may contribute towards a good outcome or its negation depending on the degree to which other key explanatory conditions (top-down support) are present and how they interact. This multifinality – where the same conditions in a different context can lead to an opposing outcome – is a common occurrence in our simplified theories about the social world. It is one commonly overlooked by some social scientists.

## Participatory budgeting and participatory budgeting research move outside Brazil

PB has diffused well beyond Brazil, across Latin America and then to Europe and beyond, roughly in that order. This turns our attention to the question of whether the innovation is indeed one that can be adopted successfully in cross-national contexts. One of the strengths of the comparative studies discussed so far is that they compare only Brazilian cases. Comparative politics was built on the assumption that states vary in numerous important respects. Using the logic of area studies, the authors mentioned previously control for the idiosyncrasies of national culture, political history and institutions of government, ensuring those factors are not determining different outcomes across cases.

One of the first things that those who engage with empirical work beyond Brazil will find is that assumptions about Porto Alegre's exceptionalism can be challenged, if not dispelled. Although differences in scale may be a point of enduring argument, similar conditions and outcomes to those in Porto Alegre are found elsewhere (Goldfrank, 2011: 260). Stephanie McNulty's comparison of six Peruvian regions, like Wampler's in Brazil, provides an impressively clear and transparent account based on extensive data collection, and utilizes case selection effectively to make logical inferences (2011). As we might expect, there are historical and cultural differences, as well as variation in state institutions, that have meant that the PB McNulty studies look different to many in Brazil. Despite examples of earlier district-level PB taking place in Peru through the 1990s, she focuses on the period following the initial democratization after the removal of Alberto Fujimori as president. Of interest here is the constitutional reform and General Decentralization Law of 2002 that mandated two participatory institutions be convened at the regional level, one of them PB. This is the first national PB law – although other countries have followed, including the Dominican Republic, Kenya, Indonesia and South Korea (McNulty, 2018: 147) – and in some of those cases guidelines, support, and therefore implementation, varies considerably (see Songmin, 2013; No, 2018). As McNulty explains, unlike the municipal PB more common elsewhere, her cases are regional-level PB covering larger territories in Peru that are quite often difficult for some participants to traverse. Participation is also organized through registered CSOs or 'participating agents' – and the degree to which more loosely organized groups were able to register seems to have had significant explanatory power in determining whether participatory democracy flourished.

McNulty's case selection provides some controls for established geographic differences across Peru. Despite cultural differences, her findings support evidence from previous studies in this alternate context. She shows that 'supportive regional leadership is a necessary factor' (2011: 132) for successful participatory institutions. In these systems, top-level political support appears crucial, and 'no case suggests that the support of lower-level officials can overcome the lack of support by a regional president' (2011: 134). She finds evidence that united and vibrant civil societies in the aftermath, but not necessarily in advance of the reform, led to successes. She also finds that the support of non-elected officials has explanatory power (2011: 133). This last factor is important, because it is often underplayed in theories of democratic deepening.

Staying in Peru, Jaramillo and Wright (2015) have contributed to the large-N studies that emerged in the mid-2010s aimed at associating PB with policy effects. They hypothesize that traditional voluntary participatory fora common in Peru, such as the *Mesas de Concertación*, may be better able to produce effective policies than the mandated PB. Their hypothesis is based on observations that the voluntary fora (which tend to be made up of elite interested stakeholders) often have greater access to technical advice through strategic interactions. Their two-wave survey of Peruvian mayors and follow-up interviews in five case studies provides evidence that participatory mechanisms are associated with increased provisions of agricultural services by municipal governments, but that voluntary fora are associated with effective agricultural policies while PB is associated with less effective policies. Their evidence seems to corroborate some of what we have seen in Brazil. They reinforce what is really an age-old lesson in political science – when politicians devolve authority without also providing for the same capabilities and support they themselves would expect when making policy, they are devolving problems and not power.

Before turning to cross-country comparisons, it is worth highlighting that systematic case-oriented comparison of PB within countries is still relatively rare outside Brazil. Along with McNulty's work, Matteo Bassoli's three-case comparison of PB governance in Italy has provided an interesting subnational comparison (2012). Bassoli takes seriously questions around the definition of PB, which I will return to in discussions of operationalization and selection of explanatory conditions for cumulation (see Chapter 4). His focus is considering PB as a type of local governance arrangement. Among European countries Italy has seen some significant diffusion of PB and some of them have had radical ambitions. However, Bassoli provides a fresh note of caution against biases that would restrict PB to an epiphenomenon of a theoretical tradition, and sees it fitting with many existing theories of local governance arrangements (2012: 1185). To understand whether PB is of any worth, we need to keep in mind comparisons with other similar and different modes of innovation and of democratic governance. Within a most-different selection of consolidated Italian cases (based on varying geography, population and the role of the global justice movement in the case), Bassoli shows that democratic outcomes, both good and bad, were generally similar across the cases. This, again, provides evidence for reducing the explanatory importance of geography in our theories. One interesting observation is that in all three cases a clear role for the political opposition within PB was not excessively supported by either the government or opposition, leading to familiar problems for PB itself.

Gaining early cross-partisan support for PB seems to have long-term benefits. Hollie Russon Gilman provides insights into the starting years of the earliest adopted processes in the US. Gilman's study includes casework in the first US case in Chicago's 49th ward, it's largest case focusing on several New York City (NYC) districts, and a case of youth-focused PB in Boston. Placing these cases side by side, she shows how necessarily different designs targeting different communities have different effects. She shows how some of the democratizing rules applied in Porto Alegre were forgone in Chicago's 49th ward during implementation, often to reflect pragmatic concerns (2016: 40–1). In this PB model budget delegates volunteered but were not elected. On the one hand, this may mean that participants can get involved as much or as little as they like, but it can also produce perceptions of patronage where long-term active 'usual suspects' do not have democratic accountability. Tensions between active members on the organizing committee and other participants developed in Chicago revealing familiar pathologies of small-scale politics (Ryan et al, 2018). Gilman shows that NYC's greater size allowed for greater devolution in roles from the steering committees and also received bipartisan support, giving less scope for perceptions of patronage. Her comparison of districts within NYC also shows differences in bureaucratic buy-in to processes and how conscious choices of organizers affect which communities are mobilized, chiming with her finding that young people had different motivations for attending PB in Boston (2016: 114). She draws a useful theoretical distinction from her empirical work between participants who are motivated by material rewards and those motivated by 'civic rewards' – the feeling of being part of a democratic process.

Larger-N comparisons outside Brazil have also made contributions to general understandings of PB and the life of democratic innovations. In Portugal, Alves and Allegretti (2012) have been among the first to analyse the death and sometimes resurrection of PB in a country that now boasts the largest proportion of voluntary uptake of PB among municipalities (Dias et al, 2018: 259). Later I make the case that considered attention to the bounds of counterfactual analysis, that is, asking what a good representation of a comparator case of 'non-PB' looks like, is one we should not lose sight of. Alves and Allegretti draw a useful distinction between abandonment and 'downgrading' of PB – where, for example, the jurisdiction or resources of the participatory budget shrink but it lives on in a less vibrant form. They offer a novel conceptual categorization and some descriptive statistics covering the 64 cases implemented in Portugal from 2002 to 2012. They report a general trend away from consultation to co-decision models in the surviving participatory budgets. Their modest inductive hypothesis is that a more empowered PB that can spend reasonable sums to make changes that matter to citizens is more likely to survive. Lack of staff capacity was also offered as an explanation for disbanding PB in some instances (2012: 13).

Much early work on PB in the English language had roots in Latin American area studies, often motivated by a concern for democratic governance in Latin America. As outlined in Chapter 1, democratic deficits are a concern throughout the 'democratic' world (Pateman, 2012; Stoker, 2017). In what Allegretti and Herzberg (2004) call a 'return of the caravels', PB was introduced from the 'new' world back to the 'old' one. That phenomenon also attracted me to studying democratic innovations. Many still find it hard to accept that radically democratic practices can often live cheek by jowl with radically clientelist ones as countries differently experience the enduring contest between democratic advancement and backsliding.[2] In my conversations with colleagues across the world, I am often struck by how even alleged experts (myself included) make erroneous assumptions based on heuristics about political cultures that they allege are 'uniquely' clientelist or plagued by democratic deficits, when the difference is often far from clear, or at best, a matter of degree. It has motivated my interest in pursuing wider cross-country comparisons despite, or perhaps because of, the warnings that it is a risky endeavour.

## Comparing participatory budgeting across cultures

Leonardo Avritzer provides a convincing argument that we ought to be very wary of assumptions that common patterns identified in designs of successful cases should lead to those designs being dragged and dropped without adaptation into other political cultures where broad enabling conditions appear (2009: 63). He shows that even within countries, different cities may benefit from different kinds of

[2] The error in logic is perhaps well encapsulated in an example from UK politics. In 2013, when Raquel Rolnik, UN special investigator on housing, as part of a wide-ranging report, criticized a particularly controversial measure to reduce Housing Benefit in the UK (also known as the 'Bedroom Tax'), a government minister and then chair of the Conservative Party, Grant Shapps, questioned why the UK government should listen to "a woman from Brazil" on the basis that Brazil had a large number of citizens in inadequate housing. I have found this a useful example for teaching students about comparative politics.

participatory institutions depending on their existing political cultures. Local knowledge for adaptation of successful designs can be key. Nevertheless, over-reliance on that truism can be dangerous if it leads us to think that PB in one context is 'incomparable' with PB in another, as if such a comparison was a fool's errand. Anything can be compared (Ryan, 2016, 2019). Of course, what scholars often mean when they invoke incomparability is that we should not make assumptions that just because something is called PB in one place or claims some effect that it should be considered to have equal effect to the same claim made elsewhere. But to understand veracity of claims and differences in effects we need to go ahead with the comparison, and systematically interrogate and document those differences rather than assume them. Although within-country or within-area work provides advantages in terms of control, these controls can be relied on too much as a logic for excluding cross-country comparisons. Comparison of wildly differing phenomena can be equally instructive (Boswell and Corbett, 2017), and assumptions about what a case is really a case of will often change in the performing of research (Flyvbjerg, 2006).

Yves Sintomer has worked with an amalgam of colleagues over the years to move in the direction of worldwide comparison and categorization of the PB landscape. This is an important body of work. Subnational comparisons and comparative designs that are drawn from an area studies background in Latin America and Europe have a sound methodological basis, but they need to be complemented by cumulative cross-regional findings for an even more ecumenical understanding of PB and participatory democracy. How else can we know and discuss the proper levels to which we can generalize? Carole Pateman considers that given the empirical evidence, 'the problem is no longer whether participatory democracy is feasible', and leaves us with the question as to whether 'in the rich countries, there is any longer either the political culture or the political will to pursue genuine democratization?' (2012: 15). Reflecting on an amalgam of empirical work covering roughly 20 cases in Europe, Sintomer et al do surmise that PB in Europe has 'little in common with the Porto Alegre model' (2015: 165). However, they also suggest some European cases achieve important degrees of improvement in citizen control of democratic decisions. I think Pateman is too quick to draw a line between the desired 'genuine democratization' as it might manifest itself in the so-called advanced economies and elsewhere. Perhaps conditions for participatory democracy may need to be different in these contexts. Only through comparison can we answer those questions.

Much like some of the work already outlined, Sintomer et al focus on delivering an overview and providing some organizing principles for understanding PB. PB may be a quickly diffusing 'moving target' (Baiocchi et al, 2011: 60), but this kind of work helps us to think about what PB is and what it is not, what the conceptual scope of PB is and what the potential for comparison within that scope might be. One of many interesting analytical contributions of their work so far has been to provide a typology of PB using the logic of Weberian ideal types (see Herzberg, 2011, for a detailed discussion). These are based on differences in design and culture, often on the origins of adoption of the innovation, that lead to differing conditions of deliberation and the role of civil society in PB. These theoretical typologies can offer useful visual aids to help understand what is at stake in PB design (see, for example, Sintomer et al, 2016: 47). Cabannes and Lipietz (2018) provide a similarly useful typological theory focusing on aims of PB. They ask who PB engages, what it engages them about, and which governance logic it applies – whether more radical or technocratic, for example. These approaches are based on inductive category development by scholars who have done impressive work since the early days of PB to keep track of cases as they arise. At points Sintomer et al suggest that there is still too much contrast for systematic comparison and analysis of many different PB types, and they eschew an empirical typology (2013: 11, 20; 2016: 45). Later they call for 'an additional effort in terms of systematic analyses and concept building' to overcome 'flaws in previous assessments and a lack of systematic cross-cutting criteria that would enable those involved to make clear choices in accordance with their margins for manoeuvre' (2016: 164). I will subsequently show that careful analysis of the properties of PB and comparisons that aim for a fully specified typological theory, even if they cannot reach it, can significantly aid judgement and understanding.

There were, indeed, many early attempts to take stock of the diffusion of PB across Latin America and then further afield, first to Europe and then beyond (Allegretti and Herzberg, 2004; Cabannes, 2004; Sintomer et al, 2005; Shah, 2007). While often providing more 'descriptive panorama' (Röcke, 2014: 8) than systematic comparative focus, these works both describe a larger number of cases than before and try and give a first sense of what is at stake in comparing emerging cases across countries with vastly varying political and cultural histories. They draw together many threads of investigation of participatory budgets, and usefully set the parameters for the kinds of questions we might want to ask in a more systematic way, to understand the effects of different combinations of conditions. They give us a sense of the rich complexity of the social and political contexts of PB experiments. These have been followed by informative volumes involving ever more scholars and practitioners, countries and cases as PB has diffused (Sintomer et al, 2013, 2016; Dias, 2014, 2018). The most impressive recent contributions are those organized by Nelson Dias and his collaborators. These provide a comprehensive hive mind of global knowledge and experiences of PB, and show that the field is blessed with symbiotic relationships among activists, scholars, critics and do-ers, many of them comfortable in any of those roles. They contain a whistle-stop tour of case studies or overviews of countries or regions from area experts. They are now collecting data for an annual atlas project to map diffusion (Dias et al, 2019). In combining this kind of data with crowdsourcing projects such as Participedia (see participedia.net) (Gastil et al, 2017), there are exciting possibilities for larger-N cross-national analyses emerging. But what of systematic cross-country comparison that explicitly employs case comparison logic for (often modest) inference?

Benjamin Goldfrank has done more than many to advance the cause of cumulating comparative knowledge of PB. In *Deepening Local Democracy in Latin America* he compares budget participation in three cities in different countries: Porto Alegre, Brazil; Montevideo, Uruguay; and the Libertador municipality of Caracas, Venezuela. Left-wing parties promising participatory reform arrived in power in these cases at similar moments, but with varying results. He introduces his work by suggesting that 'the recent boom of studies on participatory local democracy in Latin America has yet to produce compelling cross-national comparative analysis to provide an answer' (2011: 2), and 'causal analysis of why some fail while others succeed remains underdeveloped' (2011: 24). Goldfrank's question parallels the one I wish to answer using a larger number of cases: 'why do participatory experiments aid in deepening democracies in some cities but not in others?' (2011: 2). He attributes the greatest explanatory power for more open and democratically vibrant participation witnessed in Porto Alegre over Montevideo and even more so over Caracas, to greater flexibility in decentralization, and to the weakness of opposition parties. Where municipal governments had jurisdiction to govern over the things people cared about, and where they did not face entrenched and organized opposition to their reforms, they were able to prove the worth of participatory approaches. Both conditions enabled those pushing participatory programmes to achieve their goals. In his conclusion Goldfrank turns to discuss some further examples of what he says are surprisingly successful participatory budgets in other contexts in Latin America (2011: 258–60). He eventually shows that despite clear differences in outcomes in his cases, successful democratization through PB has also been characterized by equifinality – the same outcome is reached in different ways elsewhere. This finding is confirmed by further cross-case analysis presented in the following chapters.

It is food for thought that due to selecting a control group of cases where the PT had a small winning or losing margin in the 1996 election (some 10 years after the democratization of Brazil), at least some of the cases discussed by Baiocchi et al in their research (2011) might be assumed to have relatively strongly institutionalized opposition, bringing nuance to Goldfrank's conclusions. Goldfrank might counter that the cross-national nature of his research can show a relative difference in party institutionalization not present in a subnational comparison. And we should not forget that the structure of PB in Brazil has been mostly less formal and less regulated than elsewhere (Goldfrank, 2011: 256). All in all, this points to the necessity of cumulating findings across smaller-N comparisons. Any attempt will at least begin to uncover what comparisons at what levels of abstraction are robust and relevant.

Similar to Goldfrank's systematic small-N comparison of budget participation in cities in Latin America, Julien Talpin (2011) and Anja Röcke (2014) have compared PB across cities in different national contexts within Europe. Talpin's ethnographic comparative approach focuses on how individuals experience PB, and how those experiences are shaped in different environments. It is essential reading for those interested in how shock and shame brought about by some of the mechanisms of participatory engagement affect participation. His engulfment in participant observation in Morsang-sur-Orge in France brings a vivid reminder that behind the scenes of participatory experiments lie politics:

> … several actors are involved in the process, with different motives and dispositions, a complex decision-making process is created, where power is shared by different groups fighting insidiously for it, while pretending to be allied for the common good. (Talpin, 2011: 199)

His comparative approach shows that even in three relatively radical participatory experiments (in their national contexts) the opportunities for participation are conditioned by national and local political norms. Talpin is one of the earliest to provide evidence for the effects of participatory innovations like PB on the individual over time focusing on different styles, and in Talpin's cases, 'grammars' of participation.

Talpin finds that variance in participants' prior socialization and the environmental factors that limit or enable their capacity to engage are conditioned by the leading discourses, norms and experiences of disagreement and emotion within the specific participatory programmes of which they take part. Scholars of democratic innovations are still struggling to find methodologies that better understand changes in these variables over time. He repeats an important caution that is subtly present in most accounts of participation – that these instances are a drop in the ocean of any individual's overall political socialization, and we should not expect small instances of participation to mark significant punctuations in long-term individual transformations. In many cases Talpin observes citizens learning how to frame their preferences in the appropriate way to have them recognized, rather than changing their preferences in acceptance of alternative reasons. This is not to say that aggregate change from participation is insignificant, or that learning how to better articulate relatively fixed preferences is necessarily problematic for democrats, but it is to be clear about the potential of PDIs.

Röcke, for her part, finds similarly that national frames have a bearing on how participation is institutionalized. Her methods of data collection are very similar to Talpin's. She takes her case selection in a slightly different direction, choosing a most-different strategy involving the selection of an atypically strong case in one national context, an atypically weak case in another, and a typical PB case in a third. This allows her to provide answers to questions about how country-specific contexts and frames shape the diffusion of PB controlling for positive and negative cases (in terms of typicality and success). Her case-based inductive-comparative approach identifies 'the political will to introduce a new procedure and to support it against administrative and political opposition; administrative support for developing and implementing this procedure; financial means to publicize and organize the procedure; and the type of diffusion', as important factors explaining divergences in processes of implementation of PB (2009: 250).

More recently, Giampaolo Baiocchi and Ernesto Ganuza have been among the first to provide an in-depth side-by-side treatment of two cases in two different global regions (2016). They illustrate two cases that are similar but exceptional within their national contexts – both Córdoba and Chicago's 49th ward represent the first PB cases within Spain and the US respectively. Both cases produce mixed results, neither inspiring a transformational popular sovereignty. The authors report curtailment by information asymmetries when experts including both senior activists and technocrats lacked interest in breaking with entrenched roles. But the affinities Baiocchi and Ganuza draw between the cases provide a useful problematization of what we might consider pleasing outcomes of PB. The cases in themselves represent some degree of failure, but for one thing they provided a path to diffusion for more successful cases such as Sevilla and New York in Spain and the US respectively.

Even in their own right the cases opened a space for participation to take root in a way that bettered the politics that had gone before. Baiocchi and Ganuza recall that it was 'actually when participation seemed to break down in moments of ambiguity and indecision that the inquisitive dialogue most prized by democratic theorists emerged' (2016: 138). Their point is that even when participatory budgets are not outright successes on terms many of their participants would recognize, they can, in their praxis of contestation, spark imagination that enables change elsewhere in the political system. Perhaps the point is keenly reflected in the 2019 electoral defeat of Alderman Joe Moore who instigated the PB programme in Chicago and acted as a national and international advocate for PB. The 28-year incumbent was defeated by Maria Hadden, a long-term PB advocate and community organizer. Hadden was originally introduced to PB after responding to a flyer in the 49th ward, and then developed a career of her own in PB advocacy in the US, and later successfully challenged Moore as a disruptor advocating greater transparency in governance. Scholars have assumed – and I have even suggested in Chapter 1 of this book – that successful PB will beget emancipatory successes and that failures may risk disillusion. However, especially when we look back at cases and think of more distal effects, we should remember that there are a lot of possibilities in between.

A final recent evolution in PB comparisons comes from a set of studies that expand the systematic comparison of PB while also comparing other participatory designs. Françoise Montambeault (2016) compares four cities, bringing to the study of PB the novelty of a holistic framework for case comparison including more than one case per country. Two cases of participatory urban planning in Mexico – Ciudad Nezahualcóyotl (Neza) on the outskirts of Mexico city, and León – are compared along with two participatory budgets in Brazil – Recife and Belo Horizonte. Her case selection aims to control for relatively similar shared decentralization and traditions of associationism and clientelism in both countries (2016: 47). Montambeault examines cases with different outcomes within the separate participatory programmes that were shaped differently across countries. She can therefore draw associations between success and failure across two different types of PDI. Her approach emphasizes complexity of cases, treating variables – actors, institutions and contexts – as 'not isolated from one another' (2016: 62). An important contribution of her work is to recognize that the concept of 'success' in participatory programmes is under-theorized. She takes on the task more explicitly than most who have gone before, and prefers a conceptualization grounded in a combination of autonomy and collective mobilization.

Casting the net even wider, Geissel and Hess (2017) include evaluations of PB as part of large meta-synthesis aimed at explaining political efficacy arising from participatory programmes in Germany. They show that financial and structural governance support is more important than politicians' ideological commitments in explaining efficacy, and that participatory history within a locality also has strong associations with efficacy. Elsewhere Joan Font and collaborators compare many proposals arising from different participatory processes in Spain, and conclude that proposals that arise from PB when compared with other participatory designs are much less likely to be rejected by policymakers (2017: 269). Some recent studies describing the evolution of PB in Spain since that fieldwork was carried out highlight the influence of political turbulence and digitalization leading to more individualized forms of participation in larger cities adopting forms of PB, often replacing delegated forms of project prioritization and oversight (Francés et al, 2018). It will be interesting if future data collection can ascertain the impact of design change on the outputs of PB.

## Towards a systematic cumulated comparison of participatory budgeting

Comparison of participatory budgets has become ever more sophisticated, but its lessons are widely dispersed and not always contemplated together in a holistic and systematic way. In this chapter I have outlined the process of maturation of a new and significant subfield in political studies. The established fields in political studies have always benefited from early conceptual work in organizing their scope and principles (Lijphart, 1971). We are still at a relatively early stage of phenomenological development with democratic innovations. Among those PDIs, PB studies are the most advanced. Iteration among theory-led concept refinement and comparative political science is enabling self-actualization of a field of research. Developments in comparison build knowledge and build the field. In simple terms, as Mill's methodological doctrine would have it, 'We compare phenomena with each other to get the conception, and we then compare those and other phenomena with the conception ... the conception becomes a type of comparison' (1950: 298).

An important lesson to take from this story of the development of comparison of PB is that the kinds of questions that are asked by small-N comparativists and the variables they favour investigating seem to differ depending on the cases they select to compare. Campbell et al (2018), using a systematic scoping review, searched 21 electronic databases to identify evaluations of PB with the aim of assessing impacts of PB on health policy. Their work also serves to show the diversity of reporting of different aspects of cases. There is no clear reporting standard for information about cases that has developed. That, I will show, requires some innovation to allow any systematic cumulation. Campbell et al also show a wide range of outcomes investigated, many different analyses strategies and several data collection approaches across the 37 cases they identify where outcomes are evaluated. The vast majority of research that analyses political outcomes (over health, for instance) are case studies (2018: 4–8).

It makes sense when doing in-depth research on a handful of cases to select carefully those cases best positioned to answer a researcher's question of interest. But it is also clear that the choice of cases tends again to constrain the potential for testing the conclusions of one set of cases with another in favour of the potential for 'new' findings. Instead of searching for 'new' findings in 'new' cases, I offer here new and improved findings in existing case research. Let me return, then, to Goldfrank's summation of the state of research on participatory democratic processes: he contends that 'a compelling framework that integrates actors, preconditions, and institutional design remains elusive' (2011: 24–5). My approach in the following chapters is to provide a response to this that is grounded in systematic comparative analysis. Part II of the book takes the reader through that process. The goal is to understand conditions for a deeper empowered democracy by comparing cases systematically, accounting for more than a handful of cases, while retaining quality and complexity.

# PART II

In Chapter 3 we paid homage to those who have advanced the systematic study of PB. Nevertheless, the refrain remains that previous explanations of PB's achievements in deepening democracy have either relied on small numbers of cases or eschewed systematic comparison. They have produced long lists of conditions that are deemed essential for democratic deepening. If we add up all the conditions that are claimed to be necessary for any explanatory theory of deep democracy in PB, it makes a long list – contentious civil society, organized civil society, absence of co-opting strategies, political commitment, demonstration effects, rules, size, wealth, support of officials, and many intersections thereof have been offered as explanatory conditions to name just a few. What is more they have been offered to explain a range of possible outcomes from changes in state–society relations, to redistribution of wealth, increases in education, efficiency of government spending and increasing vote share for the parties implementing PB, to again, name but a few. The first chapter of this part of the book explains the considerations in specifying an inclusive, but robustly specified, examination of more than a handful of diverse PB cases.

I must begin by explaining the necessary tools for identifying necessary conditions. Bent Flyvbjerg argued that 'good social science is problem driven and not methodology driven in the sense that it employs those methods that for a given problematic, best help answer the research questions at hand' (2006: 242). In setting out on this research journey my aim was to harness the knowledge provided by existing ethnographies, drawing on single-case examples and small-N comparative work to cumulate knowledge of causes and outcomes of citizen control of spending decisions worldwide in a systematic but case-sensitive way. I was also guided by Sartori's caution regarding how comparative politics is practised. He wrote over 50 years ago that:

> … we seem to embark more and more in comparative endeavours without comparative method, ie, with inadequate methodological awareness and less than adequate logical skills. That is to say, we seem to be particularly naive vis-à-vis the logical requirements of a world-wide comparative treatment of political science issues. (1970: 1052)

I think the warning is as relevant now as it was then. Chapter 4 starts by introducing some of the assumptions and nomenclature of the QCA method used in the analysis for those less familiar with it. I explain how the research problems and data available on PB present an opportunity for learning from a QCA approach. Chapter 5 then provides a more sophisticated account of what is at stake in debates about what PB is, what it does, and how we can know when we see its effects. I present the data gathered and used to assess PB outcomes across several countries in different parts of the world.

# 4

# Comparing Participation Using Qualitative Comparative Analysis

## Why now for a cumulative qualitative comparison?

Designing social research involves trade-offs between complexity and generality. There remains an often overblown and unhelpful distinction in social sciences between strategies that standardly prioritize one over the other. For Ragin, 'it is easy to exaggerate their differences and to caricature the two approaches, for example, by portraying quantitative work on general patterns as scientific but sterile and oppressive and qualitative research on small Ns as rich and emancipatory but soft and subjective' (2000: 22). QCA sets itself up as a method that provides an avenue for assuaging some of the unhelpful tensions in this distinction.

The attractiveness of QCA as both a critical methodological approach and a novel set of techniques has led to its application across an ever-expanding group of diverse disciplines and subdisciplines in the social sciences (Thiem and Dusa, 2013: 2). It has been one of the few approaches in recent times to come from outside the methodological orthodoxy that has not been quickly chased back to the margins of social science. The number of peer-reviewed articles per year using QCA has grown gradually since the first in 1984 – up to 15 in 2005, to 35 in 2011, and then more quickly to 45 in 2012 and 99 in 2013.[1] Of those 99 articles, 16 were agenda-setting articles introducing QCA to new subdisciplines (among them, Ryan and Smith, 2012). A large and yet non-exhaustive bibliography of QCA studies on the

1 COMPASSS Newsletter, Nr 33, 10 January 2014. Available at: https://compasss.org/wp-content/uploads/simple-file-list/compasss-newsletter-33-Jan2014.pdf

COMPASSS[2] website attests to the method's continued growth in popularity, containing over 1,000 articles and 80 books at the time of writing in 2020.

There is a well-worn debate in the social sciences about the value of large-N and small-N research strategies.[3] Part of the early promise of QCA was to develop a method that makes feasible medium-N research strategies, in particular by extending the logic of small-N comparisons in a reasonable way. Ragin (2000: 25) plots the relative number of studies against the number of cases per study in the discipline producing a U-shaped curve, with several studies covering a handful of cases, several covering hundreds of cases, and a few covering case numbers that lie in between. The finding suggests that researchers are indeed quite averse to increasing the number of observations unless the number of cases can be radically improved (which might often require a significant change of research question).

Despite advances in large-N research applications, to answer many of the questions students of social phenomena would like to answer a large-N is notoriously hard to come by (Lijphart, 1971), or perhaps actually undesirable (Flyvbjerg, 2006). This can be particularly true of public policy innovation, as in the case of PB where diffusion is common but rarely universal, and intricate exemplars are valued by end-users of research. Many publications on PB have borne witness to its wide dispersal. There are in-depth accounts of celebrated exemplars, but scholars have struggled to find a unifying framework to compare cases without losing the rich substantive knowledge of context that seems so important to explaining what happened in those cases. Small-N case-based research can be attentive to the complexity of phenomena, allowing researchers to reflectively refine definitions of the elemental qualities of the things they are studying within the process of undertaking research. The trade-off is a lack of generalizability that decreases the potential for social research to be able to justify action and make an impact.

The withholding of generalization as a short-term goal is often the gambit of more constructivist approaches to research. A little bit of the generalizing discipline of existing conceptions is forsaken in the beginning, in order that it can be reintroduced later. The danger of this approach is that in allowing creative freedom, concepts become stretched

2 COMPASSS (COMPArative Methods for Systematic cross-caSe analySis) is a worldwide network for scholars interested in systematic cross-case comparative approaches to research: https://compasss.org

3 For a more in-depth treatment of my thoughts on this debate, see Ryan (2016, 2017, 2018).

beyond useful meaning. Yet, when done well, constructivist approaches can lead to accurate refinement of ideas to reflect observations.

Social science continues to divide between research that lumps the cases together while studying a handful of things that vary across them, and research that lumps the variables together and studies their intricate connections across a handful of cases. Few people venture in between. This alone is not a good enough reason to do so – people avoid risky journeys for very good reasons. However, Berg-Schlosser and Cronqvist suggest that QCA may offer a vehicle for the venture:

> Between the extremes of over-generalizing and 'universalizing' macro-quantitative approaches, on the one hand, and purely individualizing case-oriented approaches, on the other, a meaningful 'medium-range' social science can be built which, at the same time, has a higher explanatory power and a greater social and political relevance. (2005: 172)

PB is ready for a medium-N study of what PB is and what it does. QCA is a method that can grasp the opportunity provided by the build-up of worldwide case knowledge and theory but overcome the complexity and disparate nature of the data and the theories it mobilizes. It provides a set of tools to improve the interpretation of several cases where the case researchers may otherwise have their eyes close to the data such that it is difficult to zoom out and take a systematic approach to the evidence. Using QCA we can test the types of causal claims and intuitions of the researchers whose case studies and small-N comparisons have paved the way in studying democratic innovations. The following sections further elaborate the distinctiveness of the approach, and apply the lessons of recent methodological debates to substantive investigations of democratic innovation.

## What is qualitative comparative analysis?

Despite its growth in popularity, many readers may still be new to the method and approach of QCA, which comes with its own set of terms and assumptions. Introducing vast new terminology to their audience is a dilemma for those writing about fuzzy sets.[4] I try to overcome that burden for the unfamiliar reader by introducing and returning to

[4] For book-length treatments of fsQCA methodology, see Ragin (2000, 2008), Smithson and Verkuilen (2006), Rihoux and Ragin (2007) and Schneider and Wagemann (2012).

the concepts gradually throughout the examples and analysis in the remainder of the book, to highlight the advantages of the method for knowledge accumulation. Nevertheless, in this section I briefly outline some key concepts and terms as a first point of reference for readers less familiar with the method, showing where relevant how they correspond to theories in democratic innovation research.

### *Necessity and sufficiency*

QCA is an excellent method for testing the combinations of a number of conditions that are associated by set-theoretic relationships with an outcome. The logic underlying the way we try to understand the social world is often set-theoretic (see Schneider and Wagemann, 2012: 5–6). QCA explores set-theoretic relationships among variables or conditions such as relations of *necessity* and *sufficiency* (Schneider and Wagemann, 2012). The underlying logic is aimed at testing for 'If X, then Y' relationships rather than 'The more of X, the more of Y' relationships among conditions (Thiem et al, 2016).

Theorists and case researchers are particularly fond of claims of the nature 'X is sufficient but not necessary for Y'. Sufficient conditions (or more likely sufficient conjunctions of conditions) are often what many of us have in mind when we say out loud, 'X leads to Y'. We often use imperfect synonyms, which can give conditional or causal interpretations to necessity and sufficiency – such as X is 'required' or 'enough' for Y.

Take the following abbreviated passage from Gret and Sintomer's book on PB in Porto Alegre,

> A combination of a strong political culture in civil society and a strong political will in government represents the best context for initiating such an experiment. The process also requires a level of pragmatism in its implementation … formal political equality is not sufficient … true political will is required founded upon alternative action mechanisms … municipal action alone cannot hope to modify the relationship between social classes. (2005: 134)

In the space of half a page the authors suggest at least four hypotheses that are set-theoretic in nature. The hypotheses they are conceiving are based on notions of necessary (or 'required') and sufficient or insufficient ('not alone') conditions. The use of set-theoretic reasoning is ubiquitous in the social sciences, and statements about necessity and sufficiency are rife within the PB literature. These kinds of relationships among conditions can be identified analytically in *subset–superset* relations among explanatory conditions (often called *influencing conditions*) compared across cases. We can establish necessity when we observe a set of cases containing the outcome to be a subset of the set of cases displaying the cause. Similarly, for sufficiency to be established, the set of cases containing the causal condition must be a subset of the cases displaying the outcome (Ragin, 2000: 214–17).[5]

### *Combinatorial and asymmetric causation and explanation*

These hypotheses are also based on combinatorial or *conjunctural* causation. Configurative methods like QCA ascribe to an understanding of causality in the social world in which outcomes are often best explained by conjunctions of conditions. An analogy with elemental chemistry is useful where social conditions are like elements that can be combined in different ways to fashion more complex and in some ways unrecognizable compounds with very different properties. In configurative approaches to understanding cases in social science, change in the presence or absence of a single condition is understood to signify a different kind of case. It is the mix of conditions in a case that matters.

QCA provides a system of analysis that retains this complexity of cases, and yet uncovers and describes evidence for multiple conjunctural causation. The implication is that we can find relatively concise explanations across cases that still allow for *equifinality* – where the same outcome can be explained by different combinations of conditions. This equifinality assumption allows for alternative explanations (finding two or more different combinations of conditions that are sufficient for an outcome) based in different contexts. An example of such an explanatory theory might go as follows: first, that PB will fail to deepen democracy in the presence of both a very competitive electoral environment and weak civil society where supporters have to spend too much capital developing and consolidating popular support and coalitions; but second, that PB may also fail in a very uncompetitive electoral environment where government has civil society support and therefore the incentive for accountability through participatory democracy for elected leaders is absent. A QCA approach will not see such explanations as 'competing'.

5 Chapters 6 and 7 walk the reader through this process in more detail when examining the evidence.

These assumptions are not the same as those used in detecting interaction effects in regression analyses (see Schneider and Wagemann, 2012: 86–7). Using the QCA approach means we are less interested in causal effects that aim at modelling a meaningful relationship of a single cause with the outcome that is independent of the presence and absence of the other causal conditions (Ragin, 1987, 2000: 95). Rather, causes in different contexts are seen to have effects that do not 'average out' in a very meaningful way. There are two contrasting basic mathematical approaches to these logics that we can distinguish, one formed on the operators of Boolean algebra and the other on the operators of elementary algebra (Thiem et al, 2016).

The methodological assumptions may seem abstract, but they have practical consequences – not only for theories, but also for intervening in the real world if causation is assumed to be neither 'unifinal' nor 'linear'. To put it in more applied terms, I am not looking for answers of the kind: 'controlling for other factors an average 1 per cent increase in political leadership's commitment to participatory methods will lead to an average 6.54 per cent increase in citizen control of collective decisions'. Although this might be a delicious result for current fashions in journal publications if it was obtained through reasonable proxies for the concepts, the practical advice that can be construed from such a result alone is questionable. I am not hoping to subsequently drag a bunch of policymakers and activists into a room and tell them to focus their energy on increasing the participatory commitment of leaders because on average, most of them will be marginally successful. This would not be terribly convincing, and is probably a bad idea for many other reasons. Instead, the importance of context decrees that to generate an outcome it will not do to merely always reduce or increase the presence or absence of a single strong, significant explanatory variable. Increasing the interference of political leaders even committed to participation can have negative effects in certain circumstances. Politicians can derail a process that is otherwise effective where it has previously been insulated from some kinds of polarization. There is currently a burgeoning of work on mini-publics that tries to understand why input from politicians seems to work well in some contexts but not in others.

One answer to this problem of asymmetric hypothesis (where it is reasonable to assume the cause may, for example, improve or worsen democracy) is to try and express expectations about particular conditions more probabilistically. That answer is no doubt always useful. Most generalizations we make are, to some extent, implicitly probabilistic. A popular advance to explanation in the social sciences is to be more explicit about the accuracy of the probabilities based on evidence. Another (not mutually exclusive) answer is to sort through alternate potential explanations and better specify the contexts in which potential causes may act in opposing directions in relation to the outcome. The latter is the focus of the QCA approach.

QCA explanations then allow for causal *asymmetry* and also *multifinality* – Rather than the presence of a condition connected with one outcome being taken to mean that its absence must also be connected with the absence of the outcome, the same condition can be understood to contribute to, for example, deepening democracy in one context while contributing to negating democracy in the presence of other conditions. For example, we might think that a combination of strong financial backing and political leaders committed to participation will explain effective PB, but it does not necessarily follow that a weak financial position will negate PB success. Voluntary support from civil society may pick up the slack where government capacity is curtailed. And a strong financial position may actually weaken PB where leaders are not committed to participation and can freely spend funds on other projects. These are examples of hypotheses I test in the final section of the book.

### *Intersection, union and negation*

Operations based on *intersection* and *union,* as well as *negation* of sets, can help us logically interpret how different conditions combine with outcomes across cases. Intersection of sets corresponds to the logic of 'AND' statements – the intersection of set A and set B contains only all the elements of set A that are also in set B. Union corresponds to logical 'OR' – the union of set A and set B contains all the elements that are in set A as well as all the elements that are in set B. Negation corresponds to logical 'NOT' – the negation of set A (not A, sometimes written as 1-A) is its logical inverse. Throughout I adopt the common notation where the tilde '~' preceding a condition denotes absence (negation) of a condition, the asterisk '*' denotes an intersection of sets (conjunction of conditions), '+' denotes a union of sets (disjunction), '←' denotes is necessary for, and '→' denotes is sufficient for.

### *Logical cases, remainders and truth tables*

A further important aim of the QCA approach is to be transparent about the empirical relevance of the data that has been accessed vis-à-vis what data remains beyond the reach of the research. Any increase in the number of conditions examined in a single analysis leads to an exponential increase in the number of *logical cases*[6] (combinations of conditions that are logically possible; see Ragin, 2008: 24). That is, assuming our number of cases is not very high, if we try to throw more potential causes at the model we will have to admit there are lots of possible combinations of conditions we have no information about. With a small-to-medium number of cases, the number of *logical remainders* (logical cases for which we do not have empirical examples) will usually begin to outweigh the number of potential combinations of conditions for which we have empirical evidence as soon as there are more than three or four conditions in the model. Therefore, a robust medium-N QCA requires the theoretical skills to select and define three to five key explanatory or influencing conditions to be examined with the outcome condition.

Even with a few conditions and a medium-N of cases, the number of potential combinations of conditions runs too high for most researchers to analyse without good visual aids. Here, the *truth table* proves an extremely useful analytic tool. Introduced at greater length in Chapter 7, the truth table concisely maps data to concepts of interest. It summarizes the logical combinations of presence or absence of conditions in each of its rows. The truth table provides information on which empirical cases best ascribe to each logical case, including displaying the 'empty' rows that signify logical remainders. It also illustrates the extent to which cases that are logically similar in their conditions consistently lead to the outcome of interest. The truth table allows for transparent dialogue between theory and evidence.

## *Fuzzy sets, membership scores and calibration*

It is unusual in the social sciences to find that all cases under investigation can be neatly indexed to fall into discrete categories. While good social theory establishes relatively clear conceptual boundaries, we also know that it is possible to identify important differences in degrees to which some condition can be deemed to be present or absent in a case. *Fuzzy logic* allows set-theoretic analysis to account for differences in degree of presence or absence of a condition within a case. Fuzzy sets are further illuminated with the use of examples in the next chapter, but it suffices to explain here that fuzzy sets enhance QCA by allowing for cases to have different degrees of *membership* in a set representing a condition's presence or absence in the case. Where a condition is observed to be present in a

6 For each k number of conditions tested in any QCA model there will be $2^k$ logical cases.

case, the case can be said to have a full membership (membership score of 1) in the set that represents that condition. The Pope could be said to have a set membership score of 1 in the set of Roman Catholics. Where a condition is completely absent from a case, the case can be said to have full non-membership in the condition (set membership score of 0). The Queen of England could have a set membership score of 0 in the set of Roman Catholics. Other cases may have partial membership scores between 0 and 1, which better describe their degrees of membership of a set (perhaps reflecting a lapsed or 'à la carte' Catholic).

Conditions of interest are operationalized as meaningful sets by the researcher through a process of *calibration*. Calibration is the scientific process of standardizing instruments for measurement. In QCA calibration refers to the specification of the set, and in particular, the description of qualitative states that correspond to specific membership scores to reflect the different quantities of the underlying concept or condition that might be observed. Case selection is inextricably intertwined with condition selection and calibration of sets. The method of coding a variable known as calibration of conditions is that which distinguishes QCA approaches from other forms of data processing.

### *Consistency or inclusion, coverage, relevance and proportional reduction in inconsistency scores*

Finally, for this whistle-stop tour introducing QCA's main features, it is useful to briefly introduce QCA's further measures for dealing with uncertainty in set relations. In social sciences we are not running experiments in vacuums, and finding a perfect relationship represents a very high standard. There are likely to be some inconsistencies in evidence for a relationship across a number of cases. A social scientist would normally be willing to accept some minor inconsistencies to avoid disconfirming a relationship, especially when armed with a transparent measure of fit (being able to articulate the extent of uncertainty). QCA methodologists have developed several indicators of the degree to which set relationships are met. We can provide a measure of the extent to which data confirm the subset relation with an outcome, and this is known as consistency[7] or inclusion.

---

7 It is important to briefly introduce consistency to the reader here to aid understanding of the output. This explanation draws on Schneider and Wagemann (2012, Chapter 5), and a much more detailed explanation and discussion of the concept can be read there.

**Figure 4.1:** Shows two tests for necessary conditions

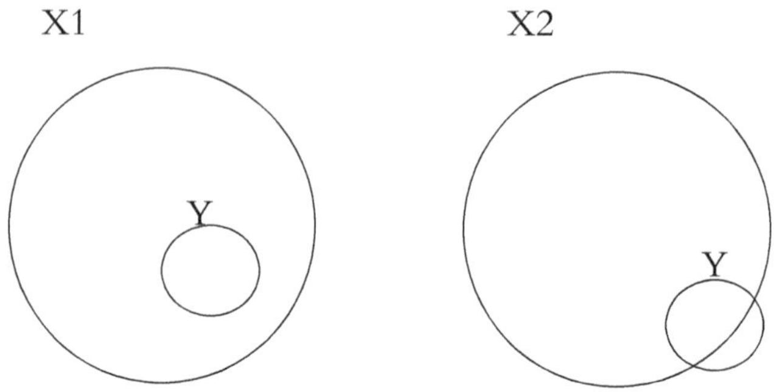


*Consistency* or *inclusion* is perhaps the most important of QCA measures of fit, and is a measure of the extent to which a subset–superset relation is confirmed across cases. Messy social science data will rarely produce clear outcomes where all cases of a certain configuration behave in exactly similar ways. For analysts, the measure provides a sense of how consistent the evidence is for a certain relation of necessity or sufficiency.

To give an example, the Venn diagrams in Figure 4.1 show two tests for necessary conditions. We can treat each of the two Venn diagrams as separate tests for necessary conditions for Y. On the left, the condition X1 is a consistent superset of Y. Whenever we see Y, we see X1. On the right, we see Y is almost but not fully covered by X2, and is not a perfect subset. Sometimes there is Y without X2. There is some inconsistency in its inclusion within the set. A social scientist might, however, be happy to say that X2 is 'almost always necessary for Y'.

Inclusion scores shown in the analysis are always calculated across all cases. The standard-used minimum consistency thresholds within the QCA literature range from 0.9–0.95 for necessary conditions and 0.75–0.9 for sufficient conditions. Thresholds of inconsistency effectively serve to avoid dismissing superset–subset relations where we have 'very few near misses' across cases (Ragin, 2009: 108). However, appropriate thresholds will depend on the nature of the inquiry (theory-testing work may require a higher threshold than exploratory work), the number of cases and the nature of the data.

*Coverage* and *relevance* of necessity are both measures of the triviality of necessary conditions (Schneider and Wagemann, 2012: 147; see also Goertz, 2006). Necessity coverage is an expression of how much smaller the outcome set is in relation to the conditions set (how much of an outcome set Y covers a condition set X). Low necessity coverage can indicate trivialness of necessary conditions (X is quite big relative to Y) and high coverage can indicate a relevant necessary condition, provided X is not too close to a constant. *Relevance of necessity* was later developed as a measure of triviality that considers the latter problem caused by a relatively large X set (see Schneider and Wagemann, 2012: 232–7). The *proportional reduction in inconsistency* (PRI) measure is useful for fuzzy analysis of sufficient conditions because it identifies how much a combination of conditions is specifically a subset of the outcome vis-à-vis the absence of the outcome. The aim is to help researchers avoid illogical interpretations of superset–subset relationships.

While I have introduced some of the key concepts and nomenclature in this section, I continue to familiarize the reader with the approach by showing how it can be applied to existing studies of PB in a cumulative way.

## Applying qualitative comparative analysis to participatory budgeting

When I began studying PB I noted several commentators asking for systematic comparisons. My attention was drawn to a report (Pratchett et al, 2009) that used a short-form QCA to systematically review 19 PB processes. Pratchett et al offer an early attempt using more rudimentary applications of QCA available at the time to try and uncover patterns of causation in PB outcomes from then available case materials. While the limitations of the time meant some results were difficult to interpret, the report showed the promise of the approach. As QCA's sophistication rapidly increased, I committed to applying it to seek to improve the knowledge base on PB.

The rapid diffusion of democratic innovations, especially PB, and the rapid increase and refinement in QCA techniques both provided me with moving targets during this ongoing research project. As I gathered data, I began to apply QCA to small samples of contrasting cases of PB across different continents, and gradually increased my dataset of cases using criteria that I expand on throughout this chapter. Over the course of this study iteration between analysis, population refinement and conceptualization often led to refinements (see, for instance, an early comparison of six cases in Ryan and Smith, 2012, and 19 cases in Ryan, 2014). Early efforts allowed me to test the effectiveness of the approach, which showed that it was worth persevering with. It also allowed me some time to reflect on population definition, calibration of conditions and presentation and interpretation of outputs. In advance of the software-aided analytic moments of QCA, if we take it to be an appropriate method for a 'medium-range' social science programme of research on PB, we are faced with a number of questions. First, what counts as a case of PB? Second, can we adequately define conditions of interest – both influences and outcomes? And third (and more practically), is the case material or data available suitable to provide enough insight to describe these conditions, both qualitatively and quantitatively?

## Iterating between cases and theory to accumulate participatory budgeting knowledge

An advantage of case focus in methodology is to allow serious thought to problems of boundaries of cases (Ragin and Becker, 1992; Byrne and Ragin, 2009). Case-based methods vary in the tools they employ and the number of cases they compare, but they hold in common an understanding of social research that is sensitive to the complexity of the case and the scope of generalizations. To allow for generalizations within a designated scope QCA requires sound theoretical specification of the population of cases and selection of key conditions for comparison. This means that case-based methods are characterized by constant iteration between inductive and deductive strategies,[8] and between evidence and theory. The approach favours ongoing problematization of the scope of populations, causes and outcomes in a piece of comparative research (Ragin, 2000; Rihoux and Lobe, 2009).

What is an appropriate way to demarcate the cases of PB we should include in analysis from those we should not? How do we recognize the phenomenon we are interested in explaining and perhaps predicting? There can be pressure to consider a relatively homogenous population, especially where observations are limited. After all, 'universal propositions may be safely applied to an actual subject matter only in so far as we are thoroughly familiar with the *type* of *object* of which the actual case is a *sample*' (Cohen and Nagel, 1934: 280–1; original emphasis). For the purposes of this research, this involves defining what a case of PB is (and what it is not). A number of challenges present themselves. PB is still a relatively young concept (compared to, say, election, parliament or protest). How exactly does it successfully distinguish itself from other traditional political processes or democratic innovations and ongoing methods of participation and/or governance? A variety of definitions of PB are to be found in the literature. Many

[8] I take induction and deduction here as common placeholders for strategies towards knowledge accumulation that prioritize hypotheses generated from empirical investigation and from theory respectively.

definitions list several features, for example, the facilitation of regular meetings, the provision of information, direct participation, self-regulation and so on (see Chapter 2). Definitions will often suggest the presence of all features in combination is essential for a case to be distinguished as PB. Many observers either explicitly or implicitly use a much lower number of conditions, or take the inclusive line that any participation in budget matters by 'ordinary citizens' constitutes PB.

A stricter approach is perhaps favoured by area scholars and those inspired by the design of the Porto Alegre case. It may also be difficult for researchers, many of whom have normative commitments to deepening democracy, to concede any ground on the attractiveness of what 'participatory budgeting' was before the concept migrated and developed, or perhaps regressed. Nevertheless, the position of the Porto Alegre case as not just a poster case, but moreover, the archetype of PB, is a challenge in many aspects for a comparative research agenda. What value is there in defining the population based on the best or first case? Polymorphism is a feature of diffusion (Porto de Oliveira, 2017: 72). PB has necessarily been implemented in different ways, as it has been adapted to different contexts. Processes that are called PB in one country would be called something else in another (Sintomer at al, 2013: 2). Röcke holds that for PB, '... the transfer or diffusion of institutions, ideas or practices always necessitates at least a minimal amount of re-interpretation with regard to personal strategies and characteristics of the new context' (2014: 28). 'Pragmatic experimentalism' across cases is also an important feature within Brazil (Baiocchi et al, 2011: 81). The question is whether this reinterpretation should represent variation in measurement, or whether there is such a variation in quality that the phenomenon is no longer recognizable.

The success of PB has led to political opportunism and promotion of the concept, but not necessarily any single model. It is difficult to know whether the adaptation of PB in new locations is a case of well thought out revision of a concept incorporating local knowledge, or the muddled product of garbled worldwide translations. It can be equally foolish to define cases based on minimal criteria. A plethora of programmes now called PB may be PB in name only, based on the fame of the original case and the allure of being seen to implement an 'innovation' (Ryan and Smith, 2012). This discussion highlights the challenge within such a comparative study of distinguishing variations in quality from variations in kinds of phenomena. The question is often asked as to whether structured comparison is a good approach given the emerging nature of the phenomenon. The answer is that structured comparison is always a good approach. If the approach can help identify and separate differences in kind and in quality, it should provide a development on previous efforts at cross-national comparison.

Scoping the population of cases and conditions of interest is never an easy task in emerging subfields of research. Yet, by its nature, a newly emerging phenomenon will be limited in its scope for comparison to a small to medium-N of cases. This is certainly true of participatory democratic innovations such as PB when compared across countries (Ryan and Smith, 2012). The field is (over)loaded with good case studies and small-N comparisons that rely on in-depth ethnography-based methodologies. This has led to a call for more systematic cross-case comparisons (Smith, 2009; Spada and Ryan, 2017). In the previous chapter I discussed how the rapid diffusion of PB has led to increased problematization and contestation of its core conditions. How, then, can a researcher adequately scope their population of cases for a valuable systematic comparison enabling modest generalization?

One obvious strategy employed in small-N case-comparative research is to limit cases by keeping key variables constant to control extraneous variance. This logic is often applied in the area studies approach or by limiting comparative designs within one country or system of government (Lijphart, 1971: 688). Yet small-N research based on researchers' in-depth case studies is often criticized because of its alleged increased risk to subjective bias. Moreover, cumulation of small-N research for comparison across studies can be difficult because of researchers' particular and differing intentions. In Peters' words sometimes it is argued that 'the researcher is the major independent variable' (2013: 169). The research I present here relies on my interpretation of the work of others. This is an advantage, because I can cumulate, compare, triangulate and cross-check. It might also be seen as the worst of both worlds – one person interpreting the subjective biases of others to suit their own. Transparency is the researcher's weapon to fight that impression, and I hope that I offer value in that respect

## The challenge of expanding the evidence base

Studies of PB have been either narrow and deep, or wide but shallow in their treatment of the cases. Up to now, description and categorization of several cases has relied mostly on induction, with several compilations that bring together descriptions of similarities and differences among cases. This is partly explained by the way in which puzzles present themselves to researchers and partly by the tools we have available. In contrasting cases across Asia and Europe, Sintomer et al bemoan that there is no 'uniform model to which the others could be compared'

(2013: 20). They offer some organizing principles – their comparison of European cases offers the closest application yet to some middle path. Working back from ideal types they offer a PB typology categorized according to different features of origin, organization, deliberation and the role of civil society (2016). Beginning from those ideals, relative distances from the ideal types can be roughly approximated and conveniently visualized. This approach does not allow for systematic or transparent measurement, and is difficult to replicate. Cases tend to cluster near types according to their national context, so there is a danger that typecasting of cases according to their national backgrounds occurs using such an approach. To my knowledge, no one has come close to expanding on a full typological theory based on evaluation of a property space in the manner suggested by George and Bennett (2005: 257).

There is also a familiar issue of accumulation of research knowledge that is biased by global power structures within the academy and research and governance professions worldwide. Despite excellent efforts in sharing of information on several interesting examples of PB in East Asia, much of the work going on in the region remains largely invisible to scholars of PB (Cabannes, 2018: 243). PB represents a 'return of the caravels' and much international exchange is done in Lusophone, Francophone and Hispanic spheres. Nevertheless, in-depth casework that reaches a global scholarly audience is always biased toward spheres where Indo-European languages dominate, and in many countries scholarly work is still rewarded by a publishing regime where English is the lingua franca. Peters warns that we should be wary that what are seen as popular generalizations are not simply artefacts of the tendency for Americans or Britons who still dominate elements of the discipline to select cases for ease of language use (2013: 171). It is one reason why we require and value the work of skilled area scholars.

Area research is a double-edged sword. Where comparisons have been more systematic, they have tended to select cases within continental bounds. Despite unquestionably high-quality contributions, most comparative work on PB has found ways to find solace in the unique and unusual aspects of the areas they control for. This can come in the form of stressing the uniqueness of the Brazilian political system and culture (Wampler and Avritzer), focusing on national framing (Röcke) or employing approaches that are more likely to uncover differences than uncover similarities across continents (Sintomer et al). The field can benefit from making fewer assumptions about the differences among PB that take place in different macro-comparative units of political organization (or at least testing these assumptions systematically across cases). To be clear on what is at stake in defining PB for comparative research – and this is very important if actors capable of having political impact are able to understand the scope of research findings – we must systematically compare the key elements of phenomena in order to define the concept. People get away with calling any old consultative event a 'successful' democratic innovation partly due to the absence of general systematic analysis and descriptive conceptual work to set things straight. By systematically comparing programmes, we can show that 'anything goes' has very different necessary and sufficient conditions to empowered PB. These differences can be observed and described across several cases and contexts, and by doing so we provide a clear vocabulary to those wishing to expose flawed participatory efforts. Only by seriously attempting systematic cross-regional comparisons will greater insight be gained into what specificity of regions and countries is lost in abstraction for comparability. We can also challenge the assumption that processes in one part of the world are different to another (at least in terms of their most important characteristics that significantly influence empowered participation).

The process of conducting QCA involves both construction and deduction, allowing constant reflexive iteration between theoretical assumptions and measurements. The method has an inimitable way of constituting clarity about theoretical assumptions involved in measurement, selections of cases, choices between parsimony and complexity in description of empirical regularities, and interpretations of results (Rihoux and Lobe, 2009: 237). Much of the procedure I illustrate will seem familiar to practised small-N researchers. This kind of careful iterative reasoning is their stock and trade. So, what's the big deal? Applying the logic of case-based research beyond conventional boundaries in the number of cases that can be compared in any one sitting can lead to unique insights. The value of a medium-range social science is that it retains the transparent conscientious reflexivity of the case researcher (Flyvbjerg, 2006: 235), and applies this contemporaneously with the expansive lessons derived from testing relationships across several accumulated instances of a phenomenon.

In case-based research, the addition of new cases one by one is challenging. This is intensified when dealing with a larger-N. Arriving on new cases may have consequences for both population definition and variable definition. New cases may present a variation in the unit of analysis significant enough to force the researcher to reconsider the population. Several new cases of PB that appear substantially different may lead us to establish new classes, concepts or types (as seen in the work of Sintomer et al and Cabannes and Lipietz, outlined previously). Another way of understanding the effect of discovery and comparison is that new cases may require re-evaluation of distinctions between scope conditions and influencing conditions (see Walker and Cohen, 1985). We might find we have to adapt our theories to distinguish certain conditions as influencing an outcome within the scope of others – finding one constellation of conditions helps to establish successful citizen participation in one context, and another elsewhere. For example, our hypothesis might be that political and financial support are necessary in poorer contexts, whereas civil society demand is an essential explanatory component in combination with political support in richer municipalities. My approach facilitates that process of judging alternative hypotheses by identifying logically sufficient combinations of conditions across contexts.

On the other hand, the understanding of how conditions are observed in new contexts may force the researcher to re-evaluate the operationalization of variables – how they have calibrated their conditions. While this iteration between cases, measurement and theory is time-intensive, its transparency in construction of the research is a key methodological advantage of QCA. I do not wish to claim that iterating between measurement, concepts and samples is peculiar to the approach. Some proponents of QCA have implied this at times, and it is unhelpful because all research involves elements of those procedures. It is better to say that the QCA approach has some heightened qualities in its sensitivity to the problematization of these issues. It is also worth pointing out that this problematization can lead to over-conscious thinking (on the latter problem, see Sartori, 1970).

Some definition is an important starting point in conceiving of a universe of cases. We saw earlier that definitions of PB tend to round on a list of key fundamental characteristics. Those provided by Wampler and Avritzer evoke some of the key design features that have contributed to distinguishing PB as an innovation in participatory governance. They are slightly abstract and tend to favour the conditions of Brazilian designs. Not surprisingly the best starting point for worldwide comparison comes with Sintomer et al's definitions listed earlier. These conditions present sensible criteria for distinguishing PB from more common 'traditional' consultations with citizens outside of the political classes.

The final sections of this chapter explain the logic in scoping and selecting cases for the analysis of PB presented in Chapters 6 to 9 of Part III.

## Differentiating PB from participatory grant-making processes: what PB is not

Sintomer et al's criteria would work to exclude from the population many of the cases named 'participatory budgeting' in England (Hall and Röcke, 2013; Ryan, 2014), and similar examples elsewhere, which tend to involve participation in the distribution of ad hoc small grants. These processes also tend to involve administrative jurisdictions that are not governed by a specific representative political body (for example, neighbourhoods, highways).

The English cases are instructive for conceptual clarity. To give an illustration, a suburb in the city of Southampton (where I live) held a 'PB' process that started in 2008 and continued well into the next decade. Thornhill, with a population of about 10,000 residents, was identified in 1999 as one of 39 exceptionally deprived areas of the UK as part of the then Labour government's major regeneration programme called New Deal for Communities (NDC). Each area was granted approximately £50 million worth of government investment, over a 10-year period (Fordham, 2010: 12). As part of a deal struck with the board controlling NDC funding allocation, the local primary care trust (PCT) agreed to make a recurring financial contribution to the area distributed via a PB process (Bonaduce de Nigris, 2008: 4). Support for the process was also provided by the city council. The process involved local residents creating projects and bidding for money from a single pot of what at its height was tens of thousands of pounds. These projects were then presented at a public meeting in the local school, and residents voted on which projects they would like to receive funding. Their votes were tallied, and project funding allocated accordingly.

This is typical of many small projects inspired by PB in the UK (PB Unit, 2008), and is similar to many described in other parts of the world (see, for example, Shah, 2007). I do not wish to suggest that these processes do not have value. From my observations, the process in Thornhill incentivized creative community-led projects, improved community cohesion, gave some decision-making control to residents, and gave participants some sense of the trade-offs involved in making decisions to allocate scarce resources. Shorter pilot programmes also mean shorter time frames for demonstration effects, which could, in theory, lead to pressure for greater empowerment – although evidence for this mechanism appears rare.

When we try to compare this process with PB in Porto Alegre, we are comparing apples with apple seeds. There is no hope for participatory grant-making processes like these to achieve empowered participatory democracy without them being planted more firmly within the legitimate democratic architecture. The process in Thornhill fails to reach at least four of Sintomer et al's criteria. It is based on a small suburb of roughly 10,000 inhabitants, no more than a portion of a local city council ward. The amount of money was set by funding schemes that ordinary citizens had no control over. Projects were limited to those aimed at improving health and wellbeing, so the agenda was set narrowly elsewhere (by the constraints of the funding stream). There was no formal public deliberation – in fact, officers felt that 'Q&A sessions would be difficult to manage, especially as contentious questions might be asked and issues of fairness might arise' (Bonaduce de Negris, 2008: 17). There was only one public meeting a year, and the continuation of the programme was completely dependent on the goodwill and fiscal priorities of funders. Those in the UK who were promoting a programmatic approach hoped that these small projects were pilots that would lead on to PB proper, but the projects' logic resembles more the 'do-ocracy' popular in the Low Countries than meaningful power-sharing between state and citizens. The prospects for programmatic 'mainstreaming' in the UK have now definitely moved north of the border into Scotland (see Escobar et al, 2018).

Other processes in England come closer to satisfying the criteria but still fall short. For example, in the London Borough of Tower Hamlets in 2009 and 2010, a 'PB' process allocated £5.04 million of council services by asking local residents to come together, deliberate and vote on priorities in their neighbourhoods (U-Decide, 2009). The Tower Hamlets process was not a grant-giving process and involved residents voting for money for their preferred service. Despite constraining its agenda to bids for 'additional' public services, it opens up a far more significant amount of public funds to local decisions than the grant-making process described earlier. However, the institutional design of this process suggests it is better described as a 21st century town meeting with a focus on local budgeting. Meetings were not regular, and there was no opportunity for the kind of civil society investment over a year-long period expected in PB. The process did not allow in its structure the development of accountability across budget delegates at neighbourhood, region or city or borough level. It was discontinued after 2010 on grounds that such funds were no longer available in a meaningful way as a result of the financial downturn. Although Tower Hamlets PB spend was drawn from a 'mainstream' budget and not based on the ad hoc 'funny-money' of one-off grants or surpluses, as is often the case in UK PBs (see Hall and Röcke, 2013: 195), its foundation was still very insecure.

This vignette invokes another important criterion for definition of the PB universe I use for comparison. Those researching democratic innovations have struggled to explain their populations by differentiating failed cases from non-cases, which partly explains a skew in publications emphasizing successes (Spada and Ryan, 2017). Like many PB scholars, I am interested in explaining how citizen control becomes institutionalized in a PB process. In the case of Tower Hamlets, a key reason why control could not become institutionalized was that the programme was discontinued after two years. The two-year criterion is one I use to differentiate a negative case from a non-case of PB. I assume that a case that is not institutionalized to recur more than once is not useful to explain how citizen control of PB processes happens. These early abandoned cases would certainly be useful for explaining why PB is initiated, and why it survives or does not. I would also not deny that one-off events can have many good democratic outcomes. My argument is that we cannot understand those processes as PB. If I had unlimited resources, I could go looking for lots of material to test the assumption that there is a complete affinity between recurrence and PB-style empowerment. I assume PB is a process involving a longer than two-year commitment with regular meetings. Processes that do not recur have very different qualities that I am not able to explore at length here.

## Cases and data for a worldwide comparison

Ever more sophisticated case selection has helped correct early narratives in democratic innovation research that relied on best-case examples. Case selection (sampling) requires judgement, and knowledge of cases and their relationship to the population will provide the grounds on whether more or less modest inferences can be made. Early monographs on QCA were keen to stress that populations could never be taken as 'given', where given meant that populations were not expected to change during the research process (Ragin, 2000: 45). The basic point Ragin wanted to make is that this process of 'casing' and determining populations is itself an opportunity for theoretical advancement (2000: 54), as cases are discarded, added, revised and refined throughout the research. One advantage of QCA as an approach is that it did not seek to artificially separate or collapse comparison as a conceptual exercise from comparison as causal analysis. That is part of its attractiveness for assessing PB.

Nevertheless, many applications of QCA have had a disappointing amount to say about case selection. When I first broached experienced

QCA practitioners with my sampling questions early on in my research, their unspoken assumption seemed to be that QCA was a home for research that involved analysis of 'full' populations that might be medium-N (for example, Western European welfare states). There remains less work, to my knowledge, that leverages transparency in information-oriented (deliberately non-random) sampling from a much larger population. There has also been a recent trend to apply QCA to so-called 'given' populations where sampling is not really practical or desirable, or to apply QCA to large-N samples. Those analyses aim to leverage QCA's set-theoretic analytic component, often producing quite useful results. The latter trend has led some to write sensible summaries distinguishing differences in QCA as both an approach and a set of techniques (Schneider and Wagemann, 2012; Thomann, 2020; Thomann and Maggetti, 2020).

Sampling is inherent in every piece of research and samples derive from a combination of population definition and case selection. I am transparent about the practical considerations that influence construction of a model to explain PB outcomes, and provide the reader with the relevant information to evaluate my inferences and to contribute their own. The decision to include or exclude cases is important because anyone evaluating the model should be aware of how sensitive model 'solutions' are to evaluate inferences based on those decisions. Therefore, I explain, particularly in Part III of this book, how cases that are not included contribute to, or might modify, general statements. The *truth table* is a useful tool here, whereas the computerized *minimization* in QCA (where an algorithm removes irrelevant terms from explanation) can be more obfuscatory if not well explained. I explain how these tools can be used in an open manner.

I set about building a dataset with enough cases to make meaningful comparisons beyond a small-N, incorporating substantial variety. I also wanted to apply fuzzy set QCA, which meant I needed to be confident that I could obtain a requisite quality of data on important conditions I wanted to test and explain for each case. When I first approached this project with some knowledge of the rapidly emerging literature, I had a sense that the field was beginning to ripen for such a task. As PB began in Latin America and has taken hold in all corners of the globe, much of the literature appears in a variety of languages. I was limited mostly to English language sources (through my own linguistic ignorance), but the research was undertaken with the premise that this 'ripening' was occurring as a certain quantity and quality of knowledge on PB was becoming available across English language sources.

For an innovation that is not a mere technical fix or upgrade, the diffusion and increase in the number of cases of PB across the globe has been staggering. Porto de Oliveira (2017) provides an impressive narration of the threads of diffusion through international relations among cities, and the pivotal role played by actors – politicians, officials, scholars and activists. It is close to impossible for even skilled, resourced and well-coordinated researchers to keep track of all the cases of democratic innovations as they diffuse and diversify throughout the world (Smith, 2009). The classification 'innovation' is itself to some extent unhealthy in that regard (Smith, 2019). Classifying something as an 'innovation' by definition requires ignorance on the part of many toward it, and nowadays almost always connotes assumptions that its solutions to problems are a fait accompli (Spada and Ryan, 2017). Inadequate conceptualization of cases of participatory governance has been blamed on some pathologies in research design in participatory governance (Spada and Ryan, 2017; Ryan, 2019). Despite those difficulties, some efforts in data collection have been impressive, such as that of Participedia (participedia.net),[9] which crowdsources information on a variety of innovations providing sometimes quite high levels of information on cases. While PB can still be considered an innovation in several contexts where it is rare, it is certainly one that is now well into stages of adoption. Another impressive data collection effort is the 2019 PB Atlas, which relies on an expert survey to estimate the number of participatory budgets worldwide (Dias et al, 2019). The collaborators estimate over 11,690 cases. That figure is based on a more inclusive definition than I provide, and comes with large confidence intervals, but nevertheless shows the breadth of influence and impressive spread of the idea.

Despite these advances, until now a medium-range study including both breadth and depth had been difficult to imagine. Retaining the value of case knowledge and comparing across more than a handful of cases is time-intensive. For some scholars of participatory governance, combining quality and quantity is a life's commitment and usually involves some research help (see Bryan, 2004, for an example of such an approach in his study of town meetings in New England in the US). In order to build a dataset, I repeatedly scoured online sources at regular intervals and gradually built up contacts across networks to access new information, recording sources and data as I went along.

9 I have worked with the Participedia project since 2009.

In the wider-ranging literature on worldwide cases I have mentioned many cases appear as cameos more so than in-depth case studies. Therefore, as I collected data on mounting claims of potential conditions that purportedly explained many important outcomes, the empty cells in my dataset were increasing exponentially rather than decreasing. I began to narrow my focus on what cases and conditions appeared most likely to bear enough information for qualitative comparison. In some literature, even a short article would provide very clear descriptions of conditions I was interested in. At other times researchers documented quirks of particular cases that were less useful for cross-cutting research questions, and did not describe a case's basic elements. In some of those cases I was able to find what I needed through cross-checking sources or clarifying an interpretation through communication with the field researchers. The 30[10] cases selected for the analysis presented in this book represent some of the sheer variety of cases and sources that any comparative study of this type must work with. Although I am limited in the main to English language sources, the cases are not biased towards the English-speaking world. The data contains 13 Brazilian cases where the innovation was strongest in its early waves and sources are several, and 6 in Peru where the first national law was put in place, and Stephanie McNulty's work provides some clear relevant evidence on those cases. These are compared with 2 cases in France, 2 in Spain, 2 in the US, and 1 each from Argentina, Canada, Italy, Germany and Uruguay. The cases and some of the main sources from which information was garnered are listed in Table 4.1. Contributions ranged from books treating a single case (for example, Abers, 2000), books treating a small number of cases in comparison (for example, Talpin, 2011; Röcke, 2014), to some mere snapshots, but these 30 cases represent those for which there was enough information of enough quality to make valid inferences about the conditions that were necessary and sufficient for citizen control of collective decisions. The list is far from exhaustive, but includes sources from which the analysis I present here could be performed to a minimally acceptable level of validity.[11]

[10] In the main analysis presented in the following chapters, the Recife case is split into two cases representing the pre- and post-PT governance eras. The approach is taken by Montambeault (2016), and its justification is discussed in the following section. Therefore I analyse 31 cases in total.

[11] I also had formal research interviews about cases with Josh Lerner, Anja Röcke, Dennis Rodgers, Julien Talpin and Brian Wampler. I tried to stay as true as I could to the descriptions in peer-reviewed materials. All errors of interpretation of material are, of course, mine and mine alone.

**Table 4.1:** Cases and main sources for the analysis presented in this book

| Case | **Main source(s)** |
|---|---|
| Ayacucho 2003–06 | McNulty 2011 |
| Belo Horizonte 1993–2011 | Nylen 2003a, Wampler 2007a, Avritzer 2009, Montambeault 2016 |
| Berlin-Lichtenberg 2005–10 | Röcke 2014, Herzberg 2013 |
| Betim 1993–2000 | Nylen 2003a, 2003b |
| Blumenau 1997–2004 | Wampler 2007a |
| Buenos Aires 2002–09 | Peruzzotti 2009, Rodgers 2010 |
| Cajamarca 2003–06 | McNulty 2011 |
| Camaragibe 1997–2000 | Baiocchi et al 2011 |
| Chicago 49th Ward 2009–13 | Baiocchi and Ganuza 2016, Pin 2017, Weber et al 2015 |
| Córdoba 2001–07 | Baiocchi and Ganuza 2016 |
| Cusco 2003–06 | McNulty 2011 |
| Gravataí 1997–2000 | Baiocchi et al 2011 |
| Ipatinga 1998–2004 | Wampler 2007a |
| João Monlevade 1997–2000 | Baiocchi et al 2011 |
| Lambayeque 2003–06 | McNulty 2011 |
| Loreto 2003–06 | McNulty 2011 |
| Mauá 1997–2000 | Baiocchi et al 2011 |
| Montevideo 1990–99 | Goldfrank 2011 |
| Morsang-sur-Orge 1998–2006 | Talpin, 2011 |
| Moquegua 2003–06 | McNulty 2011 |
| New York 2011–16 | Gilman 2016, Swaner 2017, Jabola-Carolus 2017, Su 2018 |
| Poitou-Charentes 2004–08 | Röcke 2014 |
| Porto Alegre 1988–2004 | Abers 2000, Baiocchi 2005, Santos 2005, Gret and Sintomer 2005, Wampler 2007a, Avritzer 2009, Goldfrank 2011 |
| Recife 1993–2000 and 2000–08 | Wampler 2007a, Montambeault 2016 |
| Rio Claro 1997–2004 | Wampler 2007a |
| Rome Municipio XI 2003–06 | Talpin 2011 |
| Santo André 1997–2001 | Wampler 2007a |
| São Paulo 2001–04 | Wampler 2007a, Avritzer 2009 |
| Sevilla 2003–06 | Talpin 2011 |
| Toronto Community Housing 2001–10 | Lerner and van Wagner 2006, Foroughi 2017 |

Readers familiar with the cases will already have noticed that there is a wide variety of cases in different contexts among the sample. The cases include some well-known municipal participatory budgets, but with different designs in different contexts, one focused on housing tenants, another on high school students, at least seven regional ones, some extremely large cities, and some whose jurisdiction is below the municipal level. Some of the cases are not always called PB in some of the instances where they are presented. All cases fit within the scoping criteria outlined previously.

Comparing diverse cases is an overlooked strength in much comparative research, where an obsession with mimicking control has become prohibitive to some interesting research designs. I specify the time frames covered by the data for each case. Where reasonable, I split cases into separate time frames. This is done only where field researchers suggested a clear distinction within the case. Some of the cases rely on fieldwork that was carried out some time ago, some at the height of the success of PB in Latin America in the early 2000s. Some of the North American material is more recent. Many of the earliest monographs using QCA were comparative historical analyses (Wickham-Crowley, 1991; Brown and Boswell, 1995), and there are elements of that approach in the work presented here. There are clearly different levels of information for each case. Uneven amounts of knowledge relating to each case are an accepted (if not desirable) characteristic of case-based comparative research (Newton, 2006: 851). I make every effort to be clear in analysis and discussion of cases where information was more or less lacking. Many interesting cases have been left out for lack of some authoritative information. In Chapters 8 and 9 I discuss how I imagine these cases would have contributed to the analysis.

Some readers may also question the desirability of including Porto Alegre. As the archetype of PB, it has been seen to have much influence on other cases and models of PB, and is still often seen as a yardstick for many other programmes to aspire to. It may be considered an 'outlier'. In many ways, the success of Porto Alegre is a necessary condition for any of the other cases in the dataset to exist. The question we must keep in mind here is whether this influence is an enduring significant factor affecting outcomes that vary across cases. Using QCA we can try to evaluate to what extent Porto Alegre compares with other cases – whether other cases are similar in key characteristics – and we can then return to the case and examine whether the findings make sense in light of our knowledge about it and other cases. We now turn to the substantive questions we would like answers to across these cases.

# 5

# What Participatory Democrats Expect

## 'Success'

The outcome condition I explain is *citizen control* of collective decisions in PB (ccpb): the ultimate aim is to draw on a range of cases to explain the conditions under which citizen control of budget spending decisions is effectively established. This is where democratic participation and authority over budget decisions by 'ordinary people' becomes a regular expectation. Citizen control of budgetary decision-making is understood to take place when both agenda-setting and decision-making power in budget decisions is directed by, and open to, all citizens.

This can, of course, happen to a matter of degree – different factors can contribute to check decision-making and/or agenda-setting power. On the surface these powers are easy to observe and measure by looking at the rules of the process – for example, citizen control may be affected by whether de jure vetoes for citizen groups are in place. I was interested in measuring de facto citizen control, however. This meant collecting and synthesizing a variety of qualitative information that signalled different degrees of power, including observations of what level of co-optation took place in both setting agendas and making final decisions. Wampler shows, for instance, that despite the strong rhetoric of co-governance in Santo André, government officials and the mayor's office benefited in controlling the process by having far more access to important information and the apparatus of the state. Despite a de jure veto for both sides according to the rules, the only de facto veto was exercised by the administration (2007a: 178–9). Also, decisions need to be made with the knowledge that they will be accounted for and enforced. Some system of monitoring of outcomes was more or less a constant rather than a variable across cases but, in reality, implementation of projects differs across cases. In several cases citizen control is lost in administrative prohibitions. While perfect implementation is far from expected, even for political dictators, administrators can provide numerous reasons for non-implementation, and many are tinged with a sense that power asymmetries lie unaffected (Baiocchi and Ganuza, 2016).

Chapters 2 and 3 discussed some of the variety of outcomes researchers have tried to explain, and how some have differentially interpreted 'success' for participatory innovations. Policymakers, activists, participants and citizens are all desperate to know what makes political participation 'successful'. In politics, success and failure are always contested concepts. While most actors have some vague common notions of what makes PB successful, they emphasize different elements according to their going concerns.

Many scholars have been attracted to PB to help them try to understand its potential to achieve a number of outcomes, for example, the redistribution of wealth, education or health or bureaucratic efficiencies and political gains. While many of these goals may be complementary or even conditional on one another, this study is primarily concerned with PB as a democratic innovation that effectively institutionalizes democratic participation. The aim is to explain how ownership of budget decisions by masses of 'ordinary people' becomes a convention, and what leads to that success being negated if PB becomes a disenchanting process. The key research question outlined in the first breath is 'When and how do ordinary citizens gain substantial control over important collective decisions?'

I should briefly address some alternative potential conceptualizations of success in participatory programmes to explain their relation to my focus on citizen control of collective decisions. Many have conceived success in terms of a reduction in clientelist or corrupt practices: for some, PB can be seen primarily as having been introduced in Brazil as a specific measure whose aim was to reduce patronage and shady practices in allocation of capital spending in a city. An inherited culture of clientelism has plagued (and as national scandals have revealed, continues to plague) Brazilian politics. In this context PB can be seen as emblematic of the institutional turn taken by civil society and social movements striking back against military authoritarianism in the late 1970s and 1980s (see Wampler and Avritzer, 2004: 292). Abers (1998) paints a very vivid picture of the ways in which the big patrons in some of Porto Alegre's neighbourhoods were supplanted by cooperation among citizens through the first years of PB. Certainly PB varied in its successes in this regard, with the sustained presence of electoral ward bosses at meetings in some participatory budgets (Wampler, 2007a: 250). The prevalence of a patron's supporters who do not participate regularly would 'swell' assemblies to game outcomes in places (Abers, 1998). In talking to politicians about PB, I find this fear of 'capture' of fora to be the most prominent in scepticism about PB, particularly where civil society is less vibrant. Clientelism is not unique to Brazilian politics, and even in traditionally 'non-clientelist' systems, citizens and activists have called for more transparency and control over budget spending. A number of newer cases of PB cite responses to some fiscal management scandals as an influence in their initiation, especially in the fallout from the global economic contractions of recent years. If many of these programmes consider fighting corruption and making budgets transparent a key aim of PB, perhaps an outcome we should be most interested in testing requires some measure of a reduction in corruption indicators and patronage.

Nevertheless, PB is more than just a tool for budget transparency and openness. Budget regulation and transparency has been shown to be successful in reducing incentives for politicians to benefit from information asymmetry in traditional representative political systems (Benito and Bastida, 2009). PB sets a somewhat higher standard than this. Abers (1998) shows that as citizens over time began to deliberate with one another, they moved from attending PB meetings in order to campaign for narrow localized goals, to organizing collectively to gain more control over shared concerns. Reductions in clientelism may be a symptom of, as well as a good indicator for, successful PB, but for many, PB aims not just for a better relationship between decision-makers and those affected by decisions, but also for a fundamental change in the nature of who decisions are made by and for.

Other researchers and designers of PB focus on learning and educational outcomes. Much participatory and deliberative governance has affinities with educational settings and is rooted in work of schools of democracy theorists such as John Dewey (see Dewey, 2012). There has been an increasing focus on PB in schools more recently (Dias et al, 2018). One lauded outcome of PB that was jumped on by the World Bank and others seeking to diffuse the process has been its apparent ability to increase the 'budget literacy' of ordinary citizens. Budgets, despite being arguably the legislative act with most effect on an average citizen's day-to-day life, have traditionally been less open to considered debate among ordinary citizens than, for example, moral or constitutional issues. Budgets are often referred to as the 'black box' of government – best understood and administered by economists, planners, other technocrats and, perhaps only if necessary, professional politicians. A level of budget literacy among members of an active society can be an important component of good governance. By familiarizing themselves with the jargon and technical procedures of public budgeting, citizens can come to understand the constraints and procedures faced in political decision-making with limited resources. The theory is that such knowledge can lead them to make more rational demands from the state. Similarly, when citizens can communicate with technocrats in a language they both recognize, those operating within the black box can overcome information deficits in regard to citizens' needs and wants. They may find that citizens' priorities are different to what they believed they were, as documented in Porto Alegre (Abers, 2000), or they may gain information to be able to anticipate policy failures before they are implemented.

Improved information flows through 'good governance' is often an aim of PB, and one that is desirable of any arrangement involving collective decision-making, but it only captures some of what PB sets out to achieve. Improvements in cognition, individual or collective, seen in adaptive preferences and public reason-giving are only one good that democratic theorists hope for from participation in democratic politics (Talpin, 2011: 15; see also Smith, 2009). Practices of making public arguments and changing preferences can be important in their own right, but can be far more powerful as part of a broader process of taking control of making collective decisions and even collectively reshaping the institutions of governance (see Talpin, 2011; see also Pateman, 1970).

Taking a step back from issues of implementation, those influenced by deliberation theory are often more interested in representation or inclusion of 'presence' and 'voice' of those normally excluded in fora as an outcome of participatory design. Critiques of the inclusion concept within democratic theory specify in particular the need to be sensitive to important affected and underrepresented constituencies (Phillips, 1995; Young, 2000). We might want to evaluate the success of PB by simply looking at the diversity and representativeness of participants or discourses that are brought to the fore by the process. If unequal representation remains democracy's unresolved dilemma (Lijphart, 1997), then a political process that achieves more equal representation involving more than just the 'usual suspects' is a successful one. To examine the extent to which PB achieves such inclusion might require a measurement of some shared sense of identity that results from the process. Such analyses have mainly focused on specific institutions designed for more narrow purposes (for example, mini-publics) than participatory budgets. And even where these outcomes have been measured, the focus tends to be on the collection of individual actions rather than collective outcomes as a whole (see, for example, Bryan, 2004; Steiner et al, 2004; Fishkin, 2009; Niemeyer, 2011), although this may change with the trend to greater institutionalization of mini-publics within political systems (Farrell et al, 2019). Following Smith (2009), different institutions may achieve these goods in different ways, but they are only elements of successful democratic innovation, which also requires degrees of popular control over decisions, as well as accountability and effective implementation of such decisions.

Finally, PB has not only interested those whose primary concern is the minutiae of democratic procedures or those who intrinsically value a vibrancy of political participation. Its popularity has often been driven by its promise of a more just distribution of collective resources. Many consider the aim of PB to be more concrete redistribution of wealth or other material goods to those who do not normally have it. This is the logic behind the 'inversion of priorities' rhetoric and devices included in PB. In the context of exceptionally rapid urbanization and consequential plethora of unplanned settlements, PB was very much envisioned as an instrument for inverting priorities to benefit the poor. Capital infrastructure spending was refocused away from the 'haves' in gentrified suburbs and gated communities to the 'have-nots' in the favelas or shantytowns. It is no accident that Porto Alegre became a beacon for the alter-globalization movement, the cradle for the World Social Forum, and a 'Mecca of the Left'. In Europe, too, early cases were initiated by leftist and often Communist parties. As Julien Talpin explains, these parties, reeling from the ideological consequences of the fall of the Soviet empire, saw in participatory democracy a modern idea with which to build a new positive identity and reconnect with their constituents (2011: 35). Some recent studies have compared PB and non-PB cities to show that participatory budgets in general led to improvements in the circumstances of vulnerable citizens over time (Touchton and Wampler, 2013; Gonçalves, 2014).

The level of redistribution and transformative justice achieved could certainly be expected to vary across cases of PB where it is implemented. There may be many variables that could explain these outcomes worthy of an empirical test. For example, the motives of initiators may differ – as PB has diffused, it has been accepted and implemented by parties and actors from different political backgrounds. In the UK a strong localism agenda among the Conservatives saw PB amalgamated into the new coalition government's 'Big Society' initiative in 2010; however, the overall initiative was ill received and

PB was marginalized and allowed to fall off central government's policy map. In Brazil many non-PT and even non-Leftist parties may have taken up PB in order to try and mimic the electoral rewards it saw the PT acquiring. However, Spada shows that despite abandonment of PB by PT parties after Lula's presidential victory, the number of non-PT-led participatory budgets remained stable at best (2017).

I do not attempt to explain redistributive outcomes directly. Even if the creators of PB had the ultimate goal of redistributing wealth, what makes them stand out from others who tried to achieve that goal through various means is that they trusted in an innovation in democratic institutional design. Dissecting the relationship between democracy and equality of outcomes is far beyond the scope of this book, but democratic institutions should not be judged on their ability to realize substantive outcomes that are defined as desirable a priori to the democratic decision-making process. My interest is in democracy. Rather than ask what is decided, I want to know when citizens gain control over what is decided.

## Influencing conditions

As explained, a robust medium-N QCA requires the theoretical skills to select and define a small number of explanatory conditions to be examined with the outcome condition I have conceptualized. The growing literature on PB outlined in Chapter 3 provides ample candidates for key conditions that could explain successful outcomes. A myriad of the conditions that are suggested to explain successes in deepening of democracy as a result of PB imply necessity and/or sufficiency. Plausible hypotheses include combinations of the fiscal independence of a polity, the governing ideology of the political leadership, the health of civil society, the quality of deliberation at meetings, the role of the bureaucracy, the degree of partisanship across the political spectrum, constitutional provisions for participatory governance, and more. With 31 cases the analysis needs to optimize the number of conditions we can examine across cases but also consider the limited diversity of social phenomena. Therefore, I consider four important conditions that have been considered key to explaining citizen control of budgetary decision-making in the literature, as outlined here.

### *The set of government leaders committed to a participatory governing philosophy (pl)*

People who have power rarely give it away. Debates about the role of citizens in governance or the state have raged for centuries, and are the staple of much political philosophy. We standardly indoctrinate undergraduate students by exposing them to a canon that reads from Plato through Aristotle, Machiavelli, the modern social contract theorists and theorists of representation and laterally, the likes of Schumpeter, Pateman, Dahl and many more in between, to try to comprehend what the ideal role for the individual is in making collective decisions. In some cases those writings have inspired or guided revolution, but throughout history what has been rare is for a state or other locus of power to decide to give up that power without a fight. Even where leaders talk of decentralizing power, that talk is often met with cynicism, as very few of those talkers eventually 'walk the walk'. Yet it seems the cynicism would be misplaced considering some cases of PB. Why?

If there is one issue that unites concern among political scholars of many methodological and ideological hues, it is that we seem to be experiencing a legitimacy crisis in established representative democracies (Saward, 2010; Mair, 2013; Stoker, 2017). As explained in Chapter 1, what is most interesting about the participatory fora and innovative institutional designs that have emerged since the 1980s is that democratization in these instances is governance-driven (Warren, 2009). Studies in both Latin America and Europe (see especially Röcke, 2014) emphasize the importance of the leadership strategy in putting PB onto the agenda. The leadership strategy can significantly influence the model or rules of PB, and thereby its success in practice.

This condition connects concerns about the extent to which participation is ideologically central to governing parties, the degree of support for participation across the party and political spectrum, and the instrumental incentives for government to engage citizens in decision-making. Some of the field researchers I draw on have split those conditions and analysed them independently. I treat them as elements of a higher-order construct here. All those elements and others might be operationalized separately and then combined, but it is important to be clear that in my analysis I am primarily interested in the higher-order construct that takes all into account.

In some cases, commitment to participatory ideals can be signalled in the rhetoric of speeches and policy programmes promoted publicly. In the case of Poitou-Charentes, Ségelène Royal followed a fairly radical discourse in her defence of and promise for participatory democracy, at least prior to her selection as presidential candidate in 2006/07 (Röcke, 2014: 66–7). However, despite being influenced by the World Social Forum, it was also clear that Royal recognized the strategic benefits of participation, and tempered her rhetoric in national campaigns (Röcke, 2014: 24). Therefore, this condition considers commitment to participation across political society as a whole. High-set membership values on this condition are observed where leaders sustained participatory measures in the face of challenges from opposition leaders. We also observe the condition where challenges to PB programmes were not forthcoming because there was broad support across the political spectrum, and any challenges were not strongly made or publicized. A further important indicator is whether leaders actively attempted to improve the circumstances for participation. Although I understand financial security of a municipality and bureaucratic capacity themselves to be independent conditions, the effect on the outcome of ideological commitment to participation can be observed when leaders took political risks to try and channel funds and/or human resources or other state capital to advantage PB. One conjunctural hypothesis that can be tested is the expectation that all three of those conditions will be observed in combination where citizen control is present.

### *Bureaucratic support for participatory budgeting (bsp)*

The inclusion of this condition recognizes a further source of the exercise of power that can act as a brake or catalyst for participatory reforms. Bureaucrats or other contracted officials play an important role in guaranteeing or negating the outcomes of policies. This role is conditioned by their physical capacities and competences to do the work (Lipsky, 1980). For example, the actions of officials both directly and indirectly mobilize or demobilize participants. In some cases bureaucrats exercised discretion in ways that benefited PB.

There are important differences across polities in the extent to which political leaders are able to restructure the administration (including the appointment of senior bureaucrats) to enable PB (Abers, 2000; Baiocchi, 2005). It is a little ironic that in some cases leaders were able to take advantage of the 'spoils systems' of patronage to reorganize bureaucracies such that key strategic positions as well as street-level ones were held by those who were committed to participation. As Abers points out in the case of Porto Alegre, two organizations, GAPLAN (a reorganized planning department) and CRC53 (community relations department) were initiated in this way in order to support PB (2000: 77–8). Bureaucrats were brought close to ordinary citizens, working with them towards common aims. In other cases, sympathetic bureaucrats may have been removed where leaders lost interest in participation. Rodgers gives a good account of such an occurrence in his description of the latter years of the Buenos Aires case (2010).

Therefore, this condition considers the freedom that bureaucrats have to support PB as well as their intentions and actions.

In other cases, bureaucratic support varied where politicians had either little control or little influence over which staff were involved in the project and even what they did. Lerner and van Wagner (2006) suggest that in Toronto it was committed staff in the social housing sector having been made aware of PB through diffusion channels that bypassed politicians, who, recognizing they had the capacity to act, took it upon themselves to implement a PB process. Support also varied where such reorganization as had been taken on in South America was not possible at the municipal level. We can see, therefore, that this condition suggests a number of combinatorial hypotheses that may alternate in their effect on the outcome depending on the presence of other conditions. Another expectation I test is whether a combination of support from both politicians and bureaucrats is sufficient on its own to produce real democratic outcomes in a PB process, or alternatively, whether one without the other is sufficient across cases in conjunction with, for example, the work of civil society actors.

### *Autonomous civil society demands for participatory budgeting projects (csd)*

Claims to the necessity of an active civil society for truly democratic outcomes in PB are common especially to much of the early literature in Brazil (see, especially, Wampler, 2007a; Avritzer, 2009; Baiocchi et al, 2011). Many PB scholars are sceptical of the ability of a participatory budget to become institutionalized and flourish where it is implemented only from the top down. There remains a tension within democratic theory between radical democrats and participatory institutionalists as to whether democratic deepening can emanate from the top down driven by governance imperatives (Smith, 2009; Warren, 2009), or whether that approach only reifies existing relations of dominance and pacifies the resistance to hegemony that is necessary for democracy. Both Baiocchi (2005) and Wampler (2007a) elaborate mechanisms whereby a vibrancy and activism within civil society can generate organized pressure for PB from the bottom up. In Porto Alegre, civil society activists lobbied successfully to not have the PB procedures enshrined legally precisely because they wanted the space to remain vibrant and contested. This early advantage may have become a liability when political support waned (Nuñez, 2018). So, is this bottom-up demand necessary for citizen control of PB outcomes, or are there alternative paths to that outcome?

Data collected for this condition include details on whether civil society was able to make organized and consistently strong demands invoking their rights to participate as a source of legitimating democratic decisions. This condition considers not just demand, but also capacity of civil society within a municipality or region. It tries to capture information on the extent to which CSOs were able to organize independent of government across cases. We have already seen in Chapter 4 that across Brazilian cases it was CSOs' willingness and ability to use contentious politics to hold government to account on implementing PB projects that stood out for many scholars in ensuring the relative success of programmes. However, as we will see, I find less support for this hypothesis when looking across cases.

### *Financial basis to spend (fbs)*

What spending freedom does the body organizing and implementing PB have, and is it steered or constrained by external forces beyond its control? Where diffusion has occurred across vastly different political units with different capacities and functions, the question of the degree of fiscal independence available to the instigators of participatory processes arises. The fourth and final condition I test assesses whether PB programmes have access to or can raise sufficient funds to administer the project and implement the outcomes of PB decisions. Where politicians, bureaucrats and/or civil society are committed to political reform, financial constraints may negate their ability to achieve their goals.

The participatory budgets in the dataset took place in different countries with different levels of decentralization and tax-raising powers among local governments and other subsidiary regulatory bodies. These bodies may also have different roles and freedoms with different welfare state models across the population of cases. In the early work on Brazilian cases, the fiscal autonomy of municipal mayors, including in particular their relative power to vary taxation, was frequently part of the explanation for successful implementation (Abers, 2000; Goldfrank, 2012). Onerous administrative burdens and a lack of investment can reduce participants' sense of efficiency of the process (Wampler et al, 2018: 18). However, formal powers do not tell the whole story here. In some cases, actors are constrained by historical or macro-economic problems; for example, in the Brazilian context Recife suffered from a lack of infrastructure and resources such that it struggled to implement infrastructure projects decided on by the budget (Wampler, 2007a; Montambeault, 2016). Where governments have to constantly commit funding to firefighting emergencies, they are likely to suffer more pressure to avoid rowing in with participatory decisions that are seen as risky, or they may simply be unable to fund the demands of citizens. In other cases, subsidiary bodies may have a relatively greater ability to negotiate changes in these circumstances. This condition was carefully calibrated to allow comparison across units of different size and competence.

## Why favour these conditions over others?

What very few researchers on PB have yet come close to producing is a fully specified typological theory for any combination of conditions of interest. That is, very few writers discuss all of the logical combinations of their selected key conditions that influence or shape a participatory budget. I am confident that the four conditions selected represent the most significant causal claims made within the general literature on PB and reflect field knowledge from the cases included in the analysis. I also limit the analysis to four conditions to reduce logical remainders and provide transparent assumptions about counterfactuals as much as is possible for a medium-N study. There are many other conditions that were considered and that might be included in future iterations, or other studies that try to cumulate knowledge to explain successful participatory processes. Other candidates would include a measure of the size of jurisdiction of the government or agency administering the participatory budget, returning to an independent measure of the weakness of opposition, measuring relative poverty in a municipality, democratic performance, level of decentralization in design, presence or absence of other avenues for participation apart from the PB, rules on monitoring of projects, partisanship (left or right-leaning municipality or civil society) and variances in privileges of organized interests.

In at least three instances quite convincing arguments have been made in the case literature that suggest these variables play an important role in explaining PB cases, but either the data is currently unavailable across a range of cases, or conditions were not included to avoid the problem of limited diversity. First, Avritzer makes the case that in São Paulo, PB suffered because its decisions sometimes overlapped with decisions made in other power-sharing bodies such as health councils (2009: 100). Few scholars look systematically at the effect of other decision-making fora in a municipality on the success of PB, although some hint at it. This is an underexplored important hypothesis in participatory governance. Multiple participatory venues may induce confusion or allow venue shopping. Unfortunately, discussion of this phenomenon is not rich, and data on the way different bodies involved in governance work in practice is difficult to collect and verify without conducting many interviews with people on the ground. This condition may also be a good example of alternative causation – the existence of other participatory institutions may signal experiential learning of how to do participation ('schools of democracy') in municipalities, which increases the chances that PB will be successful.

Second, my construction of the participatory leadership condition considers support for participation across the political spectrum. An important finding for Goldfrank was that the participatory programme in Porto Alegre was more successful where opposition was weakly institutionalized vis-à-vis his other two cases, because 'community organisation in Caracas and Montevideo were linked to either the opposition or incumbent parties, and they did not push for power in the new participation programmes' (2012: 7). Nylen also considers partisanship within a municipality as an important barrier to PB's success (2003b), and Wampler similarly includes the condition of 'mayor–legislative relations' as central to his comparisons. Nylen shows that even in Betim, where the PT tried to reach out across political divides, the result was relatively unsuccessful.

Opposition and partisanship on their own may be important conditions that explain the success of PB. These conditions come close to satisfying data availability requirements across cases. It would not be difficult to construct a proxy measure by investigating the historical and contemporary strength of opposition parties in each municipality, which even without rich description of how this operates in practice could be powerful as a predictor of outcomes. Nevertheless, these conditions are not operationalized separately and considered in this analysis. Including a fifth condition overcomplicates and would induce further problems of limited diversity, and the four conditions I include are slightly more prevalent as explanations of outcomes across cases, especially outside South America. It is sometimes difficult to distinguish the separate effects of opposition, partisanship and participatory leadership in qualitative accounts as the leader can adapt messages to circumstances. This is why overall support for participation across political society is favoured in the calibration of the participatory leadership condition here. Essentially, I do not conduct a strong test for weakness of opposition, but include it as part of a higher-order construct. It is important to keep these factors in mind when interpreting the results of comparative analysis.

Third, and relatedly, some might argue that size of a municipality and/or overall levels of development or poverty could mediate results of PB. In particular, Pateman questions whether there is an appetite for participatory reform in wealthy established democracies (2012: 15). This is important, and such conditions could provide 'easy wins' in terms of data availability given the quantitative measures available. However, as before, these are not the key concerns in the literature and may be more appropriately looked at in a larger-N study. In the end we have to cut our cloth to suit our means. Avenues for expanding this analysis as a mode of cumulation to enable an enlarged research agenda are discussed in Chapter 9.

## A note on comparison and time

The final important factor in casing and hypothesis formation is time – it is important to be clear about the time range for each case. PB is still an evolving phenomenon. The earliest cases began in 1989. The cases in the dataset generally represent older, more established cases of PB (at least where they have remained established). They are cases that were selected by researchers for in-depth investigation because they recognized their analytic value. In this dataset the time range for each case is set by the source material. On the whole they provide enough information for a robust comparison, and we may want to make some modest generalizations from our findings in the direction of many younger cases for which information is emerging (see Dias, 2018). Some accounts cover 15 years of a practice and in others the accounts may cover as little as 3 years of a PB programme.

We saw in Chapter 4 that Wampler highlights differences in the case of Porto Alegre over time. Baierle (2008) considers PB to be a very different beast after the 2004 elections, which left the city without a PT mayor. We might also note that in Recife, for example, PB has been governed by a number of different mayors from different parties over the years. Not only might there be both adverse and positive effects of change, but continuity may also affect PB, either positively or negatively. For instance, it might be argued that participatory learning takes place over time, allowing improvements in outcomes.

A recurring criticism of QCA is that it is too static. In a case study, researchers can trace a process, providing a mechanistic definition of causation where time and sequence are important conditions influencing outcomes. However, QCA has little to say about the difference in time between conditions observed in cases. Its analytical moment focuses on conjunction and disjunction. There have been some suggestions for remedying this. A time-sensitive variant of QCA (temporal qualitative comparative analysis or TQCA), as developed by Caren and Panofsky (2005), and later by Ragin and Strand (2008), introduces a sequence as a causal condition in the analysis. In the case of PB, for example, we might have a hypothesis that when strong bureaucratic capacity precedes a participatory governing party coming to power, citizen power in PB is difficult to achieve because the bureaucracy is strong enough to resist change. However, when a participatory governing party improves weak bureaucratic capacity, it may be able to inculcate the government ideology, and bureaucratic capacity may combine with political commitments to produce good PB programmes. TQCA is useful as it allows a test for the outcome produced when one cause precedes another, and vice versa. The sequence can then be an important part of the causal combination explaining an outcome. However, there is a pitfall in that we are adding a condition, and thus increasing limits to diversity of logical case examples.

Other work has sought to improve the treatment of time in QCA by including elements of other methods (for example, time-series QCA; see Hino, 2009). There has been renewed attention to the issue among methodologists more recently. However, QCA is still unfortunately rather unable to provide sophisticated understandings of causation that trace process and feedback. This might be seen to be a problem for the research of young, burgeoning phenomena such as democratic innovations where it is often still unclear what direction causality is taking between conditions themselves and conditions and outcomes. As I show in the analysis presented in the next three chapters of Part III, I learned that the static comparison can be a strength, especially once seen as part of a symbiotic relationship with case knowledge in a process of cumulation. Looking at what conditions consistently occur in combinations can force a researcher to re-problematize 'accepted' sequential inferences. Nevertheless, it also serves to reinforce the point that cross-case comparison cannot replicate or replace within-case methods and requires the complement. In any case, using QCA we can return to the cases with these considerations in mind to assess whether we are missing a crucial condition from the explanation and an alternative reading of individual cases is desirable. I elaborate on these in my interpretation of outcomes. I now go on to discuss the process of calibration that decides how membership values in sets are assigned.

## Conceptualization and calibration: fuzzy logic meets participatory democracy

Lamentations over social scientists' inability to conceptualize and measure phenomena discretely are not new. Sartori's words retain pertinence:

> The incessant use of 'it is a matter of degree' phraseology and of the 'continuum' image leave us with qualitative-impressionistic statements which do not advance us by a hair's breadth toward quantification. In a similar vein we speak more and more of 'variables' which are not variables in any proper sense, for they are not attributes permitting gradations and implying measurability. (Sartori, 1970: 1036)

Case-based comparative approaches assume that there is an extent to which complex phenomena can be observed and described in terms of both their elemental qualities and quantitative variations of the presence of these qualities. Descriptions when compared to idealizations and to other cases using the insights of theory can be usefully measured and mapped in terms of their set membership across cases. This lends itself to some new analytic techniques, in particular, the use of Boolean algebraic operations and fuzzy logic, to provide parsimonious descriptions of causal relationships.

Retaining some further acumens of case-based reasoning, QCA generally employs information-oriented sampling. That is to say, the case selection outlined previously is based mostly on what we know about the cases and what we know about other potential cases rather than a randomized process. Set membership of a condition is distinguished from measures of traditional variables in statistical analysis by having a meaningful maximum and minimum for set membership. Where a phenomenon is observed in a case, the case can be said to be a member of the set of that phenomenon. Cases can have different degrees of membership in a set depending on the degree to which the condition is observed. This allows comparative researchers to describe degrees of variation. Fuzzy sets are, in some ways, simply an expansion in sophistication of a crisp dichotomization where a value of 1 indicates full membership in a set and 0 full non-membership. Each case will still display a membership score either side of the crossover point (0.5), which represents maximum ambiguity between whether a case is more in the set or more out (Ragin, 2000).

Figure 5.1 reproduces an example that will be familiar to many engaged with participatory theory, and which I found useful for explaining the concept for those unfamiliar with it. Arnstein developed her well-known theoretical model of a 'ladder of participation' in critically observing efforts to include under-represented populations in policymaking in the US (1969). At one level the ladder image suggests each rung has a similar meaningful interval and interval data is an appropriate level of measurement to those interested in using the theory

**Figure 5.1:** Mapping a fuzzy set based on Arnstein's 'ladder of participation' (1969)

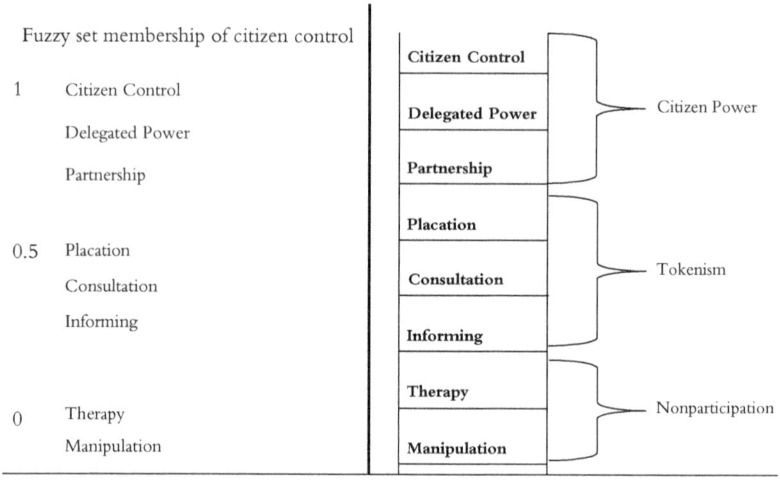


Source: The right of the figure is reprinted by permission of The American Planning Association, www.planning.org

in real world evaluation. Nevertheless, Arnstein makes important qualitative distinctions, especially between the three rungs that more represent citizen power and the other levels in Figure 5.1. This shows how the theory can be used to construct a fuzzy set to measure the concept of citizen control of decision-making, including differences of quality and quantity. Cases that display full citizen control have full membership of the set, manipulatory designs are located fully out of the set, but cases ranging up from consultation through partnership display partial membership in the set in relation to one another.

Fuzzy sets were adapted to the social sciences by Smithson (1988) and Ragin (2000). They were previously developed for use in computer sciences by Zadeh (1965). They give us the opportunity to connect theory and measurement in a constructive manner, as the example of the ladder of participation in Figure 5.1 shows. As Ragin puts it, we connect formal and verbal logic (2000: 160). A condition set is formulated by clearly defining full membership, full non-membership and other degrees of membership. In Ragin's words, 'fuzzy logic offers a mathematical system that makes allowances for the pliable nature of verbal concepts' (2000: 160). It is important to note that calibrated set scores are not a ranking. Each score is 'pinpointing a qualitative state' (Ragin, 2009: 90) that can be verbally described.

Dichotomization is only problematic where it is a byword for unreflective data processing. It can be a distinct advantage for conceptual clarification to require that research defines what constitutes the presence or absence of a phenomenon for a given study rather than sit comfortably on indeterminacy. Fuzzy sets do not allow for indeterminacy unless their users get away with obfuscation in presenting to the untrained eye. Fuzzy logic should not be relied on to help unscrupulous scholars descend into relativism. Crisp sets (where only membership scores of 1 or 0 are allowed) can be useful for theory-building and case selection in thinking through logical contradictions (where two cases appear to contain the same configuration of relevant causes but a different outcome[1]) in a property space of cases.

There are different approaches to calibration, and the approach taken for calibrating each set will depend on the nature of data and the confidence in being accurately able to attribute qualitative changes in states to recognize different levels of set membership. My analysis relies on calibration of qualitative data rather than using a quantitative proxy and directly calibrating a set using mathematical transformations. The latter method has become popular as large-N research is undertaken using QCA. For example, one could calibrate the set of a large or small municipality by specifying the three qualitative breakpoints or full membership, non-membership and the crossover point for city populations, and then use a mathematical transformation to quickly ascribe set memberships to a large number of cities based on that quantitative data.[2]

In contrast, the method of calibration I employ, straightforward in terms of understanding and conceptual clarity but not application, involves drawing candidly on rich descriptions in existing casework. Cases are ascribed fuzzy membership values in the sets 'by hand' (membership in each set represents the observed degree of presence of a condition). In my analysis, the following 7-value fuzzy set, as proposed by Ragin (2000: 156), is used.

---

1 For an applied discussion, see Olsen and Nomura (2009).

2 Ragin suggests estimates of log odds (2008: 87). There are other functional forms that can be used, but the effect of changes of functional transformation mechanisms, while measurable, remains marginal in most scenarios – it is the qualitative definition of breakpoints that matters substantively (Schneider and Wagemann, 2012: 37). Schneider and Wagemann also point to an important critique in this approach to calibration, in that it leads to 'very fine-grained fuzzy scales, thus suggesting a level of precision that usually goes well beyond the available empirical information and the conceptual level of differentiation that is possible' (2012: 37).

| | |
|---|---|
| 1.0 | Fully in (the set) |
| 0.83 | Mostly but not fully in |
| 0.67 | More or less in |
| 0.5 | Crossover point |
| 0.33 | More or less out |
| 0.17 | Mostly but not fully out |
| 0 | Fully out |

Calibrating and coding cases is an informative, inductive process. There is constant interplay here between case knowledge and theoretical understanding. On engaging in iterations of calibration it became clear that this 7-value set was an appropriate level of nuance in measurement, given the data available. To understand the iteration involved, take the example of the set of government leaders committed to a participatory governing philosophy, shortened here to 'participatory leadership'. I might have started off with the following conceptualization: full membership in this set is observed where the instigator or overseer of PB is ideologically committed to participatory politics and to implementing PB.[3] Full non-membership is where the instigator or overseer of PB is not ideologically committed to participatory politics AND[4] is actively trying to derail or revoke participatory practices. We have a number of cases that we know lie somewhere in between these points – when does a case look more like a committed participatory leader, and when does it look more like an uncommitted one? I might start by saying that the point of maximum ambiguity (or crossover point) is represented when the instigator or overseer of PB is committed to participatory politics only to the extent that it fits in with other ideological or material goals; and support for PB is present but limited and extremely fragmented across the governing ranks. Cases closer to the maximum from this point are more in, and cases closer to the

[3] The following short section draws heavily on Ryan and Smith (2012: 104–5). The research presented in the book updates that pilot study. The conceptualizations of conditions remain relatively similar, as cases have been added allowing some comparisons with that work, although I have abandoned the use of some less determinate measures.

[4] When I use 'AND; OR' in capitals I am invoking the logic of intersection and union of sets respectively. Conjunctions (corresponding to the intersection of sets) and disjunctions (union) are arithmetically calculated using minimum and maximum functions to ascertain their set membership values. The procedure is explained further when I present analysis in the next chapter.

minimum are more out of the set. I can then evaluate gradations of 'more in' or 'more out' where appropriate, given knowledge of cases and data available, and refine definitions of the concept.

Porto Alegre achieves a fuzzy membership of 1 in this set, as PB was the flagship of an explicit participatory philosophy of the instigating party. The PT proposed a programme specifically designed to involve lower socioeconomic groups in public policymaking venues to give CSOs an input into making the rules of PB, and to increase budget transparency. In comparison, we know that in Berlin the mayor is committed to participation at district level, but there is a question as to whether this justifies similar membership given that the district mayor is not the only driving force in such a federal system (Röcke, 2014). In Buenos Aires there was brief enthusiasm from those in power, but this was linked to the political opportunity structure and the contingent circumstances of the Argentine economy rather than just participatory ideals (Peruzzotti, 2009; Rodgers, 2010). Can we measure these cases using the measurement device we have constructed?

For the purpose of improving measurement and descriptions of concepts, I found it useful to visualize the cases on what I term 'fuzzy maps' (see Figure 5.2). I could then add and subtract information or move cases to obtain the best reflection of conceptual theory and observations.

The interaction between the graphical representation and the membership statements helps in the direction of confident judgements that the numerical values we ascribe cases make sense. The conception can change both in relation to the verbal definitions of key breakpoints in set membership and more tacit knowledge of the cases themselves and how they relate. Interplay then takes place where the researcher must refine the definitions of the contours of the set in light of information thrown up by the cases as coding takes place. Where cases known to have important differences on the degree to which they display the condition are found to have proximate fuzzy membership scores, this may signal a need to consider redefining membership. In this example, I can add the caveat that for full membership the instigator or overseer of PB is ideologically committed to participatory politics AND to implementing PB, AND is willing to take risky political decisions to uphold this commitment. I can then recode cases like Berlin and Buenos Aires with perhaps lower set memberships accordingly. What is sought is that the definitions of membership values will eventually make sense such that membership in the set is clearly calibrated to the theoretical meaning of the condition we wish to test.

**Figure 5.2:** Example of a fuzzy map to help calibrate participatory leadership

Participatory Leadership Strategy

| Score | Cases | Code |
|---|---|---|
| 1 | Porto Alegre,<br>Poitou-Charentes, New York<br>Ipatinga,Camaragibe<br>Rome, Lambayeque<br>Morsang<br>Recife(ii),Gravataí<br>João Monlevade, Santo André<br>Montevideo, Chicago<br>Sevilla, Betim, Berlin, Belo<br>Cusco, Moquegua<br>Córdoba | Code: 1 = The instigator/overseer of PB is ideologically committed to participatory politics and implementing PB. They are willing to take risky decisions and can build or manoeuvre support across the political spectrum. |
| 0.5 | São Paulo, Cajamarca<br>Recife(i)<br>Mauá<br>Buenos Aires | 0.5 = The instigator/overseer of PB is committed to participatory politics only to the extent that it fits with other policy goals and support is fragmented across political society in a way that makes ongoing support for the PB precarious. |
| 0 | Ayacucho, Loreto<br>Blumenau, Rio Claro<br>Toronto | 0 – The instigator/overseer of PB has little interest or is actively hostile to the PB and/or participatory politics. The PB is taking place in spite of the leadership. |

More recently I found that these fuzzy maps and similarly truth tables are particularly useful for guiding discussions with researchers in attempting to clarify the conditions of particular cases with which they are familiar. These relatively simple tools hold particular promise for aiding cumulation of knowledge from small-N case research, potentially using them in expert surveys, as more in-depth cumulation is cultivated. No researcher can have knowledge of all cases that exist, but they will have varying partial knowledge of some cases outside of their own field research. Most researchers who work on PB are au fait with the history and nuances of the Porto Alegre case, which provides an anchor for comparisons. By looking at the cases for which they have degrees of knowledge in relation to one another and in relation to an operationalization of a concept itself, researchers can engage in a dialogue with other researchers, bringing together theory and comparative knowledge at once. Colleagues can be stimulated to provide further information to help improve and refine definitions that delineate conditions, and where they think there are errors with coding, they can make arguments for change. I was worried initially that case researchers might react guardedly to my calibrations, but I need not have been (so far, at least). In almost all cases colleagues have seen an opportunity for their research to be extended in an important way. On occasion field researchers contacted me unprompted to recommend changes, and I am sure they may do so again.[5]

This process of calibration highlights the extent to which iteration is central in seeking both theoretical clarity and robust measurement for comparison of PB. Despite, and to some extent because of, the dispersion and variability of cases, measures can still be constructed that are comparable across cases and conditions. This, as I presently show, allows the use of Boolean algebraic operations to uncover relationships of necessity and sufficiency between conditions and outcomes across cases. As new cases are added, we are often forced into reassessing the nature of membership for particular sets. This is nothing new in the sense that scholars have for years been looking at how concepts travel and can be meaningfully quantified across contexts. Nevertheless, by allowing these considerations at the level of medium-N, QCA seems to provide an alternative location for robust research along the spectrum of trade-offs between complexity and generalizability in social and political research.

---

[5] Of course, there may be sample bias here. Colleagues who think your work is complete rubbish can be too polite to say so if they think issues are insignificant, or do not think it worth their engagement! Greater input and collaboration have allowed improvements in accuracy of interpretations. Nevertheless, it is important to note that texts remain the primary source on which I rely.

## A fuzzy set analysis of 30 cases

In the final analysis provided in the following chapters, sets have been calibrated according to the criteria outlined in this section. Full membership in the set of government leaders committed to a participatory governing philosophy (abbreviated to 'pl') requires that the leaders initiating the PB have committed to participation in manifestos and speeches AND that their commitment is not reduced in bargaining with non-committed parties. Leaders make decisions to support participatory projects irrespective of other political actors OR supported by them. Full non-membership requires that the instigator or overseer of PB is not ideologically committed to participatory politics; shows little interest in participation; OR is actively trying to derail or revoke participatory practices. At the crossover point the instigator or overseer of PB is ideologically committed to participatory politics only to the extent that it fits with other policy goals AND support is fragmented across political society in a way that makes support for PB precarious and political actors unwilling to take risks for the PB.

Full membership of the set of bureaucratic support for PB (bsp) requires that officials working for the governors actively support and engage with participatory processes AND those staff obstructing advances in participation are easily removed. Full non-membership is observed where officials actively attempt to derail the process, lobby for reform towards other practices and concentrate resources on other projects. At the point of maximum ambiguity bureaucratic support for participation is fragmented. Some departments may support participation while others oppose it. There is contestation over programmes within the bureaucracy, and support is contingent on important bureaucratic leaders' abilities to remain in position.

Full membership in the set of autonomous civil society demands for PB (csd) requires that civil society is dynamic and differentiated in involvement with the process AND CSOs are actively making demands for participation and projects AND are willing to use multiple resources and tactics to secure their demands, building coalitions for cooperative and contentious politics. Full non-membership denotes absence of civil society activism – often described as frail, fragile and fragmented OR an active civil society that is tied to more traditional relations between government and the public sphere within the local political culture. There is no prospect for new and diverse CSOs to get involved in the process, and low trust in alliances. At the point of maximum ambiguity there is some demand to allow civil society an ever-greater role in the governance of budgets, but the institutional designs that civil society are mobilizing for or into are not necessarily open participatory ones OR civil society is extremely fragmented and partisan mobilization is increasing rather than reducing, mirrored in disjointed support for PB.

Full membership in the set of financial basis for spending (fbs) requires that the government unit undertaking PB has independent control over substantial sums of money in relative terms to other such units of governance in their country. There is no interference from other tiers of government or authorities in the spending of the relevant budget AND the municipality is not overwhelmed by debt or other pressing financial concerns. Full non-membership is observed where funds made available for PB are paltry. This may be because the governing unit is overwhelmed by debt or unable to raise any funds, for example, through tax, charges or sales of assets. At the crossover point some money is available for PB processes and projects, but spending is constrained by decisions taken elsewhere OR PB competes for funds with closely related projects or institutions.

In the following chapters I analyse case membership in these four sets in relation to their membership in the outcome set: the set of citizen control of participatory budgeting (ccpb). Full membership of the outcome set requires a logical combination of sustained control over decision-making AND control over agenda-setting, including absence of co-optation in practice, and opportunities for monitoring and accountability. Full non-membership denotes clear co-optation and a return to clientelism, leading to disappointment and participation fatigue among citizens. The agenda for participatory decisions is set elsewhere, and decisions of the PB are only acted on where they suit governments. At the crossover point, important PB decisions are sometimes implemented, even when they are not clearly in line with government aims, but this takes place on a seemingly ad hoc basis – perhaps agendas are constrained at government level. Cases more in the set see successes, but with citizens having to struggle regularly (for example, by protesting) in order to see decisions implemented and to hold governments to account. Cases more out see some gains, but not enough to suggest even partial or temporal transformations of the logics of authority.

Settling on the descriptions of conditions and set memberships took several iterations to take into account different levels of information across cases, valid levels of abstraction for a comparison of the cases to take place, and negotiating and understanding some rival accounts of some cases. All cases were coded on the basis of the criteria previously outlined. The following data matrix (see Table 5.1) was finally produced, showing the cases' set memberships in these calibrated sets.

On presenting the data I make two important reflections before moving to present my analysis. It was noticeable in coding cases and calibrating conditions across a number of separate investigations that the study of innovative practices as they emerge exacerbates some challenges for comparison. First, Chapters 2 and 3 traced the development of PB case studies. It is now well accepted that research on participatory governance has focused too much on best cases (Spada and Ryan, 2017; Smith, 2019). The assumption implicit in much research in the field is that the true distribution of participatory governance and PB is skewed. There is assumed to be a long tail of desultory practices or a bunch of extremely positive outliers. Many of the most influential writers in the field find the touchstone for their investigations in ideal theory – they are studying 'real utopias' (Fung and Wright, 2003).

I am certainly not out to criticize that. What attracted most colleagues and myself to the field is a normative commitment to improving (or defending) democracy, so that is where my sympathies lie. Often, however, we may be too quick to dismiss 'mere consultation' than investigate properly its forms and outputs.[6] We should be mindful of the bias presented by the tension between normative commitments of democracy promotion and the reduction of normative commitments required for certain kinds of explanation. It is a useful tension to explore, but it is far from resolved in the subfield (Spada and Ryan, 2017), and is an issue for the discipline as a whole to keep under consideration in its vocational commitments (Keohane, 2009). Over-romanticizing the effects of participatory practices like PB is unlikely to be helpful (Nylen, 2003a: 149). The challenge is not to valorize certain cases too much – the lessons of Porto Alegre can remain inspirational even when some of the reality of its problems are treated in retrospect, with the benefit of hindsight. But we should also consider that conceptualizations and measures of participatory governance that may appear to be more normally distributed, can be useful for understanding democratic participation, if the relationship between the concept and the measure is clear. If we focus only on the variation at one end of the distribution of efforts in participation, we are missing a lot.

---

[6] Baiocchi et al make a similar point in their comparison of Brazilian municipalities (2011: 77).

**Table 5.1:** Data matrix of fuzzy memberships in conditions

| Case | Participatory leadership (pl) | Autonomous civil society demand (csd) | Bureaucratic support (bsp) | Financial basis to spend (fbs) | Citizen control of PB (ccpb) |
|---|---|---|---|---|---|
| Ayacucho | 0 | 0.33 | 0 | 0.17 | 0 |
| Belo Horizonte | 0.83 | 1 | 0.33 | 1 | 0.83 |
| Berlin-Lichtenberg | 0.83 | 0.17 | 0.17 | 0.17 | 0.33 |
| Betim | 0.83 | 0.33 | 0.67 | 0.67 | 0.33 |
| Blumenau | 0 | 0.17 | 0 | 0.83 | 0 |
| Buenos Aires | 0.17 | 0.33 | 1 | 0 | 0.33 |
| Cajamarca | 0.33 | 0.67 | 0.67 | 0.33 | 0.17 |
| Camaragibe | 1 | 0.33 | 0.67 | 0.17 | 0.67 |
| Chicago 49th Ward | 0.83 | 0.83 | 0 | 0.67 | 0.17 |
| Córdoba | 0.67 | 0.83 | 0 | 0.67 | 0.17 |
| Cusco | 0.67 | 1 | 0.67 | 0.33 | 1 |
| Gravataí | 0.83 | 0.33 | 1 | 0.83 | 0.83 |
| Ipatinga | 1 | 0.33 | 0.83 | 1 | 1 |
| João Monlevade | 0.83 | 0.67 | 0.83 | 0.83 | 0.67 |
| Lambayeque | 1 | 0.33 | 1 | 0.17 | 1 |
| Loreto | 0 | 0.17 | 0.17 | 0.33 | 0 |
| Mauá | 0.33 | 0.33 | 0 | 0.17 | 0.17 |
| Montevideo | 0.83 | 0.33 | 0.17 | 0.83 | 0.33 |
| Moquegua | 0.67 | 0.67 | 0.33 | 0.33 | 0.33 |
| Morsang-sur-Orge | 1 | 0.17 | 0.67 | 0 | 0.17 |
| New York | 1 | 0.83 | 0.33 | 0.83 | 0.83 |
| Poitou-Charentes | 1 | 0 | 0.17 | 1 | 0.83 |
| Porto Alegre | 1 | 1 | 1 | 1 | 1 |
| Recife (i) | 0.33 | 0.67 | 0.33 | 0.17 | 0.33 |
| Recife (ii) | 0.83 | 1 | 0.67 | 0.17 | 1 |
| Rio Claro | 0 | 0 | 0 | 0.83 | 0 |
| Rome | 1 | 0.67 | 0.33 | 0.33 | 0.67 |

(continued)

**Table 5.1:** Data matrix of fuzzy memberships in conditions (continued)

| Case | Participatory leadership (pl) | Autonomous civil society demand (csd) | Bureaucratic support (bsp) | Financial basis to spend (fbs) | Citizen control of PB (ccpb) |
|---|---|---|---|---|---|
| Santo André | 0.83 | 0.67 | 0.33 | 0.17 | 0.33 |
| São Paulo | 0.33 | 1 | 0.17 | 0.17 | 0.33 |
| Sevilla | 0.83 | 0.33 | 0.33 | 0.83 | 0.67 |
| Toronto | 0 | 0.17 | 0.33 | 0.17 | 0.33 |

Second, and relatedly, researchers engaged in small-N research necessarily have to spend a lot of time explaining assumed controls and variance of their case in relation to others. That is, how they justify their case selection and inferences they make beyond their case(s). I would be among the first to defend the robustness of those procedures (Ryan, 2017). In comparing across cases I had to be mindful of how variance is presented by different scholars (again, an advantage of cumulation is that I can take this into account). For instance, a rough and ready coding combined with a focus on maximum variation in several comparative studies could trick the secondary researcher into dichotomizing values to produce set scores with a highly negative kurtosis, thereby losing some nuance. Alternatively, a focus on controls, or simply a lack of data allowing conviction in decisions on presence or absence of conditions, can incentive the opposite – reliance on several mid-range values. The point of measurement is, of course, to accurately reflect the real world and the underlying concept as much as possible, and not to force-fit the world into a distribution that is easier to analyse. I use the image of a probability distribution here simply to show that the inclusion of a larger range of cases provides more specific information in helping us consider how our concepts reflect the real world.

In practice, fuzzy sets offer some advance for measurement by specifying three important qualitative points that will structure the distribution of cases. For the outcome I calibrate in Table 5.1, non-membership will identify irrelevant variation among the least democratic cases. Despite variation among cases coded 0, no case that scores 0 can be considered in any way to advance citizens' power. But also, at the top of the scale, full membership will identify irrelevant variation beyond a certain point where citizen control of decisions is perceptible. One case may achieve more democratic control than another. But when full membership of the set is conceived of as an ideal, and we are only measuring membership as an ideal(istic) type, that quality of having actually achieved citizen control of democratic decisions is not allowed for in empirical measurements. So, there may be two cases receiving a score of 1 that have variation above that level of success that is not considered. Despite my efforts, some may assess the matrix of set memberships in Figure 5.1 and find elements of the coding satisfactory but others objectionable. I can only hope that this will lead them to offer improvements, and in doing so we can build up the reliability of our collective understanding of the phenomenon. I discuss cases not included (and later time periods in the cases selected not covered by the data), as well as some issues of interpretation used to assign memberships to cases, at greater length in the course of presenting my analysis and results in the following chapters.

## To the analytic moments (with a return ticket)

In summary, there are multiple (and potentially overlapping) conditions that are conceptualized and operationalized by field researchers and employed in different ways to explain PB outcomes. Beyond negotiating the causal milieu, although most researchers are interested in explaining a 'success' outcome, broadly understood as empowered participatory democracy, different emphases are placed on redistributive justice, changes in the role of civil society and transparency in governance. Definition and careful scoping of research is crucial for accurate measurement and to lessen the impacts of 'travelling' problems in conceptual measurement. The advance of a QCA fully worked through, presented as it is here, is that it allows a transparent evaluation of the level of precision available in cumulating case research.

It is nothing new for researchers to have to explain their own understandings of key concepts and to operationalize them. What is new is the potential for cumulation in this approach. We should remember that the challenge for the social scientist is to provide parsimonious explanations of the real world and to make the correct choices as to what elements of that explanation are essential. The question is, are we using the right tools to do this, and what do they tell us about the substantive outcomes of participatory processes? The following chapters in Part III provide the answers to these questions.

# PART III

The identification of many potential conditions that could explain success in PB is not unhelpful. Brian Wampler's analysis of eight participatory budgets in urban Brazil, for example, has been a particularly useful contribution for scholars who wish to explain the emergence of emancipatory participatory governance through democratic innovation (2007a). Therefore, I use this as an access point in the following chapters to help explain how we might improve our theories by systematically navigating cumulation of more studies. I begin with a slightly stylized QCA of Wampler's most minimal account of deepened democracy to help establish what is at stake in set-theoretic analysis, and introduce methodological aspects gradually for unfamiliar readers. I then expand on this briefly, to show how QCA provides nuance for his most comprehensive account, before presenting the results of the more comprehensive analysis cumulating the work of several scholars.

Despite the quality of earlier work, without a more ecumenical but also systematic comparison it can be too tempting to generalize conditions particular to one context as necessary to others. In this part of the book I demonstrate to those familiar with the field the benefit of enhanced comparative approaches. I show that a more systematic comparison of diverse cases provides evidence that PB processes can be successful in very different contexts. This is a major finding because it lowers the barriers to the adoption of PB by offering policymakers options rather than a long list of requirements in policy formulation. This is not to say anything goes. I identify the most plausible conditions in alternative contexts for achieving or negating successful citizen control in PB programmes.

# 6

# Necessary Conditions for Democratic Reform

This chapter presents the analysis of necessary conditions, and shows that strong claims about finding necessary conditions in PB research have been premature. They are likely to have been an artefact of small-N research strategies where deviant cases that reduce evidence for necessity are not as obvious as they become when comparing the full range of evidence across research studies. There is quite a lot of evidence to show meaningful citizen control occurs without autonomous civil society demand and organizing, bureaucratic support for programmes, and strong financial resources respectively. That is not to say that case researchers were not on the right track with their claims, only that these claims need some further disambiguation to better identify the scope or context in which a condition becomes necessary in combination with other conditions. This is a crucial finding because it suggests that there is no context that is universally and unambiguously unable to produce some good PB outcomes, and therefore there is no place where PB will always fail (at least in the short term). Nevertheless, there is strong evidence that political leaders' commitment to participation is almost always necessary for success.

A researcher's task in presenting research is to distil excessive complexity and explain social phenomena with appropriate levels of parsimony. To this end researchers often construct typologies, and make claims about necessary and sufficient conditions based on their observations. Brian Wampler applies a familiar controlled approach in his distinguished comparison of eight cases of PB in urban Brazil (2007a). This is a useful contribution for scholars who wish to explain the emergence of emancipatory participatory governance through democratic innovation. It has been commended not only for its attentive and detailed narrative of processes within cases, but also its comparative design that moved beyond best-case examples to include variations in outcome and explanatory conditions to explain causation more systematically. In common with other examples in the emerging field of research on participatory democratic innovations, comparative work up to now has relied on more traditional small-N comparative designs. Therefore, in this final part of the book I often introduce stages of the research process by presenting a version of what a QCA replication of that study might look like. I then present wider analysis that accumulates more cases across studies. I take this approach to help readers understand and evaluate what the method achieves and what trade-offs are involved in taking on more set-theoretic reasoning over a larger-N of cases.

Notwithstanding Flyvbjerg's assertion (2006) that admonitions on subjectivity essentially misunderstand the reflexive nature of case-based research, a replication controlling even for the researcher's case choices but testing the added value of a QCA approach can be useful. Developing on increasing calls for transparency of data sources for replicability from case researchers, I implore that a QCA approach can also recover transparency at the analytic moment of smaller-N research by outlining what is at stake in decisions to highlight particular causal condition(s). I show that I can, at the very least, provide greater clarity when selecting the best trade-off between parsimony and explanatory power in small-to-medium-N case comparisons. I therefore directly address some of the possibilities of QCA as a deductive tool that aids interpretation where the case researchers may have their eyes very close to the field or data. The main model I present throughout these chapters is the result of careful reflection on which cases have provided enough information to make valid judgements for comparison.

It is important that readers unfamiliar with the method can understand the evidence base for my claims. I begin here by taking the example of a more parsimonious claim from Wampler's work to evaluate and explain the analysis and some pitfalls. Moreover, if I can add value to some of the most extensive existing studies, it provides support for the value of wider comparisons using such an approach.

Note again, then, that often Wampler's arguments are set-theoretic: 'To produce a strong PB programme, it is necessary to have high levels of mayoral support, a civil society that can engage in both cooperation and contestation, and rules that delegate specific types of direct authority to citizens' (2007a: 35).[1] To test these claims, I apply

[1] Wampler follows this quote directly with a correlational claim – 'as Mayoral support drops, as CSOs are unable to engage in both forms of political behaviour,

QCA's systematic approach, calibrating conditions based on the same qualitative descriptions used in the existing comparative study.

Table 6.1[2] is adapted from Wampler's concluding chapter (2007a: 258). It is typical of the kinds of parsimonious typological tables often presented in the findings of small-N comparative work. These tables are often used as methodological heuristics to make set-theoretic claims of necessity and sufficiency.

In Wampler's concluding chapter, he places particular emphasis on two explanatory conditions and suggests that mayoral support interacts with CSOs' willingness to use contentious politics to give four very different types of outcomes: institutionalized participatory democracy, informal and contested participatory democracy, co-opted participatory democracy, and emasculated participatory democracy. This type of table will be familiar to small-N case researchers. This is because the major advantage of small-N research is underlying familiarity with cases. This allows Wampler to verbally define each box in the table where we have an empirical example of a case. That is, he is labelling a set of cases and identifying members of the set. This is a useful process that adds plausibility and clarity to the argument; for example, it makes intuitive sense that co-optation in participatory programmes can be traced back to low use of contentious politics by CSOs, as in Table 6.1. Wampler argues from the outset that citizens need to be able to actively pursue the use of their rights (2007a: 2), and his evidence bears that out. The researcher here has helped the reader to comprehend a complex process. Prima facie, it would seem fair to conclude that the institutionalization of deep democracy can *only* occur where both these conditions are high, and that both are necessary conditions for this outcome. A simple correlation between each variable and the outcome deep democracy would be positive. From the point of view of categorical and ordinal understandings of the relationship among the conditions reflected in the data, the typology is both informative and unproblematic. But with QCA we have a further test we can use to assess the necessity claim. So what can set-theoretic comparison add?

---

and as the rules fail to delegate authority, PB outcomes will weaken' (2007a: 35). These two claims are not necessarily incompatible; what is important is that they require a different test. For the most part, both the correlational and set-theoretic inferences Wampler makes stand up well to scrutiny.

2 The adaptation includes a split of Porto Alegre into three cases reflecting three time periods, which Wampler suggests reflects better the type of PB within the case at different times.

**Table 6.1:** Types and causes of outcomes

| | | **CSOs' willingness to use contentious politics** | |
|---|---|---|---|
| | | High | Low |
| | High | Porto Alegre 1997–2004, Ipatinga [institutionalized participatory democracy] | No case |
| **Mayoral support for delegation of authority to citizens** | Medium | Recife, Belo Horizonte, Porto Alegre 1989–96, Porto Alegre 2004 onwards [informal and contested participatory democracy] | Santo Andre, São Paulo [co-opted participatory democracy] |
| | Low | No case | Blumenau, Rio Claro [emasculated participatory democracy] |

Source: adapted from Wampler (2007a: 258)

In order to elucidate the importance of calibration decisions and how our concepts affect our causal claims, it is useful to look at how differences between calibrations of set memberships used in interpreting nominal or ordinal data can affect our inferences about necessity. In Table 6.2 I calibrate some fuzzy sets to represent different interpretations of Wampler's categorical data presented in Table 6.1. Table 6.2 includes three different possible conceptualizations of measures of the outcome in order to discuss the effect of more significant differences in interpretation by applying fuzzy calibration and logic in the discussion. The first column from the left distinguishes the cases. The second to fourth columns represent three fuzzy sets for the two influencing conditions (mayoral support and citizen contentious politics), and one possible outcome ('deepened democracy A'). High presence of a condition according to Wampler's description is coded as full membership in the set (fuzzy set membership score of 1) and low as full non-membership (set score of 0). Medium membership is coded as 0.51.[3]

One might observe that the use of the word 'medium' by Wampler does not necessarily indicate halfway 'in' the concept. Equally, the word 'low' is hardly commensurate with the idea of complete non-membership of a set. This serves to highlight that there is some theory and interpretation involved in the process, and the fuzzy calibration is adding a layer of meaning. Fuzzy sets should not be confused with ordinal variables – to undertake set-theoretic analysis an ordinal variable will need to be converted to a fuzzy set. Small changes in the membership value will not fundamentally affect the subset–superset relations in QCA analysis. As a robustness test marginal changes in value can be examined to confirm insubstantial effects on the outcome.

I add some alternative calibrations of the outcome in the fifth and sixth columns to show how these choices matter. My purpose in this example is not to be precise in measurement, but to show the advantages and requirements of set-theory for understanding claims of necessity and sufficiency. For the time being, we can say that the original researcher has made a qualitative distinction of an ordinal kind (at least for the two influencing conditions), which has contributed to the calibration of a fuzzy set. For the outcome condition, Wampler's table really suggests four nominal categories, which, in some cases, I have then interpreted as ordered degrees of membership in at least three of the calibrations presented. I now show how this matters for tests of necessity.

In all cases in Table 6.2 the outcome condition representing deepened democracy codes cases having full membership (1) for those cases of institutionalized participatory democracy, and 0 for emasculated participatory democracy. The outcomes for the other cases vary. For 'deepened democracy A', I ascribe an outcome set membership of 0.51 for both categories of informal and contested participatory democracy

[3] Readers familiar with fsQCA will be aware of the logical mathematical property of fuzzy sets whereby 0.5 memberships create analytical difficulties. This is because it places the case in a logical limbo where verbal and formal logic are difficult to reconcile – the case is at the point of 'maximum ambiguity' and 'neither more in nor more out of the set'. The effect is that the coder has effectively decided that they cannot tell whether the case is a case of X or not X. The decision as to whether a case falls over or under this 'crossover point' in its set membership is a key consideration. It is normally a requirement to justify strongly the choice to choose, for example, 0.51 over 0.49, but I persevere for the sake of the example here. With this data the most significant consequences arise in analysing sufficiency relations, and are discussed in the next chapter.

**Table 6.2:** 10-case fuzzy set membership scores

| Case | Mayoral support | Citizen willingness to support contentious politics | Deepened democracy A | Deepened democracy B | Deepened democracy C |
|---|---|---|---|---|---|
| Belo Horizonte | 0.51 | 1 | 0.51 | 0.67 | 0 |
| Blumenau | 0 | 0 | 0 | 0 | 0 |
| Ipatinga | 1 | 1 | 1 | 1 | 1 |
| Porto Alegre (i) | 0.51 | 1 | 0.51 | 0.67 | 0 |
| Porto Alegre (ii) | 1 | 1 | 1 | 1 | 1 |
| Porto Alegre (iii) | 0.51 | 1 | 0.51 | 0.67 | 0 |
| Recife | 0.51 | 1 | 0.51 | 0.67 | 0 |
| Rio Claro | 0 | 0 | 0 | 0 | 0 |
| Santo André | 0.51 | 0 | 0.51 | 0.33 | 0 |
| São Paulo | 0.51 | 0 | 0.51 | 0.33 | 0 |

and co-opted participatory democracy. It is important to note that in calibrating and coding the outcome I am calibrating a set score that Wampler has not explicitly derived. Wampler is clear that Porto Alegre 1997–2004 and Ipatinga achieve the quality of empowered participatory democracy and that there is no empowerment of note in Rio Claro and Blumenau (emasculated participatory democracy), so the appropriate set-membership for these cases is easier to interpret. As his purpose is ordering and categorizing, he never quite makes a distinction as to whether his two qualitative descriptions of 'informal and contested' and 'co-opted' participatory democracy display measurable differences in how far they achieve the outcome of empowered participatory democracy – only to say that the cases form a 'wide spectrum of outcomes' (2007a: 257).

Table 6.2 shows three different potential calibrations of both of these categories. The alternate calibrations of the outcome are used to show what is at stake in interpreting the work of other researchers. In particular, it allows a consideration of how a more systematic approach can highlight the extent to which parsimony in explanations of the kind provided in Table 6.1 is warranted. The six cases that do not have a set membership score of 1 or 0 are all more or less halfway in the set of 'deepened democracy A'. 'Deepened democracy B' shows informal and contested cases as 'more in' (0.67), while co-opted cases are 'more out' (0.33). Finally, I include 'deepened democracy C' as a calibration of the outcome to allow for a model where all cases are fully out except those in the empowered participatory democracy cell. Thus, I am focused on pointing out what is at stake in measurement, and showing that QCA can be used iteratively and transparently to elucidate and match measurement and theory.

## Tests for necessity

The fundament of social science is knowing that information that reaches you is biased, and figuring out what level of uncertainty exists between evidence and theory. For necessity to be established, the set of cases containing the outcome must be a subset of the set of cases displaying the cause (Ragin, 2000: 214–17). Logically, for one condition or combination of conditions to be a subset of another condition, its membership value (the extent to which it is observed) should be less than or equal to the membership value of the superset across all cases. This is the relationship we are testing for, and that the claim of necessity or sufficiency is based on.[4]

I explained in Chapter 4 that researchers will usually seek to interpret conjunctions of conditions that pass a threshold of consistency or inclusion – 0.9 may be seen as a minimum consistency threshold for claims to necessary causation (Mendel and Ragin, 2011). In practice, researchers have usually accepted greater inconsistencies in evidence for a condition to be deemed sufficient than for necessary conditions. This is partly because necessary conditions are more often hypothesized and analysed in terms of single conditions, whereas sufficient conditions are more often evaluated as combinations of conditions. Single necessary conditions, by virtue of their presence being required in every instance of the outcome, impose more restrictions on where we might expect to observe an outcome in a way alternative sufficient combinations of conditions do not. Any number of conditions or combinations of conditions may be sufficient for a given outcome in different contexts. The assumption is that the same outcome can be reached in a number of different ways, and although some of these conditions can be more or less likely to occur, none of them is any 'better' at predicting the outcome when they do. There are, however, arguments from QCA scholars that some sufficient

[4] Ragin argues that these types of set-theoretic relations have been ignored by a focus on correlational patterns where such a relationship appears to suggest 'error' (Ragin, 2008).

conditions may be 'empirically more important' than others on the basis that we have more evidence of their occurrence. And so, there are some other measures of fit that help understand those issues, which I explain if and when I draw on them.

When we run an analysis for necessary conditions based on the superset–subset relation across the cases, as coded in Table 6.2 with the outcome 'deepened democracy A', we get the output contained in Table 6.3.[5]

We find that in a necessity analysis of these 10 cases so operationalized, mayoral support is fully consistent with the necessity superset relation across the cases, indicating that it is a necessary condition for deepening democracy. Moreover, the negation of mayoral support is equally necessary to negate the deepening of democracy (this result is logical because their set membership values are equal in every case). That is, mayoral support alone is necessary and sufficient for deepened democracy based on that data.

CSO willingness to use contentious politics does not seem to be necessary for deepened democracy on this account, contrary to Wampler's claim. Why? When we examine the cases, we see that this is because both Santo André and São Paulo show some degree of deepening democracy in this calibration. In justifying the coding, I might say that on my interpretation, Wampler acknowledges this 'medium quality' of deeper democracy when he makes the qualitative distinction between co-opted democracy, where 'citizenship rights and accountability were weakly extended' (2007a: 214) and emasculated democracy. Therefore, cases that appear to have some relevant deepening, yet low or no evidence of CSO willingness to use contentious politics, do not confirm the necessary superset–subset relationship.[6]

'Deepened democracy B' offers another interpretation of deepening democracy where Wampler's co-opted cases are more out of the set

[5] Analysis performed using the superSubset command in the QCA package for R (Dusa, 2019) and xy.plot command in the SetMethods package (Oana and Schneider, 2018). Throughout I adopt the common notation where the tilde '~' preceding the letter denotes absence (negation) of a condition; the asterisk '*' denotes intersection of sets (conjunction of conditions); and '+' denotes union of sets (disjunction). Data and replication code for all the analysis presented in this book is available at the University of Southampton Institutional Repository: https://eprints.soton.ac.uk/444081/

[6] There also seems to be evidence of some contentious politics in the cases, but it was not of a successful kind. This is reflected better in the larger-N analysis and serves to highlight the trade-offs in parsimony and complexity in explanations.

**Table 6.3:** Analysis of necessary conditions for 10 cases for outcome 'deepened democracy A'

| **Analysis of necessary conditions outcome variable: deepened democracy A** | | | |
|---|---|---|---|
| **Conditions tested** | Inclusion | Coverage | Relevance |
| Mayoral support | 1 | 1 | 1 |
| ~mayoral support | 0.581 | 0.595 | 0.717 |
| Citizen willingness to use contentious politics | 0.798 | 0.673 | 0.671 |
| ~citizen willingness to use contentious politics | 0.202 | 0.255 | 0.668 |
| **Analysis of necessary conditions outcome variable: ~deepened democracy A** | | | |
| **Conditions tested** | Inclusion | Coverage | Relevance |
| Mayoral support | 0.595 | 0.581 | 0.7 |
| ~mayoral support | 1 | 1 | 1 |
| Citizen willingness to use contentious politics | 0.397 | 0.327 | 0.498 |
| ~citizen willingness to use contentious politics | 0.603 | 0.745 | 0.855 |

of deepened democracy, but the informal and contested cases are more in the set, even if they are not fully in. The calibration of the outcome set requires the researcher to tackle the question directly as to whether the variation in democratic deepening among unempowered cases is relevant to explaining democratic deepening overall. On the crisp 'C' calibration, these middle cases are all excluded from deep democracy – on the 'C' interpretation partial delegation of authority to citizens is not enough to constitute deep democracy. Wampler suggests that the middle cases show some delegation of authority, but that this is hampered by contradictory mayoral strategies (2007a). Whether any observer wishes to allow the conceptual expansion of what deepened democracy constitutes to include more of these cases will remain always, to an extent, a judgement based in democratic theory with some normative content. What QCA allows us to do is better understand the implications of the judgement for claims aimed at causal explanation.

There is some inconsistency in all necessity inclusion scores if the outcome 'deepened democracy' is represented by the set 'deepened democracy B'.[7] With it the argument for any necessary conditions becomes less plausible. For both conditions we have cases that contradict the necessity relationship (consistency or inclusion score for mayoral

7 Not shown in the tables.

support would be 0.88, for citizen willingness to support contentious politics, this would be 0.876). The uncertainty regarding the necessity of mayoral support is introduced because with 'deepened democracy B', some cases now have greater membership in the set representing the outcome than they do in the set representing the explanatory condition, as shown in Figure 6.1. As social scientists willing to admit some uncertainty in our explanations, we might be happy with a relatively low level of inconsistency across all the cases and make generalizations with transparent reflection on this interval of confidence. As explained earlier, however, necessary conditions set a particularly high standard for causal explanation, and 0.9 may be seen as a minimum consistency threshold for claims to necessary causation (Mendel and Ragin, 2011).

The only calibration that confirms Wampler's inference that both conditions are necessary for deepened democracy is C (see Table 6.4). This is probably also the fairest interpretation of Wampler's work. This calibration sets apart the distinct category he calls institutionalized participatory democracy. Note that the necessity claim requires a conceptualization of 'strong participatory democracy' or 'deepened democracy' that excludes even partial membership to all cases of informal and contested or co-opted participatory democracy. If mayoral support and citizen contentious politics conditions are necessary, it is because our conceptualization of deepened democracy assumes that the differences between co-opted, informal and contested and emasculated participatory democracy are irrelevant to explaining democratic deepening. For purists, this interpretation might make a lot of sense. For others, it might be too restrictive.

The latter position is supported by the measures of coverage and relevance that readers can notice have been lowered significantly for the conditions that are consistently necessary in Table 6.4 compared to Table 6.3. What does this mean, and how should it be interpreted? Coverage and relevance of necessity are both measures of the triviality of necessary conditions (Schneider and Wagemann, 2012: 147; see also Goertz, 2006).[8] The 'C' calibration is restrictive and therefore deepened democracy becomes a much smaller set of elements relative to the rest of the cases within the scope of investigation – only 2 out of our 10 cases display the outcome and the rest do not. This skew means that

[8] Necessity coverage is an expression of how much smaller the outcome set is in relation to the conditions set (how much of Y covers X). Low necessity coverage can indicate trivialness of necessary conditions (X is quite big relative to Y), and high coverage can indicate a relevant necessary condition, provided X is not too close to a constant (see Schneider and Wagemann, 2012: 232–7).

**Figure 6.1:** Necessity of mayoral support for 'deepened democracy B'

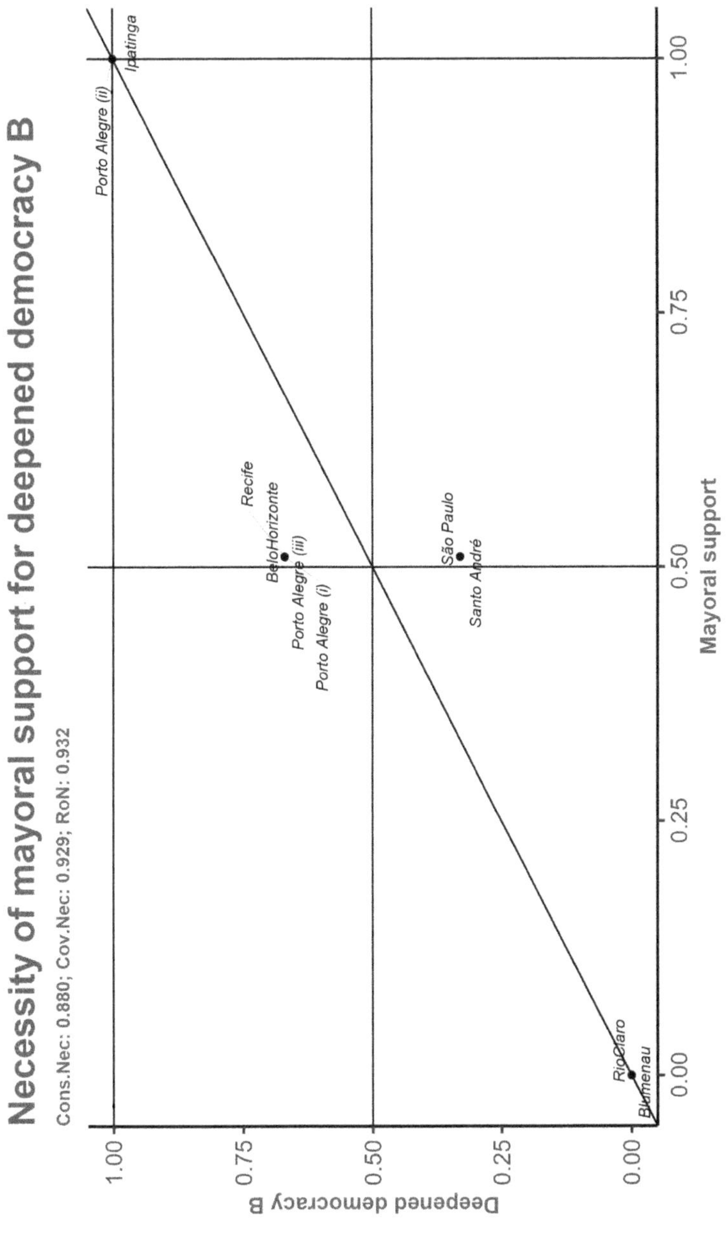

**Table 6.4:** Analysis of necessary conditions for 10 cases for outcome 'deepened democracy C'

| **Analysis of necessary conditions outcome variable: deepened democracy** | | | |
|---|---|---|---|
| **Conditions tested** | Inclusion | Coverage | Relevance |
| Mayoral support | 1 | 0.395 | 0.618 |
| ~mayoral support | 0 | 0 | 0.506 |
| Citizen willingness to use contentious politics | 1 | 0.333 | 0.5 |
| ~ citizen willingness to use contentious politics | 0 | 0 | 0.6 |
| **Analysis of necessary conditions outcome variable: ~deepened democracy** | | | |
| **Conditions tested** | Inclusion | Coverage | Relevance |
| Mayoral support | 0.382 | 0.605 | 0.712 |
| ~mayoral support | 0.618 | 1 | 1 |
| Citizen willingness to use contentious politics | 0.5 | 0.667 | 0.667 |
| ~ citizen willingness to use contentious politics | 0.5 | 1 | 1 |

it is much easier for an outcome to be a subset of causes (a necessary condition). The logic exposed is that more restrictive conceptualization of democracy will set an ever-lower bar for necessity and a higher one for sufficiency such that almost anything can be seen as necessary and almost nothing is sufficient. One can easily imagine how such a finding might expose over-conscious thinking and be deemed a trivial or less relevant finding by a practitioner looking for information on how to act to deepen democracy in a practical context.

The point of this short example is to show that the act of careful calibration of our concepts to represent the evidence and tests for superset relations can reveal something to us about our assumptions. The most important criterion for any conceptual description or measurement of the social world is that they reflect the world as accurately as possible. QCA is a tool that can entreat us to better specify what we mean when we talk about, for instance, 'success' in democratic innovations, which many have suggested is a term that is often used uncritically (Montambeault, 2016; Spada and Ryan, 2017).

A QCA approach and analytic test can provide a useful logical check on the congruence between evidence, intuition and measurement. Most analytic approaches in social science, however, are not content with stopping at the level of describing categories – their goal is to infer. If concepts (descriptions of qualities) are sets of which empirical cases have degrees of observed membership (fuzzy membership or quantitative variation), the relative degree of membership matters greatly if we want to engage in causal analysis – in this case, assessing claims of necessity and sufficiency. QCA maps the distance between the theory and the evidence, and allows transparent iteration and re-evaluation. We may conclude that QCA as an approach has added some value to the analysis in this first instance by problematizing our conceptions of democratic deepening, and forcing us to think about what substantive conclusions on causation of the phenomenon are suitable. The analysis suggests that variation in the use of contentious politics means that it can only be deemed a necessary condition if we prefer a very restrictive definition of deepened democracy, and although most readings are likely to find participatory leadership a necessary condition, that summary doesn't completely evade question based on one reasonable interpretation of the evidence. We can probably surmise that any conclusions based on a couple of conditions elide too much information, and we need to include more for accuracy.

## Extending the analysis: bringing complexity back in

This discussion is only based on a stylization of Wampler's most parsimonious conclusions and not explicitly on delving fully into his richer descriptions of the cases. While small-N research often concludes by extracting what the researcher feels are the two or three most important explanatory conditions, it can also claim advantage in its rich case description – elucidating the trail of relations and processes involving other or secondary conditions. In some large-N statistical analysis these details may be overlooked even in assessing interactions, as the compound variable represented by the interaction term is often unrecognizable from its elemental beginnings.

Wampler details any number of potential influencing conditions or variables from which other hypotheses may be formed and tested to investigate causal chains relating to deepening democracy. These include population size, social backgrounds of PB delegates, higher human development index (HDI) scores, and so on. At one point he suggests a conjunctural hypothesis whereby cities with greater HDI are more likely to be left-leaning, have broad-based CSO activity and a firmer financial base on which to administer PB, advising that they may play the role of mediating variables. In his chapters describing each case, however, he highlights and details, in particular, mayor–legislative relations, the financial basis for implementation of the programme and the rules of the game as influential in determining the depth of democracy coming out of PB processes. In fact, he affords PB rules the same explanatory primacy as CSO activity and mayoral support, although as we shall see, operationalizing it as a variable in comparative analysis is a little tricky, which is possibly why he does not highlight it as much as the latter two in Table 6.1. In short, although Wampler searches for an appropriate parsimony, his work, like that of many others discussed in this book, takes the likely complexity of causality seriously.

The key strength of traditional qualitative small-N research approaches vis-à-vis cross-sections or QCA, is that it is not bound by a 'static' analytic moment and allows fluidity in causal tracing. At the same time, this is also its weakness. A case researcher submerged in subjective determination of causal processes is in some important ways less well placed to make hands-off 'deductive' judgements about how variables combine. Wampler, in his excellent study of PB, may suggest that based on his case knowledge, these other three conditions (mayor–legislative relations, the financial basis for implementation of the programme and the rules of the game) are important but secondary in the story to the two first discussed. But in a QCA approach we can transparently analyse all possible combinations of the five conditions and potential counterfactual assumptions on an equal footing.

## An improved set calibration for a more deductive analysis?

In this section I briefly explain Wampler's conditions and provide details of how sets of conditions are calibrated for an enlarged analysis. The section draws heavily on Wampler's theoretical justifications for highlighting these conditions. His evidence is particularly useful because he often triangulates evidence from interviews (that is, subjective determinations of, say, mayoral support) with symptomatic indicators of degrees to which a condition is observed (for example, in the case of mayoral support, implementation rates of PB projects and their prioritization vis-à-vis projects decided on through other channels). This analysis showcases some of the deductive features of QCA before I present the worldwide analysis of several cases drawing on accumulated evidence from several studies.[9]

---

[9] I keep the calibration discussion somewhat brief for this analysis of one study in recognition that I have described in detail the ultimate comparison of PB worldwide in Chapter 5. The main purpose here is to show how QCA can have some advantages for theory evaluation even when working with a smaller-N.

The outcome of interest, 'deep democracy', is seen where PB programmes result in open, equal and meaningful participation of large numbers of 'ordinary citizens', and where the PB overtakes previous clientelist practices as the main method for citizens and civil society to negotiate and realize budget priorities. I do not take the most restrictive approach to conceptualization here. The cases above the crossover point on this interpretation are those where Wampler reports relatively significant delegation of authority leading to implementation of projects and high participation rates (even where results came via struggle). I give lower set-membership scores to co-opted cases where delegation of authority was more an appearance and cherry-picking of projects from PB was the norm. My interpretation is that this is a justified claim and can be read through the case descriptions. Also, the experience of co-option is more likely to reduce support for democracy and feelings of efficacy vis-à-vis the experience of contestation, which, while it frustrates citizens, can lead to some empowerment through instilling forms of efficacy over time.

In explaining how PB programmes can achieve deep democracy, Wampler puts forward five key causal conditions. The first is 'high mayoral support for PB'. Mayoral support is vital because decision-makers 'must be willing to spend scarce resources' (Wampler, 2007a: 36). There may be instrumental reasons for high mayoral support of PB programmes (as a signalling device to gauge citizen preferences, or as a political party support-building measure) as well as ideological. In the Brazilian context mayoral support is taken to be key to outcomes because strong mayoral support can lead to the implementation of projects, allowing demonstration effects (see Abers, 1998; Gret and Sintomer, 2005: 87). The argument goes that when governments are seen to be taking the process seriously by implementing the decisions of the participants in a participatory process (in particular, building capital infrastructure projects), the institutionalization of PB increases. In turn, this can give greater scope to governments to reorganize bureaucracy to administer PB constructively.

The second explanatory condition set is that of strong civil society using contentious and cooperative politics. Strong civil society can cooperate with other actors in deliberative forums, but also contest information vigorously inside and outside fora, defending rights using contentious forms of political action where required (Wampler, 2007a: 38). The types of activities CSOs are willing to engage in can often be explained by the historical density of CSOs in a municipality.[10]

For various situational and political reasons rules vary from one PB programme to another. We can talk of the set of 'rules that delegate authority' where rules allow citizens accountable and direct decision-making, which can incentivize greater and more meaningful participation. According to Wampler, 'the unintended consequence of unclear rules is a limited delegation of authority' (2007a: 39). Combining rules in an explanatory model with the role of actors using QCA (which explicitly investigates conjunctural causation) is important if we believe that institutions influence actors and actors influence institutions.

Wampler emphasizes throughout his book the combinatorial effects of conditions including how one condition may limit the degree to which any combination can be effective in deepening democracy through participation. This is another reason why the analysis may lend itself to QCA and fuzzy sets. One example is the extent to which a mayor's strategy is conditioned by the existence of a 'positive legislative environment'. The legislative environment is less favourable to an outcome of deeply democratic PB when the mayor implementing the programme does not have a broad base of support and must spend political capital shoring this up (2007a: 40). As we saw in Chapter 2, the strength or weakness of opposition and importance of broad-based political support for PB is emphasized in numerous accounts. Wampler suggests that this positive environment is a necessary but not sufficient condition for deeply democratic PB – the mayor may still not wish to delegate authority even with legislative support, but will find it difficult to delegate without. Wampler's descriptions also suggest that this condition could highlight asymmetric causation when he outlines that in the case of Santo André, a highly supportive legislature can actually incentivize the mayor to engage in many other projects, undermining the importance of PB (2007a: 209).

Finally, the 'financial basis for spending', that is, the availability of significant funds for new capital investment, is also, Wampler holds, necessary but not sufficient for PB to work effectively. This is because

[10] Note that this condition itself can be considered a conjunction – a logical combination of contentious politics and cooperative politics in CSOs. The condition representing the combination could be constructed by calibrating separately both conditions and calculating the intersection of both sets. In the example I do this implicitly (that is, in calibrating I do not compromise high contentious politics for low cooperation, and vice versa).

limited spending ability limits the power of programmes where authority is delegated to citizens.

After enumerating these conditions and explanatory hypotheses, Wampler contends that his explanations of cases will show that 'it is necessary for a PB program to have positive results in each area to produce a successful PB program' (2007a: 41). Note that these claims add a higher bar to the parsimonious claims that make up the typology discussed in the earlier example. I aim to test here Wampler's more complex claim, basing a calibration of conditions on the narrative he provides, and using fsQCA.

I calibrate sets and ascribe case membership in each case. A good starting point is to outline the verbal meanings we ascribe to set membership. As per Chapter 5, the following 7-value fuzzy set, as proposed by Ragin (2000: 156), is used.

| | |
|---|---|
| 1.0 | Fully in (the set) |
| 0.83 | Mostly but not fully in |
| 0.67 | More or less in |
| 0.5 | Crossover point |
| 0.33 | More or less out |
| 0.17 | Mostly but not fully out |
| 0 | Fully out |

This seems a feasible level of nuance to justifiably extract from the qualitative information in Wampler's book. He provides at least a few hundred words (and often a lot more) of descriptive information on each condition for each case. This rich description is necessary for an epistemologically sound QCA.

The data matrix presented in Table 6.5 discloses my calibration of the conditions.[11] I provide my most rigorous interpretation, but it is an interpretation of the work of others. While I might claim to 'control for the researcher' in my application of QCA to Wampler's cases (which I won't do when cumulating across researchers), I cannot make any exceptional claims to being able to control the ever-present problems for researchers interpreting one another's descriptions and findings. One advantage of

[11] I omit the post-2004 Porto Alegre case here because there is not the same level of description of it in this source material. For robustness I also considered the effect of slight changes to fuzzy memberships in order to help decide on appropriate consistency thresholds. Tests showed no effect on the ordering of cases within sets.

working with fuzzy sets is that it can at least lay those interpretations out in a systematic way for others to query, rather than hide them in implicit assumptions.

There are some changes from the earlier calibration based on my reading of the 'thicker' case descriptions. For instance, São Paulo and Ipatinga's scores for civil society using contentious and cooperative politics are on opposite sides of the crossover point to the data matrix in the first analysis described earlier. The introduction of more complexity can regain some anomalies that are not clear in more parsimonious conclusions. Building on the first part of the chapter, which aimed to show what is at stake in different calibrations and selecting levels of measurement, this part aims to investigate what is at stake in more parsimonious or complex causal modelling when employing case-based comparative logic.

As these measures are based on my interpretation of text and not on a ranking systematized by Wampler, as in the earlier analysis, it is also pertinent to make some comments on the difficulties involved in calibrating conditions to allow for transparency for those wishing to repeat the analysis. The rules-based condition was particularly difficult to calibrate because it requires some subjective interpretation of how even small changes in basic rules may affect participant strategies. This is often tricky to separate from outcomes in the process of PB. As rules are, in the Brazilian case, often set by the mayor, they may be better conceived of as a symptom of that support. The financial basis condition also requires decisions on how to weigh absolute and relative financial strength and include issues like inheritance of debt. By presenting these as a data matrix in Table 6.5 they can be open to scrutiny by others with knowledge of the case.

## Necessity

I am particularly interested in Wampler's claim that all five conditions identified are necessary for democratic deepening, and that a positive legislative environment and financial basis for support of PB are necessary, but not sufficient (2007a: 35). This number of necessary conditions seems a high bar. Also, if we think these latter two conditions are necessary but not sufficient, then which combinations of conditions are they necessary components of? Without any tool to analyse the consistency of this claim, case researchers are disincentivized from problematizing the combinatorial relationships between variables.

**Table 6.5:** Data matrix for Wampler's cases (5 causal conditions)

| Case | **ms** | **ccp** | **ple** | **fbs** | **rep** | **deepd** |
|---|---|---|---|---|---|---|
| Belo Horizonte | 0.33 | 0.83 | 0.67 | 0.83 | 0.33 | 0.67 |
| Blumenau | 0.17 | 0.33 | 0.17 | 1 | 0.67 | 0 |
| Ipatinga | 0.83 | 0.33 | 0.67 | 1 | 0.67 | 0.83 |
| Porto Alegre 1988–96 | 1 | 1 | 0.83 | 0.33 | 1 | 0.83 |
| Porto Alegre 1997–04 | 1 | 1 | 0.67 | 1 | 1 | 1 |
| Recife | 0.67 | 1 | 0.67 | 0.17 | 0.33 | 0.67 |
| Rio Claro | 0.17 | 0 | 0.17 | 0.67 | 0.17 | 0 |
| Santo André | 0.83 | 0.83 | 1 | 0.33 | 0.33 | 0.33 |
| São Paulo | 0.17 | 0.83 | 0.33 | 0.33 | 0.33 | 0.33 |

Note: ms is mayoral support; ccp is civil society using contentious and cooperative politics; ple is positive legislative environment; fbs is financial basis for spending; rep is rules that encourage participation and deepd is deepened democracy.

The consistency of single necessary conditions for the outcome 'deep democracy' and its negation (not deep democracy) is reported in Table 6.6.

Consistency of the necessary superset relations for individual conditions range in value for each of the five hypothesized causal conditions for deepened democracy, from 0.79 to 0.93.[12] In other words, many of these conditions come close to the criteria for construing causal necessity (an almost always necessary condition), but all suffer from some inconsistencies. A high threshold of consistency to make claims about necessity is advisable (at least 0.9). However, as Ragin, among others, repeatedly stresses, a further important test is whether it 'makes sense' based on knowledge of theory and background conditions as a necessary condition (Ragin, 2000; Mendel and Ragin, 2011). There are a number of strategies the researcher now has open, the consequences of which they choose will affect the interpretations not just of necessity but also of sufficient conditions.

As many of these conditions could be seen as 'almost' necessary, we now have an opportunity to revisit each condition and investigate how the subset relationship is contravened. One contravening

12 Rounded to two decimal points. As no condition in the analysis of the negation of the outcome (absence of deepened democracy) is highly consistent with a necessity subset–superset relation, I only discuss the analysis of the outcome (deepened democracy) in this section.

**Table 6.6:** Superset relations for single necessary conditions (5 condition analysis)

| **Analysis of necessary conditions outcome variable: deepened democracy** | | | |
|---|---|---|---|
| Conditions tested | Inclusion | Relevance | Coverage |
| Mayoral support | 0.927 | 0.784 | 0.811 |
| ~mayoral support | 0.358 | 0.727 | 0.455 |
| Civil society using contentious and cooperative politics | 0.893 | 0.589 | 0.676 |
| ~civil society using contentious and cooperative politics | 0.253 | 0.786 | 0.414 |
| A positive legislative environment | 0.895 | 0.791 | 0.805 |
| ~ a positive legislative environment | 0.391 | 0.721 | 0.476 |
| The financial basis to spend | 0.785 | 0.625 | 0.647 |
| ~the financial basis to spend | 0.466 | 0.829 | 0.65 |
| Rules encouraging participation | 0.82 | 0.805 | 0.791 |
| ~rules encouraging participation | 0.5 | 0.724 | 0.559 |
| **Analysis of necessary conditions outcome variable: ~deepened democracy** | | | |
| Conditions tested | Inclusion | Relevance | Coverage |
| Mayoral support | 0.539 | 0.551 | 0.439 |
| ~mayoral support | 0.767 | 0.94 | 0.907 |
| Civil society using contentious and cooperative politics | 0.615 | 0.45 | 0.434 |
| ~civil society using contentious and cooperative politics | 0.541 | 0.925 | 0.825 |
| A positive legislative environment | 0.539 | 0.574 | 0.452 |
| ~ a positive legislative environment | 0.767 | 0.914 | 0.872 |
| The financial basis to spend | 0.730 | 0.573 | 0.560 |
| ~the financial basis to spend | 0.539 | 0.85 | 0.701 |
| Rules encouraging participation | 0.576 | 0.642 | 0.518 |
| ~rules encouraging participation | 0.767 | 0.852 | 0.799 |

fuzzy membership value in a case may require reconsideration. For example, the condition relating to civil society only contravenes the necessity superset relationship in Ipatinga. Figure 6.2 shows it is the only case lying above the diagonal and having greater membership in deepened democracy than in citizen support for contentious politics. Can we go back and explain the deviant case? Is there a coding error? I have coded the case as more out than in the set of citizens using contentious and cooperative politics. The description of the case reports what contentious politics exists as being disagreement only within the confines of PB and only by organizations that are allies of the mayor. One could contest the interpretation. Alternatively, perhaps, if we look at the other cases in this sample, those that achieve deepened democracy appear to be large provincial capitals, and this is likely to affect the nature of civil society in the case. Therefore, one could make the argument, revisiting the case data, that for the purposes of modest generalization we could drop some cases from this particular claim and limit the scope of the generalization on the necessity of willingness to use cooperation and contention to larger cities only.

Shifting the scope of an argument in response to findings requires careful consideration. It can be all too tempting for a researcher to move away from the logic of the initial case selection to find an answer that fits the theory. In particular, for the interpretation of necessity we should set a high standard because what we interpret to be necessary has implications for what combinations of conditions we will accept as sufficient, and thereby for the theories of change we try to implement in the world.

A second consideration in seeking to establish evidence for a necessary condition would be to consider disjunctions of conditions (Bol and Luppi, 2013). We can ask which unions of two or more conditions (disjunctions) are consistent with a necessity subset–superset relation. Table 6.7 shows all the unions of two conditions with necessity consistency over 0.95. It is not uncommon to see proclamations in the PB literature that either this *or* that is necessary for an outcome. From the nine disjunctions listed in Table 6.7 we can see, for instance, evidence that either a civil society willing to engage in both contentious and cooperative politics OR a secure financial basis for spending on projects are present when we observe deepened democracy in PB programmes. Either one or the other is necessary. These can be called SUIN conditions – a Sufficient but Unnecessary part of a factor that is Insufficient but Necessary for an outcome (Mahoney et al, 2009). A researcher can say with a greater degree of certainty based on the QCA necessity analysis below that deep democracy cannot be achieved in PB programmes without at the very least a financial basis to spend OR civil society willingness to both struggle and cooperate with government. The interpretation of SUIN conditions is tricky, however, because in the same way that I discussed the perils of restrictive theories earlier, a theory that adds a disjunct logically lowers the barrier for evidence of its veracity by providing new avenues for cases to meet

**Figure 6.2:** X–Y plot of set membership in deepened democracy and civil society support for contentious and cooperative politics

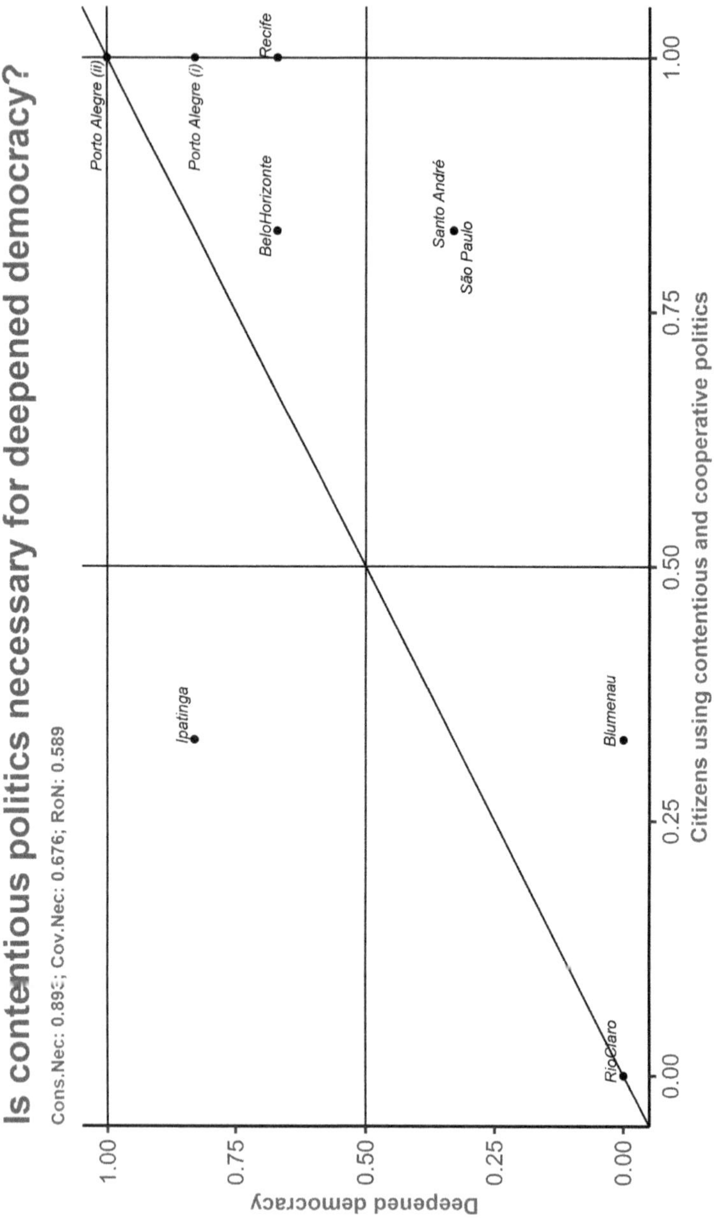

**Table 6.7:** Necessity consistency for Boolean sum expressions

| Boolean expression | Necessity consistency | Relevance of necessity | Necessity coverage |
|---|---|---|---|
| MS + CCP[1] | 1 | 0.502 | 0.683 |
| MS + PLE | 1 | 0.728 | 0.798 |
| MS + FBS | 1 | 0.385 | 0.636 |
| MS + ~rep | 1 | 0.5 | 0.682 |
| CCP + PLE | 0.966 | 0.482 | 0.659 |
| CCP + FBS | 1 | 0.194 | 0.571 |
| CCP + REP | 0.966 | 0.444 | 0.643 |
| PLE + FBS | 1 | 0.385 | 0.636 |
| PLE + REP | 0.966 | 0.627 | 0.728 |

[1] In QCA notation '+' signifies logical OR (the substitutability of two conditions) while '*' signifies logical AND (the combination of two conditions).

the required conditions. We would need good theoretical grounds to suggest that two conditions are practically substitutable to produce an outcome and represent some higher-order construct. I hope to have therefore exposed the many potential interpretations of necessity and the trade-offs that researchers should consider in making causal claims of necessity.

I hope readers will not see such exhaustive analysis as introducing unnecessary complexity. It could be seen as a terrific example of the dangers of over-conscious thinking and methodological fetishism. But my goal here is to show just what is at stake in the underlying assumptions when researchers state that X is a necessary condition for Y, and I will show that models espousing many necessary conditions will have strong implications for hypotheses about what combinations of conditions structure success in PB, and what practical action we can take to achieve success.

In terms of added value, we can at the very least say that the necessity analysis here has cast some doubt over Wampler's general contention (within the scope of his population) that all five conditions are necessary for deep democracy. Perhaps our judgement is clouded because the evidence for relationships does exist, even if they are not determining across time and space, and many of these factors can be considered substitutable necessary conditions. This adds nuance to the general claim. Is the inconsistency in claims for single necessary conditions mirrored across all the cases in our main dataset?

## Cumulating research: necessity in participatory budgeting across several cases

After introducing the analytic process as it is applied to cases that have previously been analysed together, I now turn to analyse the accumulated research of the 31 cases of PB presented in Part II of the book. Recall that these cases cover a range of studies by different researchers, and I am interested in explaining citizen control of collective decisions in PB by examining combinations of political leadership, bureaucratic support for programmes, civil society demands and the financial basis for support for programmes (fuzzy set scores outlined in Table 5.1 in Chapter 5). Are there, as has regularly been claimed in the literature, several necessary conditions including among them participatory leadership and civil society demand, for citizens to gain control of budget decisions? Table 6.8 presents all single conditions and disjunctions of two conditions that have a score of necessity inclusion that is greater than 0.9 across all 31 cases.

None of these conditions perfectly fits the necessity relationship. A political leadership committed to participation has long been considered a necessary condition for success in producing empowering programmes. The condition receives an inclusion score of 0.93 across the cases, indicating evidence of necessity. It is worth investigating further. The X–Y plot in Figure 6.3 visualizes this relationship.

Overall the evidence that participatory leadership is a necessary condition for citizen control is quite strong. The cases below the diagonal are fully consistent with necessity (X>Y). The four cases that contribute to inconsistency, placing doubt in the claim, are Toronto, Buenos Aires, Cusco and Recife (ii), that is, Recife under the PT. Going back to investigate these specific cases offers some nuance to the

**Table 6.8:** Necessary conditions for citizen control of PB with consistency greater than 0.9

| | Conditions | Inclusion | Relevance | Coverage |
|---|---|---|---|---|
| 1 | PL | 0.933 | 0.652 | 0.698 |
| 2 | BSP + CSD | 0.91 | 0.637 | 0.68 |
| 3 | BSP + FBS | 0.911 | 0.629 | 0.675 |
| 4 | CSD + FBS | 0.91 | 0.572 | 0.643 |

Note: PL is participatory leadership; CSD is autonomous civil society demand; BSP is bureaucratic support; and FBS is financial basis to spend.

necessity claim. None of these cases are what Schneider and Rohlfing refer to as 'deviant cases in kind' (2013: 581). That is, we do not have any examples in the upper left corner of the plot of strongly deviant cases that clearly achieve successful citizen control while having very little evidence of participatory leadership. Cases like Toronto and Buenos Aires might normally be considered less relevant because they are neither comparatively good examples of citizen control nor of strongly committed participatory leadership (for a discussion of how to interpret such cases, see Haesebrouck, 2015). But on this occasion they are quite instructive.

Toronto's community housing PB is a case whose membership among successful cases has been changed from the pilot studies in which I previously presented it (Ryan and Smith, 2012, 2014). This is because more recent research suggests far more mixed outcomes in the case (Foroughi, 2017). Nevertheless, early accounts of the case provide clear evidence for citizens having substantial influence over major spending decisions. Lerner and van Wagner suggested that absence of participatory leadership contributed positively to improved outcomes: 'participatory budgeting emerged when staff were passionate and prepared' and 'politicians were looking the other way' (2006: 15). The idea has some affinity with Dennis Rodgers' description of the Buenos Aires case (2010). There, politicians reeling from the *Argenitazo*[13] initiated a top-down PB, with mostly short-term instrumental goals in mind. Even when political support was abandoned as political manoeuvres within the governing coalition soon acted to undermine the PB, committed bureaucrats were sometimes able to use their skills to counteract those trying to subvert the process and allow citizens to retain decision-making power and influence spending (Rodgers, 2010: 20). The cases suggest that some democratic deepening can occur in the short term without participatory leadership, but the question remains as to whether it can be sustained.

This direction of travel seems to be confirmed by the other more successful cases where there is some degree of deviance in necessity inclusion. McNulty considers Cusco to be the most successful of the cases she studied in Peru (2011: 114), but here, also, support from the political leadership was not immediately clear. McNulty explains that the regional president won with a small margin of victory, faced strong opposition, and his behaviour did not suggest he was a fan of citizen consultation (2011: 111). Nevertheless, a combative civil society led to an accommodation of demands that seemed to later convince the leadership that participatory strategies would serve their interest. The

[13] See https://www.theguardian.com/world/2003/jan/25/argentina.weekend7.

**Figure 6.3:** Necessity of participatory leadership for citizen control

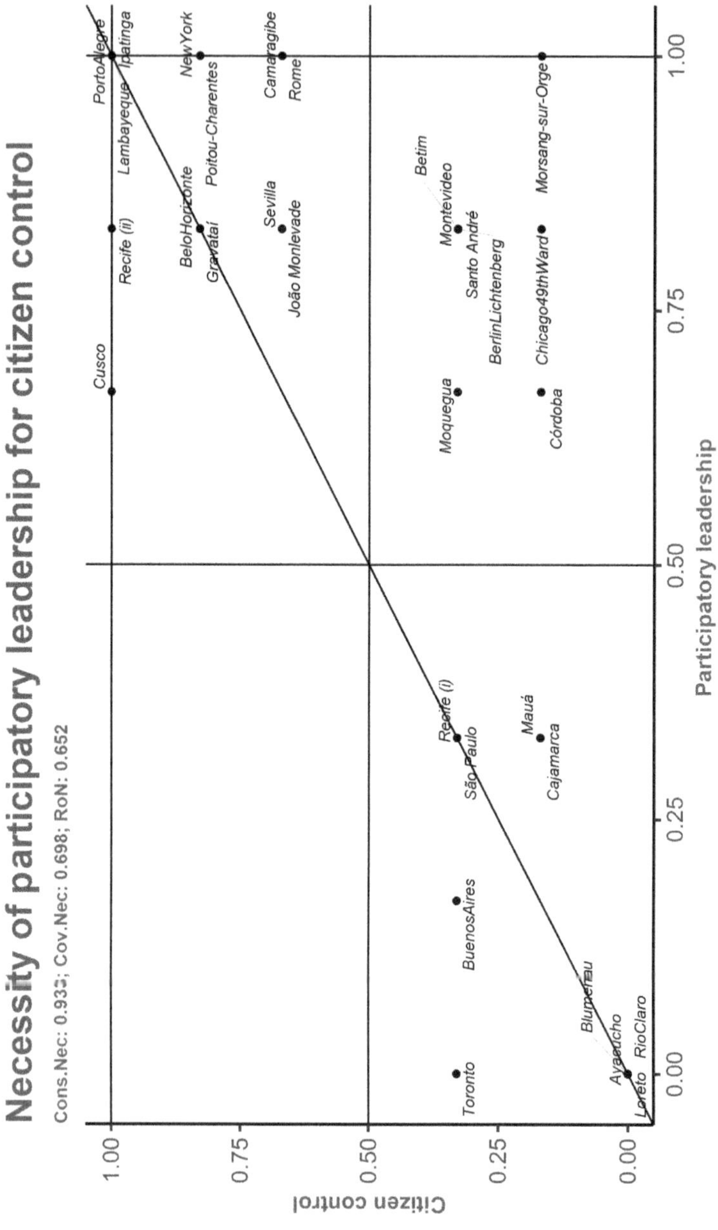

Recife (ii) case is observed to have slightly lower than full membership in the participatory leadership condition not because there is any question in the PT mayor's commitment to PB, but because he faced significant opposition to PB from within his coalition and outside it. The administration was able to ride that wave, and PB's success in Recife seems to have reached its zenith later in the decade.

This dive back into the cases on being presented with comparative evidence then suggests some nuance to the claims regarding participatory political leadership being a necessary condition for PB to achieve success in improving democracy that has been presented up to now. Participatory leadership is not a necessary condition for democratic deepening in the short run. In some cases, we can see that programmes cope with leadership absence where other actors are mobilized, sometimes providing democratic goods without political leadership for a time. But it is difficult to see any evidence of long-term good outcomes absent participatory leadership (although such cases might still be imagined). Participatory leadership comes closest to satisfying the test for a necessary condition. There is some remaining doubt, but I have shown that those issues appear to be explicable and with some nuance added, the claim gains further credibility. Future investigations of cases may be useful to test the hypothesis that a lack of supportive participatory leadership can be endured, but only for a couple of years.

On the whole, however, it is best to consider the several claims about necessary conditions for democratic outcomes in such innovations to have been somewhat premature. In early accounts the civil society condition was often held up as a necessary condition. This thesis was hardly questioned by first observers of PB. However, all conditions apart from participatory leadership show significant inconsistencies in tests for necessity. The plot in Figure 6.4 shows several pointedly deviant cases for that relationship. In some of the cases the deviance reflects successful cases where civil society was mobilized in a partisan way, but in others civil society was almost absent from the process in successful cases. The same pattern can be observed for the other conditions tested. There is a reasonably compelling amount of evidence to suggest participatory budgets are successful in providing meaningful citizen control in instances where spending is relatively constrained and where officials see the programme as a burden and fail to support it.

What of necessary conditions for the absence of citizen control of decisions in PB? Again, there is no evidence for such a strong claim, as shown in Table 6.9.

**Figure 6.4:** Fuzzy X–Y plot for necessity of citizen control: autonomous civil society demand

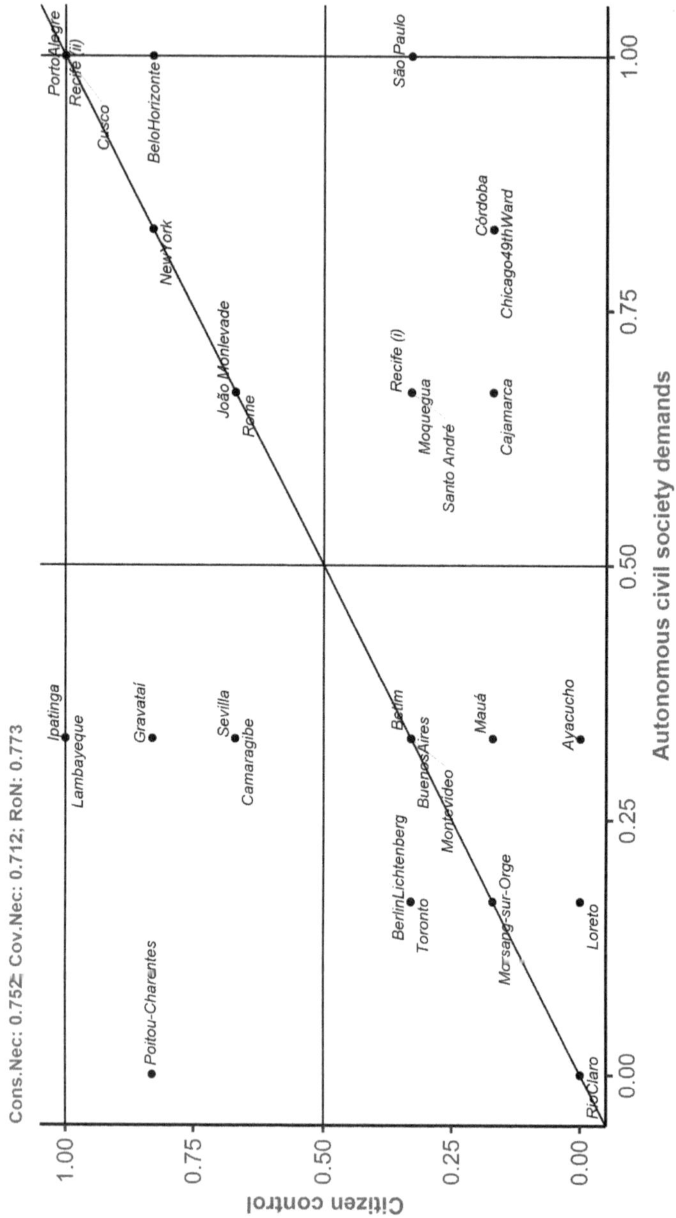

**Table 6.9:** Test for necessary conditions for the absence of citizen control of PB decisions

| | Condition | Inclusion | Relevance | Coverage |
|---|---|---|---|---|
| 1 | ~participatory leadership | 0.631 | 0.952 | 0.912 |
| 2 | Participatory leadership | 0.567 | 0.513 | 0.463 |
| 3 | ~bureaucratic support | 0.845 | 0.76 | 0.767 |
| 4 | Bureaucratic support | 0.413 | 0.733 | 0.507 |
| 5 | ~civil society demand | 0.721 | 0.81 | 0.761 |
| 6 | Civil society demand | 0.577 | 0.708 | 0.596 |
| 7 | ~financial basis to spend | 0.702 | 0.772 | 0.718 |
| 8 | Financial basis to spend | 0.517 | 0.699 | 0.551 |
| 9 | ~csd + ~bsp | 0.959 | 0.58 | 0.705 |

Note: csd is autonomous civil society demands and bsp is bureaucratic support.

One disjunction of two conditions (shown in the final row of Table 6.9) reaches greater than 0.95 consistency – that is, the absence of vibrant civil society demand-making OR the absence of bureaucratic support. It might be that one could interpret this as a useful finding if willing to consider it evidence of a higher-order construct such as 'absence of human capital', but this feels a bit of a stretch without greater recourse to theory and empirical evidence. I argue that the approach I have taken advances our theoretical understanding and provides clear signs for where future investigations should focus their interest to reduce further uncertainties.

In summary, it is better to say that the evidence presented in this chapter shows that the majority of claims, and perhaps all strong claims to necessity in PB research, have been premature. Claims about necessity are often overblown because they offer highly restrictive and sometimes contradictory accounts of democratic outcomes. It is by pushing the boundaries of what is compared in terms of the depth, breadth and variety of cases that these issues come to the fore. It is better to qualify that most of these conditions are, as I will show in the following chapters, better thought of as INUS conditions:[14] they are necessary parts of relatively consistent explanations of the successful outcomes that are valid within alternate specific contexts. The finding has important implications for practice because it means that

[14] Insufficient, but necessary part of an unnecessary but sufficient condition.

participatory innovation should not be dissuaded because a certain single condition seems beyond reach, or that all resources should be focused on some conditions because without them there is no prospect for success. There are alternative strategies for citizens to achieve democratic improvements through PB processes, and I now turn to describing them.

# 7

# Success: How Citizen Control of Politics Is Achieved

This chapter offers more specific answers to the puzzle outlined in Chapter 1. It also explains what the trade-offs are in offering more or less specific answers and what kind of answers are more or less warranted by the evidence. I bring the reader on a journey through a logical comparison of the characteristics of PB cases and present findings to inform the implementation of democratic reform. I consider again those touted necessary conditions for empowered participation such as participatory leadership and civil society demand for involvement, and outline the specific circumstances under which they can be (ir)relevant to explanations of empowered participation.

I revisit Wampler's analysis, confirming the finding that no conditions ought to be considered singularly necessary, but some are necessary in specific contexts – the evidence suggests that in a Brazilian context contentious politics must be combined with either rules enabling participation *or* a financial basis for implementation of projects to produce democratic deepening. Moreover, I find democratic deepening in challenging financial circumstances is certainly possible, but all other factors need to be pointing in the right direction – a finding that suggests that in recovering or developing economic circumstances, PB requires positive political, institutional and civil society conditions for democratic deepening.

I then focus on the wider lessons across cases, and explain that meaningful involvement of citizens in collective governance often requires a combination of will and capacity to implement programmes from political *and* administrative leaders. I explain why political commitment to participatory politics is only a sufficient condition for good outcomes in combination with bureaucratic capacities *or* financial freedoms. I revisit the question of how civil society activity may explain democratic deepening for which the evidence is mixed. Again, there is evidence across all cases that financial constraints may concentrate the mind of actors – politicians, bureaucrats and autonomous civil society activists can work together for PB overcoming resource burdens. Nevertheless, I also find evidence that more top-down approaches to developing civil society capacities developed appreciably democratic results. I can pinpoint the extent of contradictory evidence that has been presented by researchers to highlight priorities for future research. Designers and adopters of PB can note substitutable combinations of conditions that have been consistently successful in achieving empowered participation.

## Elimination using Boolean algorithmic analysis: a little helpful basics

The analysis of sufficiency relies on principles of logical elimination. Savolainen has argued that the value of Mill's methods of comparison is 'in their capacity to eliminate a limited set of alternative causal statements' (1994: 1218; see also Peters, 2013; Ryan, 2018). This element of elimination is sorely overlooked in the social sciences – unfortunately the quest for 'novel' findings often creates an incentive to add extra explanations to the ones we have. Elimination can be equally useful and novel, by reducing costs of preoccupations with less relevant features of explanations. This element of comparative research is undervalued, but I think systematic case-based comparison can have an even more subtle crucial advantage that is often overlooked. That is, it can reduce over-determination *and* under-determination in an apposite manner (Ryan, 2018). A set-theoretic approach avoids seeing hypotheses as being in strict competition but as alternative cloudy solutions that require distillation. I will again take the reader through the process using examples to explain how it works, but it is useful to briefly set out some basic principles here.

In simple terms, when two cases produce the same outcome, but differ only in one explanatory variable, the variable that distinguishes the two cases can be considered irrelevant and be removed (Caramani, 2009: 72). For example, if:

$A * \sim B * C \rightarrow Y$ (solution 1)

and

$A * \sim B * \sim C \rightarrow Y$ (solution 2)

We can deem C redundant. The outcome Y occurs when it is both present (C) and absent (~C). Therefore:

A*~B → Y (minimal solution)

We could say that the conjunction of the presence of A and the absence of B is sufficient for Y (A*~B represents the intersection of the set A and the set not B). A is an INUS condition, as is ~B.

Applications of Boolean logic to causal analysis can be used to discard irrelevant conditions while simultaneously identifying multiple parsimonious yet robust descriptions of causal relations over more than a handful of cases. This is done by testing alternative combinations of conditions for relationships of necessity and sufficiency (supersets and subsets) using Boolean logical operations such as logical 'AND' (the intersection of sets) and logical 'OR' (the union of sets). It also allows us to use simple Boolean negation operations – logical 'NOT' (negation of sets) – to show whether and when the absence of a condition contributes to outcomes.

We can therefore test the causal claims and develop the intuitions of the researchers who have advanced the field up to now using their in-depth casework. These issues of apposite determination have been far from ignored by the methodologists of social science who have come up with many ingenious ways of handling these problems. However, the QCA I disclose provides a good exemplar for an approach that incorporates these concerns in a coherent and holistic manner.

There is no conceptual difference in the way Boolean minimization is applied to fuzzy sets (Ragin, 2009: 88). Following Zadeh (1965) and Ragin (2009: 94–103), fuzzy sets directly correspond to the crisp dichotomies in the example. In crisp dichotomies where A is present (set membership = 1), the negation of A is logically absent (set membership in ~A = 0). That is ~A = 1 – A. This formula holds for fuzzy sets. A case holds degrees of membership of the negation of any set to the degree that it is not a member of the original set. For example, if a case has a membership value of 0.33 in the set of autonomous civil society demand for participatory politics (csd), its membership value in the set representing the absence of this civil society demand (~csd) is [1 – 0.33] = 0.67.

Similarly, when two sets intersect, a case is a member of that intersection if it is an element of each one of the two sets that intersect. That is, a case is present in a conjunction A*B if its set membership value for set A = 1 and value for set B = 1. If its membership in either A or B is 0, that is, less than 1, it is not a member of A*B (where either A = 0, or B = 0, then A*B = 0). The value a case's membership takes in a conjunction of two or more sets is the minimum value that it takes in each of the individual sets that make up the conjunction. That is, A*B = min(A,B). This formula holds for fuzzy sets. If a case's membership value in the set of participatory leadership (pl) is 0.83 and in the set of bureaucratic support (bsp) is 0.67, its membership in the conjunction of both conditions, participatory leadership AND bureaucratic support (PL*BSP) is 0.67 (the minimum of the two values). If we wanted to know the case's value in the conjunction of the absence of participatory leadership AND the presence of bureaucratic support (~pl*BSP), we would need to calculate the negation of the former set and the minimum value of both, that is, min[(1–0.83),0.67] = 0.17.

We can use these mathematical principles to calculate each case's membership in a combination of conditions, and then, as we did for necessity, test whether that combination holds to the superset relation of sufficiency across cases. The measures of consistency and coverage from these tests can inform us which kinds of explanations fit the data. For those combinations that do, we can then apply Boolean elimination algorithms to remove redundant determinants from explanations.

## The truth table

In Table 7.1 I present a truth table derived from the fuzzy data matrix first presented in Chapter 5. The truth table is an impressive analytical device. Each row corresponds to a logical combination of presence or absence of conditions. Although our cases have fuzzy membership in many rows, they are logically 'more in' and have greater than 0.5 set membership in only one row. That is the row to which they are ascribed in the truth table. Cases may differ to the extent they have membership in that row (making them stronger or weaker examples of the combination of conditions), but this is the row that best describes the case. Each one of the 16 rows can be thought of as an ideal type of PB (see Schneider and Wagemann, 2012: 98).[1]

The truth table is a really useful device for cumulation, both when working alone and in collaboration with other researchers in any field. It is useful in the first instance to look at it without reference

1 A truth table differs from a data matrix in that each row in a truth table corresponds to a logical case rather than a data record. In a crisp-set QCA, each case can only be a member of one logical conjunction of all the conditions under observation because a condition cannot be observed to be both present and absent at the same time – this would be a logical contradiction. Each row in a truth table represents one of these possible combinations of presence or absence of each of the observed explanatory conditions in an analysis. In the analysis presented here we have

to the outcome, and to assess how empirical cases fall in relation to key explanatory factors. The truth table is not accidently named. It lays bare the consequences of assumptions and coding in constructing comparative research. It can engineer a useful dialogue between cases in a population and the concepts we are trying to understand – in other words, between theory and evidence. The truth table can then show which empirical cases are logically identical (in terms of their properties) and which are not. That information can improve the formation of typologies and require researchers to think hard about how similar or different cases really are. Are these cases that share a truth table row really the same kinds of cases, or are they different?

I can immediately find reassurances that some cases that researchers themselves considered part of the same type coalesce here. For example, row 2 articulates the logical basis for Wampler's category of emasculated participatory democracy, and row 1 reflects McNulty's unsuccessful cases. But we also can see the sometimes surprising result that cases from far-flung parts of the world appear to have some logical equivalence when it comes to key conditions for participatory democracy. It challenges the common idea that cultural or country factors are key determinants of PB. It can, of course, also be a warning signal of some misinterpretation. The point is that the truth table organizes that information across a large number of cases so it can be transparently evaluated.

---

16 possible logical combinations and 16 rows in the truth table. Schneider and Wagemann highlight that 'Each row denotes a *qualitatively different* combination of conditions, ie the difference in cases in different rows is a difference in kind rather than a difference in degree' (2012: 92; original emphasis). This systematic approach to revealing and classifying types is overlooked by most work in comparative social science. The corresponding important logical property of fuzzy sets is that each case can only have greater than a 0.5 membership value in one of these logical combinations of conditions representing a truth table row. Another way of saying this is that each case is a good example of only one of the ideal types represented by each truth table row. Fuzzy sets allow that each case can, and often will, have partial membership in each of our 16 possible logical combinations; 1 and 0 represent the extreme values of full membership and full non-membership in the set representing presence or absence of a condition. In the four-dimensional property space created by four conditions, each case can only be found closest to the vertex representing one of these ideal types. Empirical cases have partial membership in all kinds of logical cases, but they have strong membership only in one. This highlights that the cruciality of the conceptual definition of the crossover point in calibration cannot be undersold. In calibrating, the researcher makes an important decision as to whether a case is more in or more out of the set.

**Table 7.1:** Truth table for 31 cases

| # | Participatory leadership | Autonomous civil society demand | Bureaucratic support | Financial basis to spend | Cases | Outcome: citizen control of PB |
|---|---|---|---|---|---|---|
| 1 | No[1] | No | No | No | Ayacucho, Loreto, Mauá, Toronto | No |
| 2 | No | No | No | Yes | Blumenau, Rio Claro | No |
| 3 | No | No | Yes | No | Buenos Aires | No |
| 4 | No | No | Yes | Yes | No cases | Unknown |
| 5 | No | Yes | No | No | Recife (i), São Paulo | No |
| 6 | No | Yes | No | Yes | No cases | Unknown |
| 7 | No | Yes | Yes | No | Cajamarca | Yes |
| 8 | No | Yes | Yes | Yes | No cases | Unknown |
| 9 | Yes | No | No | No | Berlin-Lichtenstein | No |
| 10 | Yes | No | No | Yes | Montevideo, Poitou-Charentes, Sevilla | Contradiction[2] |
| 11 | Yes | No | Yes | No | Camaragibe, Lambayeque, Morsang-sur-Orge | Contradiction |
| 12 | Yes | No | Yes | Yes | Betim, Gravataí, Ipatinga | Contradiction |
| 13 | Yes | Yes | No | No | Moquegua, Rome, Santo André | No |
| 14 | Yes | Yes | No | Yes | Belo Horizonte, Chicago, Córdoba, New York | Contradiction |
| 15 | Yes | Yes | Yes | No | Cusco, Recife (ii) | Yes |
| 16 | Yes | Yes | Yes | Yes | Porto Alegre, João Monlevade | Yes |

[1] Yes = present, No = absent. Each row can be considered a logical case or a type of PB.
[2] Contradiction here signifies that the two or more empirical cases that are strong members of the row do not agree on the outcome. In some it is present and in others it is absent.

The truth table invites us to consider affinities that we might have easily assumed away. It is a useful prompt for case researchers to think more ecumenically than perhaps they are comfortable with, and to consider their cases as similar to those looked at by other researchers with slightly different research strategies. For example, in row 14 we see that cases from three different regions all show evidence of political support for the project, autonomous civil society demand, and relatively good financial situations compared to other such governing units in their countries. Nevertheless, in each case there are reports that administrators or technical teams were often actively working against implementation of either PB programmes or projects. Although each case – New York, Chicago, Córdoba and Belo Horizonte – fits this type to a different degree, the description of the cases in the literature suggest they all fit this type quite well.

A second advantage of the truth table is it can tell us which logical types of PB (combinations of conditions) we have empirical examples of and which we do not. When we make general claims about necessity and sufficiency we implicitly engage in counterfactual analysis of these unobserved combinations. With the truth table we can engage in that analysis explicitly and transparently. Rows 4, 6 and 8 represent what are called 'logical remainders'.[2] The diversity of our cases is limited. Is this because such cases are unlikely to exist or because we are blind to them? One explanation is that these rows represent hypothetical cases where financial resources are high, but some impetus from a combination of key actors is absent. It may be that participatory programmes are less likely to present under those conditions. Perhaps because their variation from more ostensibly successful scenarios is not as obvious as that provided in rows 1 and 2, the type of case is more likely to escape the attention of social scientists where it does exist. We have no strong empirical evidence for outcomes in these circumstances. Truth tables that cumulate research can therefore be used to justify later case selection strategies.

2 Researchers must be clear about the assumptions they make about counterfactuals. An awareness of limited diversity can allow the researcher to make good transparent decisions about what key variables should be tested for causal relationships across cases. QCA researchers cannot hide away the exponential increases in the number of logical possible combinations of conditions where a new one is added. The discipline of calibration ensures the researcher still cannot escape tough decisions and theoretical justification of what is fully relevant, partially relevant or completely irrelevant variation. Such decisions will, in turn, be dictated by the richness of data and the number of cases. The methodical approach poses challenges and takes the analytical brain in a reflective direction.

Finally, we can consult the outcome condition in the right-hand column to begin to understand which combinations produce the outcome of interest. In some rows all cases agree on the outcome and it is clearer where the combination is associated with citizen control of PB decisions or its absence. In other rows, cases present a logical contradiction. The same conditions lead to different outcomes in the cases. We might want to look at those cases that disagree and see if we can resolve the contradiction if there is some miscoding, or we are missing a key explanatory condition. However, this dichotomous data represents something of a simplification. We have in hand more fine-grained fuzzy memberships. With fuzzy sets there is almost always some inconsistency in each row, and we have measures of fit that can inform us as to whether the outcome ascribed to the row is supported by the evidence from all cases. Using the truth table researchers can transparently investigate, contribute to and challenge the construction of a medium-N comparison.

## Investigating sufficient conditions

We can now use the algorithms developed for Boolean reduction to assess, based on the cumulated evidence presented, what combinations of conditions are sufficient to produce our outcome or negate it. Explaining logically the absence of the outcome is one of the most undervalued and underemphasized strengths of case-based research designs.

Recall in Chapter 6 that we introduced the QCA approach initially by looking at how it might model Wampler's most parsimonious conclusion. Before returning to the 31-case analysis, the example is again used to help understand how conceptualization can affect analysis of sufficient conditions, and when strong or even weaker claims of sufficiency of conditions are warranted. We observed the effect of different set calibrations, representing different interpretations of deepened democracy in Table 6.2 on the analysis of necessity. Minimized sufficient conditions for the outcome 'deepened democracy' are presented in Table 7.2. The comparison of different potential interpretations is again instructive for exposing some of the pitfalls in analysis. It is important to understand how accuracy of set-theoretic inferences can depend very much on how we conceptualize and measure the evidence, and is aided by an understanding of how conceptual and causal theories can be mathematically represented.

In Chapter 6 we showed that the 'C' calibration was the only one to confirm both mayoral support and support for contentious politics

**Table 7.2:** Analysis of sufficient conditions for deepened democracy across 10 cases

| | Outcome tested | Sufficient conditions | Inclusion | PRI | Coverage |
|---|---|---|---|---|---|
| 1 | Deepened democracy (A) | **Mayoral support** | 1 | 1 | 1 |
| 2 | Deepened democracy (B) | Mayoral support* **Citizen contentious politics** | 1 | 1 | 0.757 |
| 3 | Deepened democracy (C) | ∅ | – | – | – |

Note: Analysis performed using truthTable and minimize commands in the QCA package in R (Dusa, 2019). Measures of fit are reported for the conservative solutions only. Bold = core condition. The inclusion threshold was set at 0.8.

as necessary conditions for deepened democracy. I argued that the importance of this finding needed to be examined because highly restrictive standards for deep democracy often lead to a skewed distribution of set memberships. While a restrictive conceptualization of democracy logically lowers the requirements for necessity relationships, it logically increases the bar for sufficiency. If the set representing the outcome is restricted to a relatively small one in scope, it is ever more difficult to find a relevant smaller subset to fit that same set (a sufficient condition). In this example, we indeed find no evidence of sufficient conjunctions of the two conditions tested for relationships with deepened democracy 'C', as reported in row 3 of the table. Note, again, that the finding alone does not invalidate the argument about necessary conditions for deepened democracy or the conceptualization of deep democracy itself. What it identifies is the mathematical foundations that explain how restrictive conceptualizations of deep democracy (or any outcome) will lend themselves to long lists of necessary conditions and little evidence to explain what conjunctions of conditions might be sufficient for that outcome.

What of the alternative conceptualizations of deepened democracy? In Chapter 6 'deepened democracy A' was shown to necessitate mayoral support only. The finding rested on assumptions about what differences in quality signified key differences in kind that distinguish deep democracy from its negation. In Table 7.2 mayoral support alone is confirmed as sufficient under this interpretation (row 1). Citizen contentious politics is eliminated and assumed irrelevant. Again, the neat finding masks some thorny issues of assumption, which, if misunderstood, undermine that simple interpretation.

**Table 7.3:** Truth table for outcome 'deepened democracy A'

| | Mayor support | Citizen conten-tious politics | Deep democracy | Number of cases | Inclusion | PRI | Cases |
|---|---|---|---|---|---|---|---|
| 1 | 1 | 1 | 1 | 6 | 1 | 1 | Belo Horizonte, Ipatinga, Port Alegre (i), Porto Alegre (ii), Porto Alegre (iii), Recife |
| 2 | 1 | 0 | 1 | 2 | 1 | 1 | Santo André, São Paulo |
| 3 | 0 | 0 | 0 | 2 | 0.329 | 0 | Blumenau, Rio Claro |
| 4 | 0 | 1 | ? | 0 | – | – | – |

The example shows how conceptual (un)clarity can result in potentially erroneous elimination of causes. The assumption relies on an interpretation that the middle-of-the-road cases in Table 6.2 – Belo Horizonte, Port Alegre (early and latter versions), Recife, São Paulo, and Santo André – are slightly more in the set of deepened democracy, and equally slightly more in the set of mayoral support. The truth table is also an extremely useful tool for understanding conceptual and measurement choices in case research. The truth table for the outcome 'A', minimized in row 1 in Table 7.2, is now reproduced in Table 7.3. This truth table includes measures of fit. We can observe that two truth table rows are completely consistent with the subset relation (inclusion score of 1). These include row 1, where mayoral support combines with support for contentious politics, and row 2, where mayoral support combines with the absence of support for contentious politics. A logical minimization has taken place, to produce the output in row 1 of Table 7.2, where citizen support for contentious politics has been eliminated by being deemed an irrelevant factor. The outcome is observed regardless of variance in support for contentious politics, and that condition is eliminated from explanation. Thereby we arrive at the parsimonious solution

**Table 7.4:** Truth table for outcome 'deepened democracy A' with alternative coding

| | Mayor support | Citizen contentious politics | Deep demo- cracy | Number of cases | Inclusion | PRI | Cases |
|---|---|---|---|---|---|---|---|
| 1 | 0 | 1 | 1 | 4 | 1 | 1 | Belo Horizonte, Port Alegre (i), Porto Alegre (iii), Recife |
| 2 | 1 | 1 | 1 | 2 | 1 | 1 | Ipatinga, Porto Alegre (ii) |
| 3 | 0 | 0 | 0 | 4 | 0.338 | 0.02 | Blumenau, Rio Claro, Santo André, São Paulo |
| 4 | 1 | 0 | ? | 0 | – | – | – |

that mayoral support for contentious politics alone is sufficient for deepened democracy.

Nevertheless, the minimization here masks an important choice made (or in this case, mostly ignored) at the moment of calibration. As already explained, the difference between 0.49 and 0.51 in fuzzy set theory represents the important difference in quality that organizes a case as being more in a set or more in its negation. In Chapter 6 I rather uncritically ascribed many cases with medium mayoral support 0.51 membership in the relevant set (more in the set) to avoid ascribing them the indeterminate membership score of 0.5 in this example. What if I had ascribed some of them a score of 0.49? In Table 7.4, I observe the difference if the middle-of-the-road cases are ascribed a score of 0.49 (more out of) the set of mayoral support. This significant reinterpretation of cases' membership in an influencing condition pushes a number of cases into different truth table rows. Rather than eliminate citizen willingness to support contentious politics, the minimization will now eliminate mayoral support as a sufficient condition. The example shows the sensitivity of the theoretical distinction between what cases are more in or out of a set (either side of the 0.5 crossover point).

It is important to understand that this sensitivity does not extend in the other direction within the fuzzy set. If I had recoded all those middling cases with a mayoral support set membership of 0.52, the substantive interpretation and the truthTable (Table 7.3) would not change (only to show some very minor inconsistency in the inclusion score).[3] This sensitivity of calibration around the crossover point is a strength and not a weakness, and shows that conceptual clarity is paramount in evaluating necessary and sufficient conditions. The elimination would have been entirely reasonable had the coding been justified using a theoretical standard. The example of deep democracy 'A' shows that fsQCA, when applied appropriately, is not a journey into indeterminacy but one that interacts with data to improve the ways in which the researcher can better understand their cases and relationships among them.

I have shown that conceptions 'A' and 'C' of deep democracy offer either somewhat underspecified or very strictly specified versions of the concept respectively. We saw in Chapter 6 that the 'B' calibration revealed inconsistencies in claims about necessity. Row 2 of Table 7.2 reports the minimal sufficient conditions under the 'B' calibration, and explains that the conjunction of mayoral support and citizen willingness to support contentious politics is entirely consistent with the sufficiency superset–subset relations across the cases. Even if neither condition is necessary or sufficient on its own, in the cases where they both occur in combination, that combination is sufficient to produce deepened democracy. Citizen contentious politics is highlighted in bold (Table 7.2) because it can be considered a core condition (Fiss, 2011). Mayoral support might be eliminated from this conjunction to form a more parsimonious solution if we were willing to make the counterfactual assumption that cases where mayoral support is absent but citizen willingness to support contentious politics is present would lead to deepened democracy. We do not have any empirical examples of those kinds of cases (row 4 of Tables 7.3 and 7.4) in this circumscribed dataset, and this appears a very difficult counterfactual assumption to accept based on theory. It might lead the researcher to search out such a case for their next research project.

3 Note also that if I had ascribed all those cases the same scores in both mayoral support and deepened democracy at 0.49, the original result would also not change. What is at stake is a clear qualification rooted in qualitative evidence of when a condition is more absent or more present across cases.

In the example it is crucial to note that the result is a function of the measurement calibrated to concepts we choose. We always make these implicit judgments when we infer. The method is used to make those judgements more explicit. If Wampler had observed using an ordinal scale that some of the cases were medium rather than merely low or high in terms of the observance of contentious politics, there might have been ground to calibrate degrees of membership differently and have a different result.

A critic might now observe that this only goes to show the perils of inferring with a small-N, using secondary data, but as I have previously argued, that criticism misunderstands the approach that rests on exploiting the advantages of intense engagement with conceptual clarity and casework itself. Transparency about what is at stake can be liberating rather than debilitating. At another extreme, with all this method and maths, should we now expect to have lost the sympathies of Sartori who would pour scorn on the over-conscious thinker 'who refuses to discuss heat unless he is given a thermometer' and is paralysed by 'logical perfectionism' (1970: 1033)? I hope not. Sartori famously champions the 'conscious thinker' who 'manages to say a great deal simply by saying hot and cold, warmer and cooler' (1970: 1033). I argue that despite the value of numerical reasoning to QCA, it is more a tool for the conscious than the unconscious thinker.

Another criticism could be that measures here for the outcome set are simplistic. The point I want to make, however, is that it may only be in the undertaking of this analysis that such decisions are highlighted. Rihoux and Lobe have shown that a stepwise QCA approach properly applied allows an iteration between maximal parsimony and complexity that arrives at a greater explanatory power (2009: 238). What this analysis of Wampler's typology shows is that applying QCA tools to existing research and its conclusions can highlight what is at stake in considering whether our summaries are overly complex or parsimonious.

## Expanded reproduction of Wampler's Brazil analysis

What of the sufficient conditions for deep democracy in the wider analysis of Wampler's five conditions? What combinations of conditions are consistently sufficient for deepened democracy in Brazil? The truth table based on the data in Chapter 6 is produced in Table 7.5. It contains a row representing each logical combination of presence (1) or absence (0) of a condition. Each possible row is identified by the number in the first column. With five conditions there are 32 logical

**Table 7.5:** Truth table showing sufficient conditions for deepened democracy (5 conditions)

| Row | MS | CCP | PLE | REP | FBS | Out: DD | Incl. | PRI | Cases |
|---|---|---|---|---|---|---|---|---|---|
| 31 | 1 | 1 | 1 | 1 | 0 | 1 | 1 | 1 | Porto Alegre (i) |
| 32 | 1 | 1 | 1 | 1 | 1 | ? | 0.936 | 0.853 | Porto Alegre (ii) |
| 14 | 0 | 1 | 1 | 0 | 1 | ? | 0.899 | 0.667 | Belo Horizonte |
| 29 | 1 | 1 | 1 | 0 | 0 | ? | 0.815 | 0.5 | Recife, Santo André |
| 24 | 1 | 0 | 1 | 1 | 1 | ? | 0.776 | 0.595 | Ipatinga |
| 9 | 0 | 1 | 0 | 0 | 0 | 0 | 0.709 | 0 | São Paulo |
| 4 | 0 | 0 | 0 | 1 | 1 | 0 | 0.378 | 0 | Blumenau |
| 2 | 0 | 0 | 0 | 0 | 1 | 0 | 0.338 | 0 | Rio Claro |

Note: MS is mayoral support; CCP is civil society using contentious and cooperative politics; PLE is positive legislative environment; FBS is financial basis for spending; REP is rules that encourage participation and DEEPD is deepened democracy. Incl. is the inclusion score and PRI refers to Proportional Reduction in Inconsistency.

combinations of presence or absence of each condition. In this table I have shortened the truth table to only display those eight rows that have empirical cases that are members (more in than out) of the row. A full table would include all the other 24 combinations – the 'logical remainders'. The row that cases are ascribed to is the combination of factors that best describes the case.[4] We then also get a value for how consistent the superset relationship is for the combination described in the row (the inclusion score). It is important to understand that the consistency score for each row includes all the cases, memberships in that row. The truth table does what it says on the tin and reveals some truths. It neatly summarizes concepts and measurements ascribed (calibrated) across all our cases

What can we understand from this summary? The first thing to notice is there appears to be good variety across the cases as they fall into different rows, which reflects the rich information and diversity of cases Wampler studies in Brazil. Only two cases (Recife and Santo André in row 29) have the exact same combination of the five conditions. Even though they may display these conditions to varying degrees, their set memberships agree on being more in (or more out) of each

[4] With fuzzy sets, cases have partial membership in numerous rows but they will only have greater than 0.5 membership in one row. See footnote 1.

influencing condition. Perhaps more interesting is that although they agree on all those inputs, the cases diverge on whether deep democracy occurs. Those cases even landed in different categories in Wampler's categorization described earlier. This could be an important finding. As before, we may want to investigate potential errors in coding or specification of the explanatory conditions we chose to include in the model. We should also think about whether the cases are more similar than expected. Recife had several changes to its mayor and the rules of PB over the time period. This might be evidence that it was worth considering splitting Recife into two cases covering separate time periods, as was done with Porto Alegre in these examples. Montambeault favours such a within-case comparison of Recife in her work separating the pre- and post-PT mayors (2016), which is a large influence on why I adopt the approach in my larger-N comparison. To solve that contradiction, we need to consider deepened democracy to have occurred in the 2000s but not in the pre-PT PB of the 1990s in Recife. Such a consideration would place the new 'Recife (ii)' case into a separate fully consistent row. We should be cautious, however, not to simply make the data fit our theories, and consider whether, in fact, these inconsistencies reveal a need to expand theories, but it would be a reasonable strategy here.

As we saw in the first analysis in the chapter, the second key step of the QCA following the identification of the truth table is to provide minimal Boolean expressions – parsimonious solution terms that explain the relationship among (combinations of) conditions and outcomes. This requires the analyst to decide on how much inconsistency in the sufficiency relation they are willing to accept to declare a combination of conditions (truth table row) sufficient to produce deepened democracy. Guidelines range anywhere upwards of 0.75. By accepting some inconsistency we are, in effect, modifying our claim to one that these conditions are 'almost always' sufficient for the outcome, which is good enough for most social scientists. I have placed a '?' in the outcome column for values in this range in Table 7.5. The transparency of the choice of consistency adds a very useful measure of fit to case-based inferences that can help colleagues evaluate the evidence base for empirical generalizations.

In Table 7.5 there is very little inconsistency in the first two rows. They differ only on whether the financial means to spend on PB projects was present or not in the case. For example, in Porto Alegre funds for PB and project implementation were not as plentiful in the early days in comparison, but the participatory budget still managed to deepen democracy, and by the mid-1990s the PT had reorganized finances such that they were in a quite healthy position. If we took a more conservative threshold of 0.9 (considering only cases with an inclusion score greater than that to be sufficient for the outcome), it would result in a solution term that immediately eliminated financial explanations as redundant. We would declare the presence of all other conditions in combination sufficient for the outcome:

S1) MS*CCP*PLE*REP → Deep democracy

Further minimization, making no concrete assumptions about the logical remainders[5] not shown in the table, can lead to a parsimonious expression suggesting the intersection of just two sets explaining deep democracy:

S2) CCP*REP → Deep democracy

In other words, we can make assumptions about cases for which we do not have data that would allow us to drop the mayoral support (ms) and positive legislative environment (ple) conditions from the solution formula – we do not know much about what happens when they are absent in the presence of the other conditions. But we already have data in the other rows that prevent us from considering citizen contentious politics (ccp) and rules encouraging participation (rep) irrelevant – we know better what happens when those conditions are absent in similar contexts. That is to say, the data provides evidential grounds that the combination of citizens' willingness to use both cooperative and contentious political action along with rules that enable participation is core[6] to any reasonable explanation of sufficient conditions for deep democracy. We might, however, need to be more or less cautious in theoretical assumptions about those rows for which we have less information. Concentrating focus on the eight rows of the truth table (Table 7.5) with strong empirical exemplars holds to the more conservative solution term containing more elements (see S1). Good

[5] These are the combinations for which there is no or low levels of empirical data. The algorithm will simply use any logical combination for which we have no cases to help eliminate conditions from the solution.

[6] On the idea of core conditions, see Ragin (2008); Fiss (2011); Misangyi et al (2017).

knowledge of background theory and cases is, as always, paramount in general explanations that will include multiple assumptions.

There are three rows in Table 7.5, identified as 14, 29 and 24, that have inconsistencies within the range of 0.75–0.9. What should be thought of them? We can take them in turn. I think most analysts would include row 14 as sufficient for deep democracy. It has strong measures of fit and a strong case exemplar in Belo Horizonte. It is more difficult to make an argument for the other two. Row 29 as it appears currently contains a true logical contradiction – to include it as sufficient would be to ignore the absence of deepened democracy in the Santo André case. This row is as much an example of deep democracy as it is of not deep democracy, and therefore it is not that useful for explaining deep democracy. I would not consider there enough evidence to consider this combination sufficient. Finally, row 24 is worth considering. The inconsistent evidence for sufficiency here comes not from Ipatinga, which is the clearest example of this combination of conditions occurring in practice, but from the partial membership of two least successful cases of Blumenau and Rio Claro. The plot in Figure 7.1 visualizes the relationship between cases' memberships in row 24 and the outcome. The two cases lie below the diagonal, having greater membership in X than in Y.[7] In those cases, this combination of the presence of most influencing conditions, along with the absence of civil society use of cooperative and contentious politics, is at least perceptible to a minimal degree, whereas deepened democracy is not at all perceptible. This is the source of inconsistency. One reading of this data would argue that we should not draw inference about a combination of conditions from examples that are more or less 'irrelevant' because they are not strong examples of the combination of conditions, as opposed to truly deviant cases that would fall much further to the right of the X–Y plot in Figure 7.1 (see Schneider and Wagemann, 2012). On another reading this points to an advantage of fuzzy sets – the analysis shows that very minimal levels of the conditions that occurred strongly in Ipatinga are not associated with strong democratic outcomes – in fact, quite the opposite. The discussion highlights again that comparative analysis of this sort is about better learning the relationships between cases, data and theory.

[7] Note the logical property that more INUS conditions added to any conjunction will tend to increase consistency by lowering the value of case membership in a conjunction (lowering the value of X). The more we add caveats to a theory the more it ought to explain the cases (although perhaps not always for the better).

**Figure 7.1:** Sufficiency of row 24

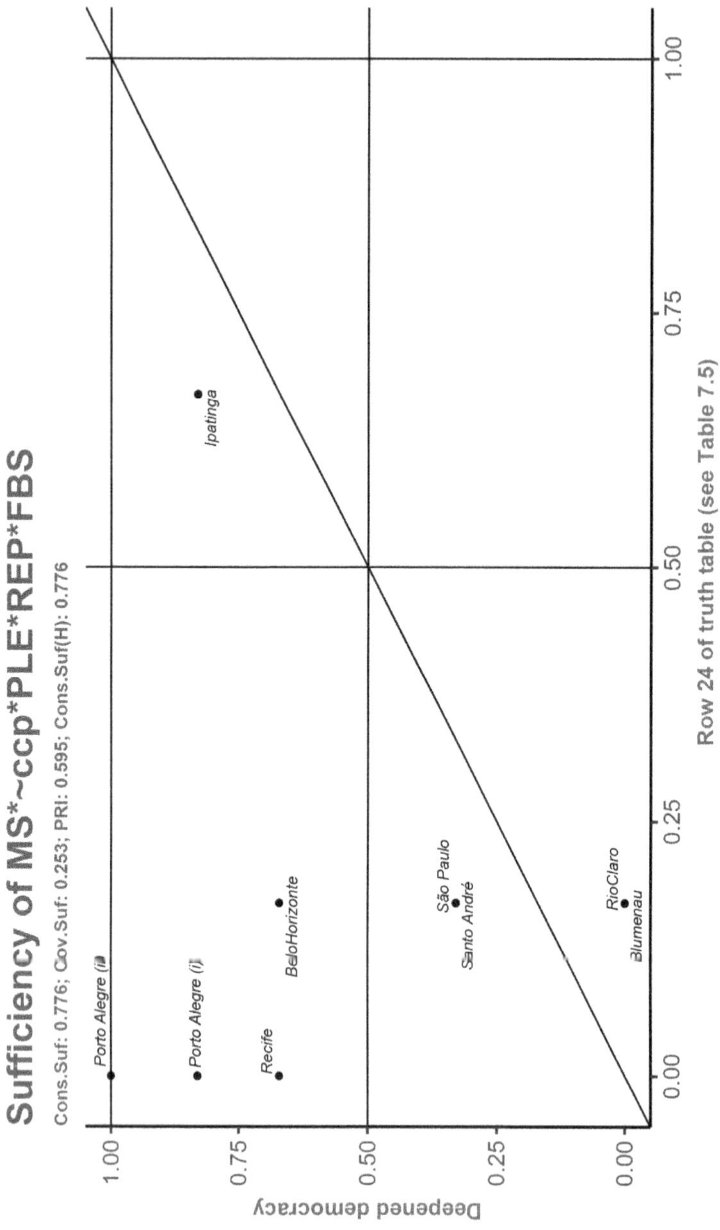

Even though the internal validity of the individual accounts of cases is sound, we might be conservative and wait for more information to be confident that the findings in Ipatinga and Recife generalize. QCA also provides good clues as to where we should go looking for new cases or further fieldwork (Schneider and Rohlfing, 2013). Table 7.6 reports the solution taking a consistency threshold of 0.89. Considering what we know about the cases, the strength of expectations and precision of the measurement from the material, including the top three rows as sufficient is, in my judgement, an appropriate interpretation. It means the most parsimonious solution retains only the conditions in bold in Table 7.6.[8]

The final analysis of Wampler's Brazilian data alone then presents the following model of necessary and sufficient conditions to explain deep democracy:

**CCP***PLE* MS***REP** → Deepened democracy (I)

**CCP***PLE*rep***FBS** → Deepened democracy (II)

Alternatively, the model is factorized as:

**CCP***PLE*[MS***REP** + rep***FBS**] → Deepened democracy

At an absolute minimum, the evidence suggests that in Brazil, use of contentious politics must be combined with either rules enabling participation or a financial basis for implementation of projects (core conditions in bold). Actually, the evidence suggests that municipalities in poor financial circumstances may need all the other conditions present in combination for deepened democracy. Alternatively, as in Belo Horizonte, even where rules chop and change and mayoral

[8] The specific parsimonious solution highlighted utilizes the row dominance argument. Otherwise four logically equivalent models are produced. This is an intermediate solution. The conservative solution would retain ~ms in the second term. However, I specify that no logical remainders include the absence of mayoral support as a sufficient condition for the outcome. The discussion of this condition and its high consistency with necessity provide extremely strong grounds for this theoretical expectation. In QCA the conservative solution allows no minimization using logical combinations of conditions for which we have no empirical assumptions (logical remainders). The parsimonious solution makes whatever assumptions lead to the most parsimonious solution. In the intermediate solution the researcher holds some theoretical expectations constant in the counterfactual analyses.

**Table 7.6:** Truth table showing sufficient conditions for deepened democracy

| Expression | Inclusion | PRI | Coverage | Unique coverage | Cases |
|---|---|---|---|---|---|
| MS***CCP*** PLE***REP** | 0.949 | 0.898 | 0.676 | 0.356 | Porto Alegre (i), Porto Alegre (ii) |
| **CCP***PLE* ~rep***FBS** | 0.915 | 0.746 | 0.393 | 0.073 | Belo Horizonte |
| Model | 0.954 | 0.915 | 0.749 | | |

Note: MS is mayoral support; CCP is citizens using contentious and cooperative politics; PLE is positive legislative environment; FBS is financial basis to spend; REP is rules encouraging participation. Bold = core condition.

support waxes and wanes, significant democratic empowerment comes when money is available, civil society demands responsive spending, and the legislative environment is not hostile to PB. This conclusion is not a million miles from Wampler's. It adds nuance. It is important to note that the absence of rules enabling participation is an INUS condition that cannot easily be removed from this explanation. This invites us to an interpretation that perhaps informality or updating of rules can be read in a positive light in certain circumstances. QCA requires a few machinations, for sure, but they are worth it if they give us extra accuracy in our empirical generalizations.

## Larger-N comparison of cases

The truth table for analysing the main dataset of 31 cases is presented again in Table 7.7. This resembles that previously presented in Table 7.1, but now includes measures of fit.

Again, the top two rows are highly consistent subsets of citizen control of PB (>0.97). Those constellations of conditions should be considered sufficient conditions for citizen control of PB decisions. It is worth noting that the small inconsistency in those cases, which is a minor contributor to inconsistency in each row that I discuss here, comes from the Cajamarca case. The case is worth highlighting because it represents one that has no extreme set membership values for its influencing conditions.[9] We might call it a middle-of-the-road

[9] Truth table rows were investigated using the pimplot command in the SetMethods package for R (Oana and Schneider, 2018).

**Table 7.7:** Truth table for citizen control of PB for 31 cases

| # | PL | CSD | BSP | FBS | Out-come: CCPB | N | Incl | PRI | Cases |
|---|---|---|---|---|---|---|---|---|---|
| 16 | 1 | 1 | 1 | 1 | 1 | 2 | 0.975 | 0.946 | João Monlevade, Porto Alegre |
| 15 | 1 | 1 | 1 | 0 | 1 | 2 | 0.971 | 0.913 | Cusco, Recife (ii) |
| 10 | 1 | 0 | 0 | 1 | ? | 3 | 0.904 | 0.701 | Montevideo, Poitou-Charentes, Sevilla |
| 12 | 1 | 0 | 1 | 1 | ? | 3 | 0.9 | 0.728 | Betim, Gravataí, Ipatinga |
| 11 | 1 | 0 | 1 | 0 | ? | 3 | 0.873 | 0.605 | Camaragibe, Lambayeque, Morsang-sur-Orge |
| 7 | 0 | 1 | 1 | 0 | 0 | 1 | 0.826 | 0.427 | Cajamarca |
| 14 | 1 | 1 | 0 | 1 | ? | 4 | 0.822 | 0.59 | Belo Horizonte, Chicago 49th Ward, Córdoba, New York |
| 3 | 0 | 0 | 1 | 0 | 0 | 1 | 0.8 | 0 | Buenos Aires |
| 9 | 1 | 0 | 0 | 0 | 0 | 1 | 0.797 | 0 | Berlin Lichtenberg |
| 13 | 1 | 1 | 0 | 0 | 0 | 3 | 0.791 | 0.431 | Moquegua, Rome, Santo André |
| 5 | 0 | 1 | 0 | 0 | 0 | 2 | 0.647 | 0.215 | Recife (i), São Paulo |
| 2 | 0 | 0 | 0 | 1 | 0 | 2 | 0.505 | 0 | Blumenau, Rio Claro |
| 1 | 0 | 0 | 0 | 0 | 0 | 4 | 0.501 | 0 | Ayacucho, Loreto, Mauá, Toronto |
| 4 | 0 | 0 | 1 | 1 | ? | 0 | – | – | |
| 6 | 0 | 1 | 0 | 1 | ? | 0 | – | – | |
| 8 | 0 | 1 | 1 | 1 | ? | 0 | – | – | |

Note: PL is participatory leadership; CSD is autonomous civil society demands; BSP is bureaucratic support; FBS is financial basis for spending; CCPB is citizen control of decisions in PB.

case. Its membership of the outcome is lower because it is described as having a number of less than satisfactory elements, and it appears that participants played a less influential role overall than elsewhere (see McNulty, 2011: 103). The one other case in the dataset that has a similar middle-of-the-road profile is Moquegua, McNulty's other moderate case. Cajamarca is, on my reading, of slightly more use in explaining the absence of citizen control of PB. It is a good example of a case whose evidence, although it contributes to some degree of deviance from the general relationship of sufficiency, is more easily overcome as one of more minor degrees of measurement rather than a difference of kind.

The variance in set scores and number of conditions means we can expect many rows to show some consistency with the outcome. The proportional reduction in inconsistency (PRI) measure can be used here to identify how much a combination of conditions is specifically a subset of the outcome vis-à-vis the absence of the outcome. We can discard all rows with <0.75 inclusion consistency and all those having low PRI scores <0.5 as insufficient for the outcome. This leaves four rows with more complex degrees of inconsistencies of evidence for consideration (10, 11, 12 and 14). These are indeed the four rows labelled as contradictions in Table 7.1. Each of these rows has some level of inconsistency but also contains at least one 'true logical contradiction'. That is to say, although the subset relationship of sufficiency holds up quite well across all cases (>0.82), in each row there is a deviant case contributing to inconsistency that is a good empirical example of that particular combinations of conditions.

These contradictions are not easy to resolve using any single method – for example, by adding another variable or by changing a set definition. If there were an easy way to do it, I would be presenting the resolution rather than the contradiction! However, these contradictions are usefully revealed by that data to raise important questions about causal theories in PB and point to areas where further research on PB may be most useful. The rows themselves offer options for good small-N research designs in order to try and better understand what explains opposing outcomes. But there is also an argument that they signify a slightly foggier portion of the research communities' PB map. Many of those rows differ from one another on single alternative conditions and exist in the same general area of the overall space of properties of participatory budgets. They agree on political leadership and vary a little on the combinations of other conditions. Therefore, blunt remedies such as recoding would simply push cases around the rows rather than solve contradictions. The five contradicting cases are Montevideo, Betim, Morsang-sur-Orge, Chicago and Córdoba. I duly considered coding errors, and returned again to the source material, but the calibration and evidence hold up quite well on reflection – in terms of outcomes, each of these cases disappointed in the long run where there tended to be evidence of growing co-optation or reduced implementation of programmes. The only borderline decision was to recode Morsang-sur-Orge's score on bureaucratic support, which would place it instead in the same row as Berlin-Lichtenberg. I decided to retain it as is, at it offers a more instructive presentation of the analytic process.

Another consideration would be to reintroduce an explanatory condition that distinguishes the contradictions from other cases. Something that captured the formality of rules might seem appropriate but in practice is not salutary. Formalizing new rules over time seemed to undermine successes in Montevideo, Chicago and Córdoba, but has been interpreted as helpful in places such as Belo Horizonte and Poitou-Charentes; it is therefore not clear that it is a condition that resolves the uncertainties. Until other evidence is brought forward to resolve the issue, our favoured general theories based on the evidence will depend on the levels of uncertainty we are willing to accept. Therefore, I produce the solutions that include or exclude these combinations of conditions as sufficient, and address the implications of each.

In this book I have argued that scholars of participatory democracy have erred perhaps too much on the side of constructing their outcomes of interest in more ideal and narrow terms. They are influenced by noble normative goals and want to set high standards. It is an easy position to defend in that sense. But it has significant drawbacks if it inadvertently lowers a fog over some avenues of empirical understanding. I, and I hope many other scholars, am willing to accept some contradictions and uncertainty where they are presented in a transparent manner. Including these four rows as sufficient yields the following minimal parsimonious solution for citizen control of PB.

**participatory leadership (PL)*bureaucratic support (BSP) →** citizen control (CCPB)

\+ (OR)

**participatory leadership (PL)*financial basis for spending (FBS) →** citizen control (CCPB)

which can be factorized to:

**PL*(BSP + FBS) →** CCPB

This minimal solution lends further credence to the necessity of political leadership as it is INUS for all solutions. Participatory political leadership cannot be removed from any reasonable explanation of citizen control of the participatory programme based on the evidence.

The overall model retains strong consistency and coverage for such a parsimonious one. Table 7.8 shows that the two alternate explanations of citizen control both uniquely account for some cases, but also account for a significant number of cases of PB.

We can reason that the empirical evidence reveals two broad types of successful PB. First, in row 1 of Table 7.8 participatory leadership combines with strong bureaucratic support for the programme. This solution uniquely explains Camaragibe and Lambayeque. In Lambayeque the officials were 'extremely flexible with the rules' to encourage broad participation (McNulty, 2011: 88). Camaragibe is a somewhat special case with an alternative form of 'participatory administration'. Participatory delegates elected for longer terms worked almost as an auxiliary phalanx of voluntary administrative staff, connecting the administration to the societies and neighbourhoods. The explanation also resonates in places like Gravataí, Cusco and Ipatinga, where a more top-down type of PB with strong administrative buy-in led to strong citizen influence on government even where it was a more managed process, sometimes when the funding environment is less forgiving.

**Table 7.8:** Sufficient conditions for citizen control across 31 cases

| # | Expression[1] | Inclusion | PRI | Cover-age | Unique coverage | Cases |
|---|---|---|---|---|---|---|
| 1 | PL*BSP | 0.898 | 0.834 | 0.686 | 0.191 | Camaragibe, Lambayeque, Morsang-sur-Orge, Betim, Gravataí, Ipatinga, Cusco, Recife (ii), João Monlevade, Porto Alegre |
| 2 | PL*FBS | 0.803 | 0.706 | 0.687 | 0.192 | Montevideo, Poitou-Charentes, Sevilla, Betim, Gravataí, Ipatinga, Belo Horizonte, Chicago 49th Ward, Córdoba, New York, João Monlevade, Porto Alegre |
| | Model | 0.813 | 0.728 | 0.878 | | |

[1] The expressions and solution are derived using the minimize command in the QCA package for R (Dusa, 2019) and esa command for truth table construction in setMethods (Oana and Schneider, 2018). All solution types are the same. PL is participatory leadership; BSP is bureaucratic support; FBS is financial basis for spending. PRI refers to Proportional Reduction in Inconsistency.

Alternatively, bureaucratic activity is less relevant to successes in the second PB type. Here, what is needed to allow the participatory politicians to achieve their desired intentions is the relative absence of tight fiscal constraints. The combination uniquely explains New York and Belo Horizonte. It suggests some advantages for bigger cities and regional hubs. As in Porto Alegre, which is also a good example, even when faced with constraints on finances in the early days, administrations had more levers to pull to be able to build finances from different sources. Finance could also be a proxy for size in that size of city may allow some initial leeway in fiduciary support for the programme, allowing demonstration effects to occur and for the process to build over time.

## What has happened to civil society?

Although this neat parsimonious model seems the most appropriate one to derive from the data, it renders civil society irrelevant to explanations of citizen control of PB. As I said at the outset of the book, this is a controversial finding. In fact, anyone reading the early accounts of PB covered in Chapters 2 and 3 would find it alarming. If anything, in many of those accounts strong contentious civil society support for participation was valorized as the necessary condition above all others. There might be succour in the finding for those who believe in the possibility of governance-driven democratization and emancipatory outcomes where participation is initiated from the top down. Yet deviations from existing strongly held hypotheses always require a greater standard of evidence. Therefore, it is important to revisit the analysis. It is useful here to look again at the inconsistent truth table rows included in the solution.

If we look at rows 10, 11 and 12 in Table 7.7 together, these are all cases where committed participatory leaders operate in a context of either low, narrow or mollified civil society activity. Each row has one truly contradictory case, but pretty much all other evidence points to the rows' sufficiency for the outcome. The cases represent some mid-sized Brazilian cities, often commuter towns on the outskirts of a larger metropolis, as well as some of the more successful cases where PB has travelled and been adapted outside Brazil. Ignoring for the moment the three contradictory cases, all these cases have had some clear results in terms of providing empowerment to citizens. In general, however, they may be thought to represent a different kind of empowerment, which returns us to questions about the role civil society should play in democracy. The nature of the empowerment in these contradictory rows tends to be more top-down, aimed at building civil society capacity through the state. Either cases focus on specific policy areas where civil society is constrained, such as the Poitou-Charentes regional high school budget, or elsewhere, in municipalities with a weaker civil society where clientelism was normalized, civil society becomes mobilized in more positive ways, as in Gravataí and perhaps Ipatinga. These are examples of states trying to build civil society in a symbiotic relationship. The contradictory cases may then be understood as places where that gamble did not pay off. In Morsang-sur-Orge, Montevideo and Betim, it seems that for various reasons efforts to empower wider sections of the community hit stumbling blocks and fell flat.

What happens if we exclude all these types of cases and hold a higher consistency threshold of 0.95? We will now only include the first two rows in minimization and arrive at the following sufficient solution for citizen control:

**PL*CSD*BSP** → CCPB (Inclusion = 0.98, PRI = 0.96, Coverage = 0.539)

This solution suggests that financial constraints are, in fact, irrelevant to explanations of empowerment. Where all three actors – political leaders, bureaucrats and autonomous civil societies – are dedicated, and none is acting to veto or downgrade participation, we see good outcomes that sometimes overcome real financial constraints. Porto Alegre, Recife under the PT, Cusco and João Monlevade are the best examples of this explanation, but it is consistent across pretty much every case. The solution suggests that regardless of fiscal limits either due to constant bargaining with other tiers of government or a pressing need to firefight dire poverty, participatory democracy can still be successful when committed PB leaders work together with civil society and have bureaucratic support. The finding is important because it provides strong evidence to rebut claims that within successful cases the ability to spend freely is a necessary part of the explanation of good PB outcomes. The fear of a situation of scarce resources often leads to winding up of successful participatory practices. It can be surmised here that where finances were tight, participatory leaders, administrators and civil society were keenly aware of the need for coordinated action, and this was sufficient to allow the institutionalization of programmes with high levels of citizen control. There is almost no available evidence across all cases to reduce that explanation.

## Summary: successful conditions for citizen participation

In this chapter I have shown that the conditions we consider essential to explaining citizen control in PB depend on what standards of evidence we favour and, to some extent, on what conceptualization of PB success we hold to. Some things are clear. If participatory political leadership is a necessary condition for empowered participation, it is not, on its own, sufficient. Where we go from there depends on our attitude to risk and unexplained uncertainty.

The evidence suggests participatory entrepreneurs would do well to try to ensure bureaucrats can support or at best comply with and not have incentives to resist or derail participatory programmes. Combining bureaucratic buy-in for participatory programmes with political buy-in is a path to success in both more and less restrictive accounts. A less restrictive account suggests the combination alone is sufficient, but it is less restrictive because it fails to explain unsatisfactory outcomes in three cases where those conditions were present. Future studies might do well to revisit and compare the cases in those rows, or identify similar cases of participatory governance where those conditions occur with diverging outcomes to see if the contradictions can be explained through comparison between deviant and typical cases.

The most restrictive account requires that civil society remains autonomous, can engage in contentious politics, and continues to provide the countervailing power to state activity where needed. Those who prefer this account will have to be transparent that it is more restrictive, and such characteristics of civil society are less likely to occur in harmony with committed politicians and bureaucrats who are open to making use of invited and contested spaces. These instances where politicians, public servants and critical civil society actors are comfortable with one another are perhaps the real utopias, and therefore less likely to exist for many reasons, but we do have evidence for them here. Where they happen, it is almost impossible to dispute that democracy is significantly enhanced and policies and infrastructure projects proposed and chosen by ordinary citizens are implemented.

Nevertheless, a less restrictive answer to the question of what conditions are sufficient for success in citizen participation offers some uncertainty but more options. If we are willing to live with some unexplained inconsistency in our theories, we can also say that where bureaucratic support and civil society autonomy is lacking, participatory leaders who are able to leverage financial resources almost always produce significant gains in citizen empowerment.

These nuanced findings brought about by cumulation across cases provide a significant advance in our understanding of PB and participatory programmes. They have practical implications for those who wish to act to improve democracy. Implementers of participatory programmes should be aware that there is low risk of their programmes having insignificant effects on democracy where three conditions exist simultaneously to create a positive symbiosis – autonomous and active civil societies, committed politicians, and bureaucrats motivated to serve the public in innovative ways. However, I think democratic innovation scholars and practitioners of participation should also be aware that if they hold too tightly to these conditions, they are failing to explain numerous instances of democratic enhancement. There is plenty of useful evidence for action in between critiques of an 'anything goes' mentality and high standard bearing. Where some conditions seem out of reach because of the barriers in local contexts, as long as willing political leaders can be identified, support from either the bureaucracy or financial freedoms can suffice to produce citizen control of decisions.

# 8

# How Citizen Control of Politics Is Negated, and the Puzzles That Remain

According to Porto de Oliveira, 'there are still no significant studies on negative cases of PB, that is, where the following question has not been answered: What happened with PB, in certain cases, for it not to be successful?' (2017: 240–1). It is a criticism levelled at scholars of democratic innovations in general (Spada and Ryan, 2017). In explaining success across cases I have not yet exhausted the evidence base. We can learn much from independently explaining the absence of citizen control. In this penultimate chapter before concluding I focus attention both on this question and on unearthing some final stones by considering cases and theories that did not make their way into formal analysis. I show that where programmes have failed to empower, there are at least two sufficient explanations. One is the absence of participatory leadership alone, which resonates with the idea that participatory leadership is a necessary condition for success. The other is the combined absence of bureaucratic support, autonomous civil society and financial freedoms. Designers or adopters of participatory programmes are reminded that the otherwise beneficial features of political leadership can be immaterial where civil society and organizational staff participation is desultory, and where funds are lacking.

I then identify the key puzzle that remains – what distinguishes citizen control from its absence in cases where participatory leadership is present? The answers to this question remain inconclusive. Future research may need to investigate more closely whether the presence of some conditions is beneficial in the early stages of development of PB but less so later, and vice versa. For example, where political leaders instigate participatory reform, absence of critical civil society in the presence of strong bureaucratic support could allow administrators to develop positive mobilization strategies that reach out to new publics early on, but in the long run, exclusion of civil society leaders will encourage an exclusive technocracy. I cannot test these ideas with the data I have here, but offer some plausible hypotheses based on case knowledge for future research.

Let us first return very briefly, as we have in previous chapters, to our initial examples of QCA approaches to PB data to iron out some final methodological assumptions. Although I assume asymmetrical causal explanations, this does not mean I can analyse sufficiency for the negation without regard to the analysis of either preceding necessity relations or the analysis of sufficiency for the outcome's presence. That is, the analysis in Chapters 6 and 7 is relevant, and I need to be able to present results that are coherent across the piece. Table 8.1 shows the outcomes of sufficiency analysis for the three different conceptualizations of the absence of the outcome of 'deepened democracy' implied by initial efforts to represent Wampler's final summary of cases in his 2007 study. On this occasion we get the same substantive conclusion in each test – that the absence of citizen willingness to support contentious politics is sufficient for the absence of deep democracy. We can immediately note the asymmetry of this explanation to any of those offered in Table 7.2 in Chapter 7. We did not think that the presence of contentious politics was sufficient for deep democracy. Despite the same sufficient condition being named for each row in the table, the different answers rely on different (and sometimes problematic) assumptions. Revealing those assumptions again helps reveal coherence of claims.

Given that in Chapter 6 using calibration 'C' it was held that both mayoral support and citizen support for contentious politics are

**Table 8.1:** Analysis of sufficient conditions for the negation of deepened democracy across 10 cases

| Outcome tested | Sufficient conditions | Inclusion | PRI | Coverage |
|---|---|---|---|---|
| 1 ~deepened democracy (A) | **~citizen contentious politics** | 0.745 | 0.662 | 0.603 |
| 2 ~deepened democracy (B) | **~citizen contentious politics** | 0.835 | 0.802 | 0.717 |
| 3 ~deepened democracy (C) | **~citizen contentious politics** | 1 | 1 | 0.5 |

Note: Bold = core condition.

necessary conditions for deep democracy, we should logically deduce that their absence is sufficient for deepened democracy's absence:[1]

Absence of mayoral support AND

Absence of citizen support for contentious politics → ~ deep democracy

Wampler makes a version of that claim in his conclusion (2007a: 281), and it is confirmed here. In fact, row 3 of Table 8.1 reports that the absence of citizen contentious politics alone is sufficient to negate deep democracy under the most restrictive calibration. What has happened to mayoral support?

Similar to Chapter 7, a minimization has taken place, where mayoral support has been eliminated as a relevant explanatory factor. If we consult the truth table for this outcome in Table 8.2, we see that both the first and second rows are consistently sufficient for the outcome (~deep democracy). And therefore, because the outcome is seen regardless of variance in mayoral support, that condition is eliminated. This leaves us with us a more parsimonious solution that absence of citizen support for contentious politics alone is sufficient to negate a deepened democracy.

Nevertheless, as we saw, the minimization here masks a coding issue where 0.51 was chosen as a membership score without much thought to its relation to theory and cases. Again, a reinterpretation across the crossover point would push a number of cases into different truth table rows and lead to a different minimization.

The solution presented in row 1 of Table 8.1 also hides an important uncertainty for interpretation created by the conceptualization and measurement of deepened democracy 'A' – that of simultaneous subset relations for an outcome and its negation (see Schneider and Wagemann, 2012: 238). The combination of the presence of mayoral support and absence of support for contentious politics is fully or almost fully consistent with the sufficiency superset relationship for absence of deep democracy. Nevertheless, that combination is also fully or almost fully consistent with sufficiency for the super–subset relation for the presence of deep democracy. To hold to both claims is illogical. The scenario is always made possible when accepting some inconsistency

[1] Logically, if X is necessary for Y, then ~X is sufficient for ~Y. This should not be confused with an erroneous causal symmetry statement that if X is sufficient for Y, then ~X is sufficient for ~Y.

**Table 8.2:** Truth table for outcome '~deepened democracy C'

| | Mayoral support | Citizen contentious politics | ~Deep democracy | Number of cases | Inclusion | PRI | Cases |
|---|---|---|---|---|---|---|---|
| 1 | 0 | 0 | 1 | 2 | 1 | 1 | Blumenau, Rio Claro |
| 2 | 1 | 0 | 1 | 2 | 1 | 1 | Santo André, São Paulo |
| 3 | 1 | 1 | 0 | 6 | 0.505 | 0.505 | Belo Horizonte, Ipatinga, Port Alegre (i), Porto Alegre (ii), Porto Alegre (iii), Recife |
| 4 | 0 | 1 | ? | 0 | | | |

in fuzzy sets while also declaring conditions that reach a threshold of consistency lower than 1 to be deemed necessary or sufficient. The cases of Santo André and São Paulo here represent the true logical contradictions of the super–subset relation that are relatively good examples of a truth table row but are not actually consistent with the sufficiency subset relationship. Normally we can use the proportional reduction in inconsistency (PRI) measure, as mentioned briefly in Chapter 7, to adjudicate which interpretation is more appropriate, but because in 'A' we used a fairly arbitrary calibration of the 'medium' cases, that PRI measure is not really interpretable. It is, yet again, an example of the importance of conceptual clarity in calibration.

## Wider analysis of five conditions

I have already discussed at length the considerations involved in calibration for the wider analysis incorporating five conditions. The truth table and chosen minimization are reproduced in Tables 8.3 and 8.4. The explanatory model can be written as:

~ms***~ple***(~ccp*FBS + ~rep*~fbs) → ~deepened democracy

Note the causal asymmetry with the solution presented for sufficiency – this is not the mirror image of the explanation of deepened democracy

**Table 8.3:** Truth table for outcome (5 conditions)

| # | MS | CCP | PLE | REP | FBS | OUT: ~DD | Inclu-sion | PRI | Cases |
|---|---|---|---|---|---|---|---|---|---|
| 2 | 0 | 0 | 0 | 0 | 1 | 1 | 1 | 1 | Rio Claro |
| 4 | 0 | 0 | 0 | 1 | 1 | 1 | 1 | 1 | Blumenau |
| 9 | 0 | 1 | 0 | 0 | 0 | 1 | 1 | 1 | São Paulo |
| 29 | 1 | 1 | 1 | 0 | 0 | 0 | 0.815 | 0.5 | Recife, Santo André |
| 14 | 0 | 1 | 1 | 0 | 1 | 0 | 0.798 | 0.333 | Belo Horizonte |
| 31 | 1 | 1 | 1 | 1 | 0 | 0 | 0.727 | 0 | Porto Alegre (i) |
| 24 | 1 | 0 | 1 | 1 | 1 | 0 | 0.671 | 0.405 | Ipatinga |
| 32 | 1 | 1 | 1 | 1 | 1 | 0 | 0.628 | 0.147 | Porto Alegre (ii) |

Note: MS is mayoral support; CCP is citizens using contentious and cooperative politics; PLE is positive legislative environment; FBS is financial basis to spend; REP is rules encouraging participation; OUT: DD is ~deepened democracy (the outcome).

**Table 8.4:** Sufficient conditions for ~ deepened democracy (5 conditions)

| Expression[1] | Inclusion | PRI | Coverage | Unique coverage | Cases |
|---|---|---|---|---|---|
| ~ms*~ccp* **~ple***FBS | 1.000 | 1.000 | 0.426 | 0.272 | Rio Claro, Blumenau |
| ~ms***~ple*** ~rep*~fbs | 1.000 | 1.000 | 0.346 | 0.191 | São Paulo |
| Model | 1.000 | 1.000 | 0.618 | | |

[1] Bold = core condition. Intermediate solution with consistency cut-off of 1. ms is mayoral support; ccp is citizens using contentious and cooperative politics; ple is positive legislative environment; fbs is financial basis to spend; rep is rules encouraging participation. PRI is proportional reduction in inconsistency.

provided in Chapter 7. This relatively conservative solution is highly consistent and produced by holding theoretical explanations that the presence of mayoral support, citizen use of cooperative and contentious politics or a positive legislative environment should not be included in minimizations. The absence of political support is clearly key to any explanation of the avoidance of democratic improvements in these Brazilian PB programmes. Any explanation of PB failure on the evidence of this data must include within it the absence of a positive legislative environment. When political willingness is absent in the mayor's office and the legislators' offices at the same time, there are two further conjunctions of conditions which, when fulfilled, will suffice for negation of success. First, when this absence of political will meets a tame civil society AND money is available, deeper democracy through PB is negated. This makes a lot of sense – where politicians are not really interested in participatory politics, civil society is not holding them to account, even though money is available it will be spent elsewhere in these circumstances. This fairly well describes Blumenau and Rio Claro. Alternatively, where money is not available, and the rules act against flourishing of participatory programmes, the actions of civil society are rendered redundant. The explanation fits the case of São Paulo.

The first finding combining absence of political support with absence of appropriate civil society tools in the presence of available funds can help explain why sponsoring organizations such as NGOs and the World Bank have moved to combine their focus on civil society capacity with greater attention to local politicians. Donor organizations have moved in the direction of identifying investment areas where they have local 'participatory champions'.[2] The QCA here has confirmed much of Wampler's work, but it also adds some nuance as to what conditions are more necessary parts of explanations in different contexts. The structured approach to comparison is useful even for small-N researchers to help them know if their face is too close to the page to systematically consider all permutations and to summarize them effectively.

One of the advantages of traditional qualitative research that compliments QCA is the ability to refer to case-specific causal explanations that can qualify results and point to the need for further cross-case analysis, including new variables. For example, we could turn to investigate, now, the combination of development and financial situation conditions in a more sophisticated analysis across cases. Or, based on the less conclusive analysis of evidence for necessity, we might wish to investigate the impact of alternative participatory fora on PB, such as Future City in Santo André, which Wampler mentions had influential effects. The idea that PB may suffer when it is not the only game in town or where other participatory mechanisms are more appropriate to a city's political culture is a recurring rather than prevalent theory in the literature (see Avritzer, 2009, for a good discussion of this), and would benefit from greater data collection. What comes out of the QCA on this reading is a clearer indication of where one needs to make more detailed explanatory arguments. Schneider and Rohfling (2013) have made contributions that detail

[2] My thanks to Brian Wampler for this suggestion in personal correspondence.

exactly how researchers can use QCA to make decisions about which cases should be selected for within-case analysis, and where QCA is best combined with process-tracing.

## Negating participatory budgeting over a larger number of cases

Do those explanations chime across our larger sample of cases? To some extent, yes, but more cases add the evidential basis for greater clarity. Table 8.5 presents the truth table for the negation of the outcome.

The analysis of the negation of the outcome (that is, the absence of citizen control in PB) is neater than others I present in some ways. If we take a consistency threshold of 0.84 here and explain all rows containing good examples of failed participation, we introduce only one true logical contradiction, which is the case of Rome XI district (row 13). The Rome case is not the strongest example of successful outcomes in that Talpin reports evidence of informal exclusion and considers it a 'marginally empowered' case (2011: 149). It is considered more in the set of citizen control because he reports mobilization with good demographic participation, high autonomy and co-decision-making. PT-Recife (ii) and Cusco also provide evidence of some inconsistency in degree to the sufficiency of the same truth table row, because they resemble its conditions to a small extent, despite being extremely poor examples of PB failure. The row represents the combination of relatively strong leadership in political and civil society with a more resistant bureaucracy and financial constraints. It characterizes well some of the more mediocre cases of PB – Santo André and Moquegua fit that description. It is the most ambiguous row in the dataset. Therefore, I exclude it from the explanation here, but later report the one noteworthy change including it would bring to the solution.

Taking a sufficiency exclusion threshold of 0.87, the following solution containing two sufficient conjunctions for negation of citizen control in PB decisions is produced from the truth table:

**~pl***(~fbs + ~csd*~bsp) → ~ccpb (i)

\+

**~csd*~bsp*~fbs** → ~ccpb (ii)

Table 8.6 reports relatively strong measures of fit. It reports the most parsimonious solution that makes use of the three logical remainders

**Table 8.5:** Truth table for negation of citizen control of PB

| # | PL | CSD | BSP | FBS | OUT: ~CCPB | N | Incl. | PRI | Cases |
|---|---|---|---|---|---|---|---|---|---|
| 1 | 0 | 0 | 0 | 0 | 1 | 4 | 1 | 1 | Ayacucho, Loreto, Mauá, Toronto |
| 2 | 0 | 0 | 0 | 1 | 1 | 2 | 1 | 1 | Blumenau, Rio Claro |
| 3 | 0 | 0 | 1 | 0 | 1 | 1 | 1 | 1 | Buenos Aires |
| 9 | 1 | 0 | 0 | 0 | 1 | 1 | 0.967 | 0.837 | Berlin-Lichtenberg |
| 5 | 0 | 1 | 0 | 0 | 1 | 2 | 0.904 | 0.785 | Recife (i), São Paulo |
| 7 | 0 | 1 | 1 | 0 | 1 | 1 | 0.87 | 0.573 | Cajamarca |
| 13 | 1 | 1 | 0 | 0 | 1 | 3 | 0.842 | 0.569 | Moquegua, Rome, Santo André |
| 11 | 1 | 0 | 1 | 0 | 0 | 3 | 0.805 | 0.395 | Camaragibe, Lambayeque, Morsang-sur-Orge |
| 10 | 1 | 0 | 0 | 1 | 0 | 3 | 0.775 | 0.299 | Montevideo, Poitou-Charentes, Sevilla |
| 14 | 1 | 1 | 0 | 1 | 0 | 4 | 0.744 | 0.41 | Belo Horizonte, Chicago 49th Ward, Córdoba, New York |
| 12 | 1 | 0 | 1 | 1 | 0 | 3 | 0.733 | 0.272 | Betim, Gravataí, Ipatinga |
| 15 | 1 | 1 | 1 | 0 | 0 | 2 | 0.697 | 0.087 | Cusco, Recife (ii) |
| 16 | 1 | 1 | 1 | 1 | 0 | 2 | 0.555 | 0.054 | João Monlevade, Porto Alegre |
| 4 | 0 | 0 | 1 | 1 | ? | 0 | – | – | |
| 6 | 0 | 1 | 0 | 1 | ? | 0 | – | – | |
| 8 | 0 | 1 | 1 | 1 | ? | 0 | – | – | |

Note: PL is participatory leadership; CSD is autonomous civil society demands; BSP is bureaucratic support; FBS is financial basis for spending; CCPB is citizen control of decisions in PB; N is number of cases, Incl. is Inclusion score. PRI refers to Proportional Reduction in Inconsistency.

in rows 4, 6 and 8 to eliminate the more peripheral factors from the first solution term (i). On this occasion, these are relatively easy counterfactual assumptions to make. First, we were unable to use logical remainders in the analysis of the outcome in Chapter 7, so there is no fear of making contradictory assumptions. Also, based on what we have learned so far, it would be difficult to assume that citizen control could be easily negated where participatory leadership is not also

**Table 8.6:** Parsimonious solution for negation of citizen control in PB (31 cases)

| | Expression | Inclusion | PRI | Coverage | Unique coverage | Cases |
|---|---|---|---|---|---|---|
| 1 | **~pl** | 0.912 | 0.868 | 0.631 | 0.299 | Ayacucho, Loreto, Mauá, Toronto, Blumenau, Rio Claro, Buenos Aires, Recife (i), São Paulo, Cajamarca |
| 2 | **~csd*~bsp*~fbs** | 0.979 | 0.952 | 0.454 | 0.122 | Ayacucho, Loreto, Mauá, Toronto, Berlin-Lichtenberg |
| | Model | 0.914 | 0.859 | 0.753 | | |

Note: pl is participatory leadership; csd is autonomous civil society demands; bsp is bureaucratic support; fbs is financial basis for spending. PRI refers to Proportional Reduction in Inconsistency.

absent. There is no empirical case in the whole dataset that is more out of the set of participatory leadership and more in the set of citizen control of PB. This is why we have good grounds to make the claim that absence of participatory leadership is not necessary but is alone sufficient for failure of PB. The discussion of the Toronto and Buenos Aires cases in Chapter 6 offers the one minor caveat to this claim, but it remains a strong one. The absence of long-term commitment to participatory politics from political leadership uniquely explains the cases of Blumenau, Rio Claro, São Paulo, Recife pre-PT, Cajamarca and Buenos Aires. In building on the previous analysis of Wampler's data alone, this more parsimonious explanation might seem a drastic reduction of explanatory conditions, but it shows the advantage of leveraging a larger number of cases.

The alternative conjunction is an intriguing one because it provides a window to perhaps the major outstanding puzzle that I have yet to solve. This conjunction combines the absence of financial freedom and the absence of bureaucratic buy-in to participatory processes with the absence of active and autonomous civil society. The explanation has relatively low coverage and much of its coverage comes from the fact that it explains cases we have already explained with the first solution term. While Ayacucho, Loreto, Mauá and Toronto are covered by both alternative explanations, this second sufficient conjunction uniquely explains less. The best example of such a case is Berlin-Lichtenberg, and even there the case's minimal but perceptible successes provide some source of inconsistency in the explanation. In Lichtenberg an activist mayor promoted PB and pushed it as a radical democratic project along with help from some agencies, despite some opposition and indifference from other political leaders. However, many city officials did not seem to trust citizens and looked at the programme through a new public management and public sector reform style lens. There were some important civil society activists pushing the programme, but they were a narrow group; these Berlin districts were fairly constrained in their jurisdiction and had no opportunity to raise funds. In the end, despite some good outcomes and being held up as one of the more radical early German experiments, it is characterized as a good consultation model but not an empowered co-decisional one (Herzberg, 2013; Röcke, 2014). Potential for accountability was lost as oversight committees were disbanded. If there is only one good exemplar case, why is the conjunction so intriguing?

This conjunction of conditions is in a similar part of the property space to many of our true logical contradictions in the dataset and no more than two differences in presence or absence of a condition from all of them. For example, if we chose to include in our minimization row 13, which contains a true logical contradiction, as discussed earlier, the only effect would be that the absence of autonomous civil society demand would be eliminated from this conjunction. In fact, all the contradictory rows agree on the presence of political leadership committed to participation.

The major outstanding question, then, is how we can explain cases where political leaders are committed to participation but the participatory programme fails. This is the case, to an important extent, in Lichtenberg, Montevideo, Morsang-sur-Orge, Chicago, Córdoba, Betim, Moquegua and Santo André, and, at a stretch, could be read to cover Rome. Figure 8.1 plots this relationship to show how those cases cluster.

These cases very much represent middle-of-the-road cases, or perhaps less than good but not awful outcomes. They all combine participatory leadership with some combination of presence or absence of the other three influencing conditions, and tend to contradict logically similar cases on the outcome. The Lichtenberg example represents the characteristics of a least likely case to have participatory leadership and also citizen control of PB because all the other hypothesized influencing conditions are absent.

**Figure 8.1:** Participatory leadership and absence of citizen control

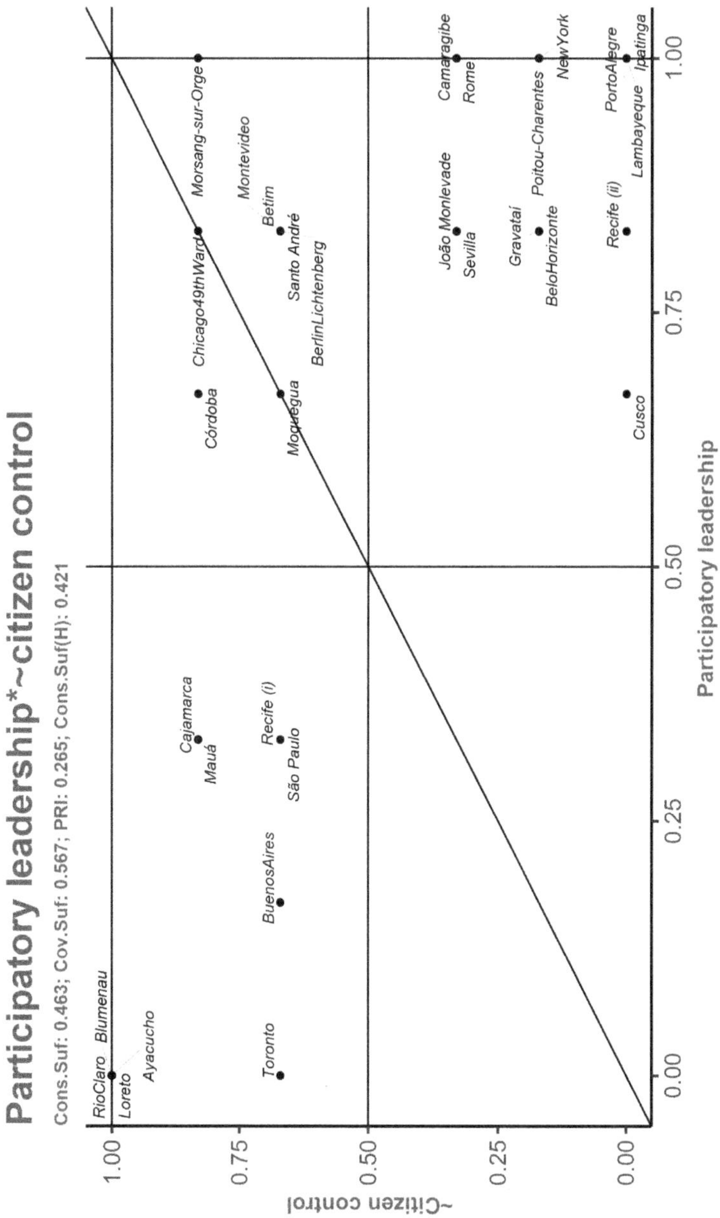

Following Schneider and Wagemann, the pattern in Figure 8.1 where all cases fall far from the bottom left of the X–Y plot, just goes to show that all these cases are consistent with the statement that participatory leadership is necessary for citizen control and the absence of participatory leadership is sufficient for the absence of citizen control (2012: 246). But what is more interesting is that these mid-range cases make the significant contributions to lowering *coverage*[3] of those set relations. The presence of participatory leadership on its own is not a good explanation for this category of cases' relationship with citizen control. We know that participatory leadership distinguishes the cases in the left of the graph from those on the right, but we do not have yet a grasp of the explanatory condition that better distinguishes those cases in the top right from the bottom right. As we add any of the conditions I have tested here to the explanation, any increase in their coverage is offset by some increase in their inconsistency. The conditions I have included cannot determine this more fine-grained divergence in outcome. By corollary, the hypothesized conditions then explain quite good and quite bad participatory programmes succinctly, but they do not explain middling outcomes well at all. We lack evidence of a variable that differentiates success and failure within the scope of the cases where politicians are actively looking to support citizen participation.

## Why participation fails and where explanations fail (so far)

This analysis has shown that there are two definite scenarios in which participatory programmes will fail to empower citizens to be authors of public spending decisions. As supported by the analysis of necessity, there is little evidence to suggest that where a leader's commitment to participatory democracy is absent, PB can still find success. The absence of participatory leadership can be considered a sufficient condition for the absence of citizen control of PB decisions. Based on the evidence of these cases, any remaining uncertainty about failure in the scenario of vacuous leadership is removed when either finances are squeezed or where both strong civil society action and bureaucratic support for participatory programmes is in short supply.

Failures where politicians commit strongly to participation are more difficult to explain. While a combination of poor outcomes across

[3] This is somewhat analogous to contributing to a low r squared value in correlational analysis.

the other three conditions modelled here is almost always sufficient, different combinations of these three conditions in the presence of participatory leadership more often explain successes than failures. Cumulation of evidence has pointed out the relevant direction of cases we need to re-examine. A quick look at the cases and other hypotheses advanced in the literature does not provide an obvious answer to the question identified. More data collection and comparison with similar kinds of cases is needed to answer that puzzle.

A comprehensive answer is beyond the scope of this book, but there are interesting insights in the literature that highlight the most likely avenues for advances in future research. Several cases of PB and some hypothesized explanatory theories were not included in the comparisons detailed previously owing to a lack of data, or because they did not quite meet the scope conditions. The case of Dong-gu, Ulsan, for example, is one of the more successful cases in Korea (Songmin, 2013), and although I could not confirm some details to include it in the analysis, it seems most similar in type to Rome where relatively strong civil society autonomy and political leadership led to some good outcomes despite fiscal constraints and inconveniences to bureaucrats. It is worth considering if there are any insights from cases that may vary outside what I have captured thus far to understand how further analysis can complement those findings. In order to begin to provide some tentative ideas for further consideration, I now zoom out again and consider those cases and conditions to try to understand what has not yet been understood.

## Evolving analysis for the longer-term

The QCA approach is useful for indicating different types of PB associated with alternate paths to outcomes. The order of cause and effect has also been a source of controversy in PB activism and scholarship. Ganuza and Baiocchi (2019) explain how administrative reform may erroneously be understood as an outcome of success, when it is better understood as a condition for PB reform in Porto Alegre. There is some evidence that PB can lead to improvements to administration, especially where it is used in a state reconstruction context such as in Dondo (Cabannes and Lipietz, 2018: 76). The approach I have taken may be able to distinguish the alternative paths to success in different such contexts, but despite the clear advantages, one of the limitations I have discussed is that approaches to considering change over time are blunt. Temporal antecedence is the key necessary condition for causal analysis. It is preserved in the separation of outcomes and influencing conditions in the analysis and the case material, of course, but it may be that a sequencing of some of the influencing conditions that is not preserved actually explains the divergence in outcomes.

For example, it might be that strong civil society demands in the absence of bureaucratic support early on in programmes lead to administrative burdens and implementation delays, or opportunities for the politicization of the bureaucracy. Civil society actors most willing to hold government to account may grow disillusioned and exit the process, as seemed to happen in Chicago, or alternatively, politicians may be pressured more into rule changes that undermine the openness of the process, as seemed to happen in Córdoba and perhaps Montevideo. Even if the presence or absence of the conditions switch later, the damage may be done, and processes may continue but only in a co-opted form. Alternatively, early bureaucratic support for programmes in the absence of strong civil society contributions may incubate processes for a time, allowing them to develop positive mobilization strategies that reach out and establish demonstration effects. I do not have the data to test the relationship systematically, but it seems both an appealing and plausible hypothesis (although contradictory cases are far from unimaginable).

We can also see variance in the trajectory of cases, some of which are characterized by radical reform and incremental decline, as in Porto Alegre; others with punctuations of improvements and retrenchment, such as in Belo Horizonte and Recife. We should not be surprised that participation declines where outcomes of PB are not easy to demonstrate to citizens. Coleman and Sampaio (2017) provide some time-series data to show that declining participation in Belo Horizonte in e-participatory budgets can be partially explained in this way.

It can be similarly useful to abstract from a singular innovation and take a look at participatory culture over the longer term. For a start, those observers focused on civil society have been keen to highlight the importance of associational histories in their accounts of PB, which seem at least important for explaining whether participatory programmes are instigated at all, never mind their successful outcomes. The evidence from João Monlevade may provide indicative signals here of the contribution of participatory innovations over time in developing cultures more amenable to democratic innovations. Nylen (2003b) documents an early PB programme in the city that failed to produce the required changes in society, and was abandoned when the PT lost the administration, but Baiocchi et al's description of the later process suggested it benefit from learning after the PT regained the mayor's office four years later (2011: 90). Learning can also inspire improved successes elsewhere, of course, as diffusion studies have shown – among the cases examined, the Chicago case paved the way for a more successful case in New York, while the case of Poitou-Charentes had some influence on the take up of PB in Paris (Sintomer et al, 2016).

The emergence of studies that can track the fragility and volatility of innovations are useful here (Alves and Allegretti, 2012; Spada, 2017; Dias et al, 2019). The period in which much fieldwork takes place tends to represent the height of PB's adoption in a country, but despite its prevalence falling away in some regions, PB is still mostly a growing innovation worldwide (Dias and Júlio, 2018: 31). Latin America and Brazil in particular have seen changing modes of participation (Lüchmann et al, 2018), which is, to some extent, explained by political upheaval in those countries. Further collection of data across cases over time may confirm how previous experiences with participation pave the way for later successes. It can also confirm indicators of within-case change such as change in governing regimes, or whether changes in rules and responsibility for PB moving from central cabinet offices to more peripheral ministries is an indicator of change in outcomes.

Democratization programmes have often been thought of as coming in 'waves'. There is a long history of different degrees of imbalances of power in politics. Some waves erode a little of the edifice of power imbalances and sometimes they create a cavern, or whole cliffs fall into the sea. Each participatory programme may simply represent a drop in the ocean. In the same way that physical scientists cannot predict exactly which wave will cause erosion and when, we will always have to satisfy ourselves with some uncertainty about certain conditions leading to transformative outcomes.

Data collection over the long term may also help us better understand the relationship between different types of democratic innovation. The decline of many participatory budgets over the long term, despite their clear successes in democratizing politics, points to the need for programmes to remain agile (see Gilman, 2016: 119). There are significant challenges in keeping commensurate the goal of institutionalization of participatory democratic norms, while avoiding a routinization that closes down the necessary creativity of fresh ideas that sustain democratic politics. Lüchmann et al put it nicely, arguing that as:

> … institutions which challenge what is already instituted, PBs carry with them a need for constant renewal as

> a condition for their own survival. And when such institutions become a routine, they in many cases lose their innovative and daring character, beginning a slow descent to extinction. (2018: 103)

It may be that a more nuanced understanding of devices within participation rather than a focus on named programmes is useful. One potential explanation of failure where the conditions for participation are in place is that the spaces for citizen participation can become cluttered. PB partly worked in Porto Alegre because it was the main venue for demands and an appropriate one for the civic culture of the city at the time (Avritzer, 2009). Understanding these long-term trajectories of participation will take us back to taking conceptualization seriously, understanding how we should distinguish different democratic devices and how they can be usefully sequenced and combined (Saward, 2003). As PB has travelled, we increasingly see hybrid models emerging that incorporate different devices from other models of participation.

In Australia, where randomly selected deliberative mini-publics have been popular, those designs have been effectively applied to public budgets (Hartz-Karp and Weymouth, 2018). Rather than focus on inclusion through mass mobilization, those designs aim to achieve equal opportunities through more systematic exclusion, avoiding partisan mobilization and mobilizing usual suspects (although, like PB, the extent to which mini-publics have achieved that in practice varies). The key advantage of those designs, which is often forgotten in the clamour to demonstrate long-term empowerment and institutionalized democratic learning, is that they rotate participants back out of power, so that new elites cannot form. PB processes were actually more conscious than most other democratic innovations in striving to achieve a rotation of delegates in their procedural rules, but often the pool of potential delegates becomes more homogenous over time. It would be interesting to compare innovations that hold strong to principles of rotation and those that do not to understand the effects of that design choice.

Expanding cases and scope of designs may bring insights. PB and participatory democracy have become prominent in countries at different stages of regime change and governance modernization, or with varying understandings of democratic citizenship. Cabannes and Ming (2014) describe quite an empowered case in rural Chengdou, where training materials encouraged participation to question traditional authority, and where the long-term planning often elusive in PB was encouraged by allowing citizens to apply for loans above the nominal PB funds (Cabannes, 2018: 248). Co-financing PB projects with donors or business groups investing in PB is also popular in models in Eastern Europe and Russia (Shulga and Vagin, 2018). These cases may be considered quite different in kind to those I compare systematically, but the focus on innovative funding mechanisms entreats us to think about whether the financial variables could be further disaggregated to better capture differences in administrative decentralization vis-à-vis alternative funding models.

Invoking decentralization may also again raise the question of whether size or jurisdiction is an important explanatory condition for success in PB. There are several arguments that small-scale democracy lacks some level of alienation that is actually necessary for positive elements of contentious politics to flourish (Mansbridge, 1983; Ryan et al, 2018). Those familiar patterns of dominance of fora by the usual suspects can be seen in descriptions of cases in Morsang-sur-Orge, Chicago, and to some extent in Rome, and in the gender and class differences reported among elected delegates and speakers in assemblies. Nevertheless, the prevalence of these factors in itself seems to be evidence that size is too simplistic an explanatory factor, and the failure of thousands of years of effort to explain the optimum size of a polity (Ryan et al, 2018) leaves me less confident that it is an avenue for fruitful investigation.

A further trend prominent in some large cities since the 2010s is the increase in the use of multichannel participation (Spada and Allegretti, 2017). Here cities may offer a range of more or less demanding opportunities of participation to citizens. The approach is sometimes justified on the basis that citizens will engage in ways that make sense to them or where their personal resources will best be used. A presumed advantage is that agility can reign, and unused channels can become redundant. However, the temptation can be to rely on the more popular, less demanding channels that are cheaper in terms of their financial and in-kind costs, and suffer the fate of a lack of vibrancy and demonstration effects over time.

A final potential confounding variable linked to the length of participatory programmes that has escaped significant attention is the question of communication. Following the failures of the British Columbian Citizens' Assembly to have their recommendations accepted in referendum, advocates and organizers of randomly selected mini-publics have made strong efforts to promote their work in the media. In Porto Alegre it was also clear that the administration got communication right early on. Politics is always a game of communication campaigning, and deliberative and participatory democrats have only more lately returned their attention to how invited spaces communicate with the wider public sphere.

In summary, there are at least three future strategies for understanding these mid-range cases better. One is to investigate more systematically whether they are part of a longer-term trend and have more distal effects (Jacquet and van der Does, 2020). A second is to more clearly separate different devices the cases employ and not treat them as simply one model, allowing more fine-grained analyses. A third is to follow up in future comparative studies on the several alternate hypotheses I have briefly outlined – from understanding the role of media, the style of mobilization, or use of alternate avenues of participation in the case, to identifying better indicators of change in within-case analysis.

Of course, we will have to live with outliers too – 'Sometimes, the situation can be significantly affected by a single individual' (Sintomer et al, 2016: 163) – but the research I have presented has at least helped remove a lot of uncertainty and explained the potential for future analysis. The final chapter looks forward to the practical implications of the analysis presented, and potential future analyses suggested for deepening democracy more generally.

# 9

# Conclusion: Democratic Innovations after the Beginning

To understand why citizen participation in politics succeeds and fails, this book has focused on participatory budgeting, probably the most well-known democratic innovation worldwide. I have traced the development of comparative work on PB as the innovation has diffused and as knowledge of the field has developed. I was motivated to figure out under what circumstances citizens involved in programmes designed to engage them in governance gain meaningful control of important collective decisions. I have shown that as the field of democratic innovation, and in particular, PB, matures, significant steps have been taken in the direction of a more systematic comparison providing ever better answers to that question.

Parts II and III presented and discussed practical issues involved in undertaking advanced QCA across cases. I argued that we can better understand participatory democracy by allowing an assessment of the value and potential of cumulating existing knowledge using systematic formal logic. My aim was never to undercut other approaches or extol the virtues of one approach, but rather to provide a new complementary approach. Up to now research has focused on in-depth qualitative small-N research, or large-N studies that either focus on individuals as the unit of analysis or on breadth at the expense of depth. The value of robust and general findings is that they can allow relevant actors – civil society activists, political leaders and even academics – to plan their actions with a degree of confidence in the lessons of evidence. My work offers notable improvements in our understanding of participatory democracy, and I identify complementary tools of analysis that should be of use to those interested in furthering their knowledge of PB. The QCA approach to cumulating and systematically reviewing the evidence of previous research reveals redundant elements of causal claims or identifies oversimplification. I conclude here by outlining the key findings and their implications for the theory and practice of democracy.

## Looking back before looking forward

In introducing the book, I outlined a set of key wider debates that the work presented here will contribute to. I certainly did not need to demonstrate that highly democratic outcomes are achievable in PB programmes – that has been done before – but I have shown that these democratic improvements are relatively widely spread, varying in both their number and qualities. I have argued throughout that we need to take the conceptualization of participatory programmes, including PB, seriously, and we should not be afraid of understanding the full range of cases and their outcomes. I outlined the consequences for causal interpretation of narrower conceptualizations of successful outcomes in PB. Of course, our understanding of what constitutes a success is grounded in normative as well as conceptual theory, and cannot simply be understood by measurement. It can help us, however, if we can articulate more systematically what is at stake in different conceptualizations. I have shown that some standards may be too high – contrary to what is implied by much of the previous literature on the topic of PB, there are few, if any, single necessary causal conditions that explain successful citizen control in participatory decision-making.

Instead, the most important contribution is in explaining how PB programme outcomes vary across cases. My comparison provides some specific combinations that may alternatively produce good outcomes. Instigators and adopters of participatory programmes should think about the contexts in which they innovate and what they know works in such contexts. Political leaders' commitment to participation in words and deeds is a necessary condition for citizens to gain meaningful control of collective decisions (accepting some minor caveats that the absence of leadership can be overcome in the short term). By corollary, where this commitment is absent, failures are almost ubiquitous. Any hope for successful programmes where politicians' commitment is absent is extinguished completely when either other relevant actors are not minded to support the process or where the entity running the programme faces financial constraints.

Where civil society retains autonomy and acts both in contention and concert with willing political leaders, and bureaucratic staff are able and willing to support the process, this combination of factors is sufficient for success, regardless of financial challenges. Where key actors are able to work together, they can find ways to overcome challenges. I would also hold that this is the best opportunity to break through the 'glass ceiling' where a critical mass of power transfer can lead citizens to really consider the injustice in existing institutional relationships. This explanation sets a high standard for successful participation, and will be favoured by those who prefer solutions where risks are more clearly articulated. These are, perhaps, the 'real utopias' once envisaged by Erik Olin Wright and colleagues.

Nevertheless, and perhaps controversially, there is also relatively good evidence that civil society may be less relevant to explanations of successful outcomes. In almost all cases where leaders commit to programmes, a combination with a strong financial position alone, or with strong bureaucratic buy-in alone, is sufficient for empowered democratic decision-making. The caveat comes in that there are a small group of cases that strongly contradict this last statement, but they do so in very idiosyncratic ways. These represent middling cases where leaders are committed to inculcating participatory norms but end up with less than good but not egregious democratic outputs. They provide an important puzzle for future research. In particular, theory-generating or clarifying studies may want to revisit the question of what role the state can play in shaping civil society through participatory politics.

The cumulation of cases can serve to increase the options available for democratic reformers who wish to bring about transformational outcomes by helping them to consider the most effective potential strategies for changing the contexts they wish to intervene in. Future studies will also want to build on this research to accumulate data on cases over the long term. I have outlined a set of wider questions that will provide avenues for more specific data collection that can complement existing findings. The cumulative qualitative approach I favour here has been useful in furthering development of a field of study and outlining what is at stake when scoping concepts. I harnessed the strength of previous casework and accumulated that knowledge to try to provide a more parsimonious statement about what causal processes are at work in a sample of some of the most well-known and well-studied cases of PB.

## Expanding comparisons of democratic innovations

The question of comparability of cases is one that constantly troubles researchers in the emerging field of democratic innovations. That inquisition is a good sign. Lijphart notes that comparative politics makes progress 'as a result of the efforts of the field's innovators to fashion universally applicable vocabularies of basic politically relevant concepts' (1971: 686), and as Mill put it, the 'general conception is itself obtained by a comparison of particular phenomena' (1950: 298). The most transparent way to know the relevant level of abstraction at which phenomena are comparable without resorting to conceptual stretching is to examine and list their key properties and to compare them. This basic method of identifying the intension and extension of a concept should be no different for social or physical scientific research. What is different in social research is that the observation of these characteristics is more usually a matter of degree, and we often have to live with greater levels of uncertainty. This difference in certainties should not hamper efforts unduly. When it is more difficult to pin down and clearly observe these characteristics, especially in the early stages of phenomenological development, in order to progress our understanding, we need to cumulate knowledge systematically by comparison. A cumulative comparison can be conscious of the accuracy of conceptual delineation. We require a research agenda that marries sensitivity to theory and conceptual clarity, with sensitivity to accuracy in observations of practices, and with sensitivity to appropriate methods of inferential comparison. My work here can plug some gaps in such a research agenda.

I have been interested in testing hegemonic claims about what kinds of democratic innovation best achieve democratic outcomes (see, for example, Fishkin, 2009), with claims that plural approaches to democracy may achieve comparable combinations of democratic goods (Smith, 2009). Democratic theorists have been prone to hegemonic claims about whether mass participation can or cannot work in this or that context. I have shown that successful participation is not a matter of absolutes, but a matter of context. This is not to introduce 'matter of degree phraseology'. It may be that 'competing' theories of democratic empowerment are, in fact, not really competing but try to explain different specific contexts without a tool for identifying adequate trade-offs in parsimony and complexity. Only through comparative analysis can we iterate between and assess these claims effectively. My analysis of key factors used to explain democratic PB outcomes suggests that they are characterized by equifinality. I think we should expect democratic outcomes to vary within and across designs, but hope that we can continue to reduce uncertainty around factors that may predict those outcomes. The successful cases here can, in some instances, confirm or deny a number of 'competing' theories of democracy and governance and show that others are not in competition. Yet, as I have detailed, even a 'within-type-of-innovation' comparative design ran up against important revealing questions of a definition of what PB is and what we should expect from it. If anything, we seem to be biased as a social research community to lay the burden of proof such that the comparativist must prove that two or more cases are comparable rather than incomparable. For comparativists there is a certain pressure not to compare 'the incomparable' – to narrow the scope of their research and to favour case-based research on most-similar systems. While there is much rationale in these ideas, they should not dominate at the expense of more ecumenical or abstract comparisons that seek answers to interesting questions. It is by regularly comparing across cases that we actually find out how far apart things are (and challenge received wisdom in a changing world).

There are, for example, ongoing questions of what is or is not a mini-public (Fishkin, 2009; Ryan and Smith, 2014). Warren (2009) speaks of possibly over 100 named processes of governance-driven democratization, and many more have emerged since Warren's work was published. The pressure to innovate can lead so-called innovators to be keen to distinguish this or that as an invention. There is a worry that incentives for action in such a direction come at the expense of identification of devices that are common to good outcomes and therefore prevent replication of best practice across cases, or understanding of broad contexts where one design might (not) fit. It is essential that when we build a field of research as social scientists, we, too, are aware of biases that work to privilege methods that highlight the uniqueness of events. As an antidote we need methods that cumulate research in a way that is sensitive to holistic case research and ideally involves bringing researchers together efficiently to produce robust research. QCA approaches are at least relatively transparent in their operationalization of concepts and the ways in which they are seen to transverse. We should look for methods that can supplement such an approach.

There are several opportunities now to build on the knowledge provided and to see if the findings that hold for PB across these cases also hold across others. Further work might also be able to apply some of the time-sensitive QCA methods being developed to test sequencing of democratic innovations and/or the use of technology in PDIs. Deviant cases or new cases that mimic deviant conditions should be investigated, and there may also be interesting opportunities to integrate large-N data collection with case research to explain the death and resurrection of participatory projects.

## Methods and methodologies in research on participatory democratic innovations

The number of cases I have studied here is still relatively unusual. I found that refreshing. Most researchers have a fairly strong unifying theory about how small-N or large-N research contributes to theory formation, but their presuppositions can sometimes crack if you push them into medium-N territory. Research on PDIs has been quite commendable in its conscious efforts to continue dialogue between ideas and evidence. The perhaps unusual road I have travelled, taking on the study of a medium-N of cases, is not one that provides a 'best of both worlds' for research approaches, but it does provide some correctives and enlightening insights that may not otherwise be easy to come by. The QCA approach allowed for interplay between induction and deduction and a flexible but robust theoretical framework. The problematization of concepts and qualitative variation was evidence-based, but at the same time concerns about replicability, logical calculation and extrapolation were accounted for with relative transparency. The approach can only ever be part of a broader collaborative research effort. I have highlighted kinds of cases that need further attention from ethnographers or conditions that need to be tested across a larger-N, perhaps through systematic correlation using more accessible proxies.

I have shown that a procedure that uses systematic Boolean logic when constructing research design can be useful to derive typologies similar to the method envisaged by George and Bennett (2005: 257). This had not been tried before to such an extent in the field of participatory innovation. The presentation of the calibration and truth table also prompts thought experiments and theoretical work that can try to explain why we do not have empirical instances of key factors or many contradictory instances of others. I have even shown that the logical approach that QCA provides could be effectively utilized by researchers studying a small number of cases in order to check whether their conclusions rely too much on intuition. QCA seems a good method for systematically reviewing the best evidence we have on a given phenomenon. I suggest that expert surveys might avail of some of these tools to incorporate qualitative evaluations of cases in a more systematic way.

Yet many things remain unclear. There may be a worry that constructing research in the way I have done still falls foul of subjectivity – an unsympathetic critic might say I mask uncertainty and subjectivity behind a veneer of unfamiliar language and mathematical operations. I think that would be to go too far; I certainly thought hard about whether I was sterilizing qualitative research, but I cannot make any special claims to have interpreted raw materials any more objectively than another capable reader might. It is important to open up a discussion about how we can improve the accuracy and transparency of inferences. We cannot remove judgements but we need to make our reasons explicit in a way that allows others to engage with them.[1] Transparency, I have argued, is paramount for research, but is particularly important when interpreting the work of others. In some ways there can be an initial cost to transparency in using QCA, as with any method that introduces new information and jargon, because there is some cost to others to identifying its message. Moreover, I often rearranged cases' memberships according to the requests made by case researchers where they saw me present my work. Building on the fuzzy maps, I would, in future, like to develop tools that may allow crowd interaction among researchers while sorting and discussing case calibration with swift recourse to the evidence. In the end it will require further engagement among colleagues to answer some of these questions.

There may be good arguments for avoiding these research strategies. Lieberson (1994) is quick to point out that Mill himself, on whose lucidity the comparative method is grounded, was sceptical of using such a method in the social sciences.[2] Thoughtful critiques from this school have shot difficult charges at case-based research strategies, perhaps most convincingly when rounding on their perceived inability to distinguish random from real data and adequately consider measurement error (Hug, 2013; Lucas and Szatrowski, 2014; Krogslund et al, 2015; Paine, 2016). Such critiques of case-based research have helped improve our understanding of their value immensely, but their dismissal of small-N strategies is based on a focus on technique over approach. The lasting criticism of King, Keohane and Verba's work (1994) is that it tries to impose variable-oriented thinking on case-based research strategies. 'Variable-oriented' and 'case-based' are really shorthand here for different underlying assumptions about the nature of the world at any one time, or at least what kinds of uncertainty we are willing to prefer in explanations of the social world. Critiques are not ignoble, and their lessons provide a useful check on unreflective 'small' thinking. The contributions of Schneider (2016), and Thiem

1 My thanks to David Owen for helping me clarify this point more eloquently.

2 For a simple explanation of Mill's methods and a connection to Boolean logic, see Ryan (2018).

and Baumgartner (2016) have, however, helped to clarify and elucidate the intrinsic value of case-based and analytical set-theoretic research strategies. Neither is the QCA approach immune from critique. Stark differences among QCA's defenders on that score testify to it. Certainly case-based approaches can incentivize an over-reliance on designs that too easily latch on to a particular pattern in a case, which influences how a researcher considers variance that is only perceived. But this is a similar psychological issue for modelling in large-N research; it just manifests a little differently. We need to better understand our own biased anchors that we cling to in all research approaches.

As I hope I have shown, small-N research can create incentives that restrict researchers too quickly to claims of exceptionalism. Analyses that highlight exceptionality are not necessarily problematic and can be quite powerful, but they should not be the norm. The true explanation for avoidance of medium-N strategies is not difficult to imagine. Small-N approaches rely on a high quality of information about and familiarity with cases in a study. And it is simply very difficult for a researcher, possessed with only one brain, to have a deep understanding of many cases. Trade-offs are necessary. Lijphart's words still ring true: '... awareness of the limitations of the comparative method is necessary but need not be disabling' (1971: 685). The question, then, becomes one of developing coping or enhancement strategies for small-N research, or at least applying the comparative method in a way that has potential to contribute to generalization. Collaborations among small-N researchers are often a good idea, and I have highlighted some very successful ones among PB researchers. Perhaps I can persuade them to make use of tools for more systematic comparisons.

The research presented in this book does two things that are not fashionable, but should be. Rather than search for 'new' examples of public policy innovations, it tries to bring together existing research and, in the end, provides new insights. Second, it produces research in a way it can be added to transparently, and easily replicated. In fact, it tries to replicate some previous analyses, testing them with a new method. I will welcome wholeheartedly ongoing critique from case researchers and others as the point of this work is to prompt that discussion.

## The future for participatory budgeting and participatory democracy

Participatory democratic innovation has matured as a field of study, but this is the end of the beginning. A large industry of innovators and public participation professionals has developed who both advocate for and implement processes like PB. Moreover, all over the world, several administrators, civil society activists, politicians, and, of course, citizens who never engaged in politics have had experiences with PB both good and bad. Like many democratic innovations in this era of governance-driven democratization, the number of PB processes worldwide continues to grow. It seems for now that PB is here to stay as a phenomenon, even though it has not remained in many places. PB still faces many opponents and a lot of uncertainty.

An important long-term challenge I have not been able to focus on up to now is worth highlighting. The challenge of long-term financial planning has not yet really been overcome. Many participatory budgets seem to run into difficulty when returns to scale reduce and implementation failure increases. Efforts to involve PB participants in some kind of long-term decision-making, for example, in Santo André, did not really work. Long-term decision-making can be disappointing if it simply means kicking the can down the road. Designers should consider this issue, particularly with the unsustainability of human life based on our current decisions becoming an ever more alarming prospect. Participatory programmes often seem to suffer because monitoring and implementation is an afterthought, and when that point of a cycle is reached, funds have already been used up. Where processes fail in delivering accountability and long-term security for participants, one cannot blame them for wondering whether the joke is on them for believing these processes can deliver. But perhaps we should not be surprised – few, if any, political decision-making procedures have a good record in making decisions for the long term, or on monitoring and implementation. The last point, however, also highlights how overclaiming the potential of any programme to deliver can be dangerous.

Democratic innovation is often seen as a response to democratic deficits, but it is not yet clear that it has actually responded. Politics in general appears increasingly characterized by populism and polarization. Frankly, participatory innovation has failed to really engage the disengaged in a way that elections and referendums have continued to do. While some participatory budgets are good examples of including otherwise disengaged voices, others exacerbate alienation and anger with political process. The reality is that populism is engaging more citizens than participatory and deliberative democracy right now. Perhaps in my bleakest moments I felt I was writing a history book. PB has been wound down in many places where it was transformational. In many places where it is still being ramped up it is far from transformational. Engaging the poorest and hardest to reach sectors of society is a high bar, and often proves difficult (Grillos, 2017). But we should also not confuse softening of the waves with a change in the tide. The positive effects of participation are likely cumulative. This is why it is so important to make sure we know how they happen.

Even if PB morphs as it travels, the aims of its core design are important to keep in mind because they sought to overcome issues of very simplified audience democracy. We should be mindful when designing democratic innovations, in particular where we are engaging a microcosm of the population, that we are also communicating in innovative democratic ways with the wider demos. PB's approach to mass mobilization has shown in some instances the possibilities where hard work on that dimension of buttressing democracy pays off. PB cannot fix everything, even at a local level, and its impact on real transformational outcomes towards a participatory public culture cannot easily be judged. However, it is a significant innovation and does drive us further in the right direction. Many participatory experiments will fail. What I have tried to do here is show the contexts in which important conditions will combine to explain this failure or to explain success. Policymakers and activists will want to take note of the evidence. If you are sitting at home in your city right now, wondering what steps to take to improve citizen participation, what should I tell you?

First, set your expectations. Politics is hard, and while we should aim for the stars, falling short is not the end of participation. If we try to sell clear failures as successes, we are only kidding ourselves (Ryan and Spada, 2017). It is better that we are transparent about the uncertainty with which we operate. But the evidence is clear. You can make participation work in your city or neighbourhood. You may need patience, and you will need representative political leadership committed to participation over the longer term, but successes have come in multiple contexts.

Second, keep informed. One of the reasons PB has been most well received in the academic literature is that it does not shut out interest from those studying development, political economy, area studies scholars, public administration, local government studies, and so on. My point is not that we should all know everything about these diverse literatures; it is more so that academics tend to silo and are the poorer for it. Data collection, methodologies and the creative ideas of normative theorists are improving all the time. Social science can actually help solve problems in the world. Some academics working in this field can actually lay claim to positive impacts!

Third, try to engender the conditions for multiple key actors to support programmes. In particular, bureaucrats and agency staff have been overlooked in some of the literature, and they tend to appear as important INUS conditions in explanations. But you cannot focus on one variable alone. The analysis and theory both suggest it is certain conjunctions like participatory political leadership and bureaucratic buy-in to participation that produce participatory programmes where authority is transferred from representatives to citizens.

Fourth, be patient and do not scorn middling outcomes so easily. Contradictory outcomes may not always spell doom either. Sometimes democratic behaviour emerges because processes seem to break down (Baiocchi and Ganuza, 2016: 138). We do not know what the long-term distal impact of these projects is yet. Our concepts still need refinement and our causal theories are still uncertain. Changes in power relationships are still difficult to achieve but worth it. Keep going.

# References


Abers, R.N. (1998) 'From clientelism to cooperation: Local government, participatory policy and civic organizing in Porto Alegre, Brazil', *Politics & Society*, 26(4), 511–37.

Abers, R.N. (2000) *Inventing Local Democracy: Grassroots Politics in Brazil*, London: Lynne Rienner.

Allegretti, G. and Herzberg, C. (2004) *Participatory Budgets in Europe: Between Efficiency and Growing Local Democracy*, Transnational Institute and the Centre for Democratic Policy-Making, TNI Briefing Series No 2004/5. www.tni.org/reports/newpol/participatory.pdf

Almond, G.A. and Verba, S. (1963) *The Civic Culture: Political Attitudes and Democracy in Five Nations*, Princeton, NJ: Princeton University Press.

Alves, M.L. and Allegretti, G. (2012) '(In)stability, a key element to understand participatory budgeting', *Journal of Public Deliberation*, 8(2), Article 3.

Andeweg, R. and Farrell, D. (2017) 'Legitimacy Decline and Party Decline', in C. van Ham, J. Thomassen, K. Aarts and R. Andeweg (eds) *Myth and Reality of the Legitimacy Crisis: Explaining Trends and Cross-National Differences in Established Democracies*, Oxford: Oxford University Press, 76–94.

Arnstein, S.R. (1969) 'A ladder of citizen participation', *Journal of the American Planning Association*, 35(4), 216–24.

Audickas, L., Dempsey, N. and Loft, P. (2019) *Membership of UK Political Parties*, London: House of Commons Library. www.parliament.uk/business/publications/research/briefing-papers/SN05125/membership-of-uk-political-parties

Avritzer, L. (2002) *Democracy and the Public Space in Latin America*, Princeton, NJ: Princeton University Press.

Avritzer, L. (2005) 'Modes of Democratic Deliberation: Participatory Budgeting in Brazil', in B. De Sousa Santos (ed) *Democratising Democracy: Beyond the Liberal Democratic Canon*, London: Verso, 377–403.

Avritzer, L. (2006) 'New public spheres in Brazil: Local democracy and deliberative politics', *International Journal of Urban and Regional Research*, 30(3), 623–37.

Avritzer, L. (2009) *Participatory Institutions in Democratic Brazil*, Baltimore, MD: John Hopkins University Press.

Avritzer, L. and Wampler, B. (2005) 'The spread of participatory democracy in Brazil: From radical democracy to good government', *Journal of Latin American Urban Studies*, 7, 37–52.

Baierle, S. (2008) 'Shoot the citizen, save the customer: Participatory budgeting and bare citizenship', *Soberania Popular Sovereignty*, 1(1), 190–223.

Baiocchi, G. (2005) *Militants and Citizens: The Politics of Participatory Democracy in Porto Alegre*, Stanford, CA: Stanford University Press.

Baiocchi, G. and Ganuza, E. (2016) *Popular Democracy: The Paradox of Participation*, Stanford, CA: Stanford University Press.

Baiocchi, G., Heller, P. and Silva, M.K. (2011) *Bootstrapping Democracy: Transforming Local Governance and Civil Society in Brazil*, Standford, CA: Stanford University Press.

Bassoli, M. (2012) 'Participatory budgeting in Italy: An analysis of (almost democratic) participatory governance arrangements', *International Journal of Urban and Regional Research*, 36(6), 1183–203.

Beck. U. (1992) *Risk Society: Towards a New Modernity*, London: SAGE Publications Ltd.

Benito, B. and Bastida, F. (2009) 'Budget transparency, fiscal performance, and political turnout: An international approach', *Public Administration Review*, 69(3), 403–17.

Berg-Schlosser, D. and Cronqvist, L. (2005) 'Macro-quantitative vs macro-qualitative methods in the social sciences – An example from empirical democratic theory employing new software', *Historical Social Research*, 30(4), 154–75.

Blaug, R. (2002) 'Engineering democracy', *Political Studies*, 50, 102–16.

Bohman, J. (1997) 'Deliberative Democracy and Effective Social Freedom – Capabilities, Resources and Opportunities', in J. Bohman and W. Rehg (eds) *Deliberative Democracy: Essays on Reasons in Politics*, Cambridge, MA: MIT Press, 321–48.

Bol, D. and Luppi, F. (2013) 'Confronting theories based on necessary relations: Making the best of QCA possibilities', *Political Research Quarterly*, 60(1), 205–10.

Bonaduce de Nigris, F. (2008) *Your Health, Your Community, Your Vote*, Thornhill Plus You Evaluation Report.

Boswell, J. and Corbett, J. (2017) 'Why and how to compare deliberative systems', *European Journal of Political Research*, 56, 801–19. doi:10.1111/1475-6765.12205

Brown, C. and Boswell, T. (1995) 'Strikebreaking or solidarity in the great steel strike of 1919: A split labor market, game-theoretic and QCA analysis', *American Journal of Sociology*, 100(6), 1479–519.

Bryan, F.M. (2004) *Real Democracy: The New England Town Meeting and How It Works*, Chicago, IL: Chicago University Press.

Byrne, D. and Ragin, C.C. (eds) (2009) *The SAGE Handbook of Case-Based Methods*, London: SAGE Publications Ltd.

Cabannes, Y. (2004) 'Participatory budgeting: A significant contribution to participatory democracy', *Environment and Urbanization*, 16, 27–46.

Cabannes, Y. (2018) 'Highlights on Some Asian and Russian Participatory Budgeting Pioneers', in N. Dias (ed) *Hope for Democracy: 30 Years of Participatory Democracy Worldwide*, Faro: Oficina, 235–54.

Cabannes, Y. and Ming, Z. (2014) 'Participatory budgeting at scale and bridging the rural–urban divide in Chengdu', *Environment and Urbanization*, 26(1), 257–75. doi:10.1177/0956247813509146

Cabannes, Y. and Lipietz, B. (2018) 'Revisiting the democratic promise of participatory budgeting in light of competing political, good governance and technocratic logics', *Environment and Urbanization*, 30(1), 67–84. doi:10.1177/0956247817746279

Campbell, M., Escobar, O., Fenton, C. and Craig, P. (2018) 'The impact of participatory budgeting on health and wellbeing: A scoping review of evaluations', *BMC Public Health*, 18, 822.

Caramani, D. (2009) *Introduction to the Comparative Method with Boolean Algebra*, Quantitative Applications in the Social Sciences, Beverly Hills, CA: SAGE Publications Ltd.

Caren, N. and Panofsky, A. (2005) 'TQCA: A technique for adding temporality to qualitative comparative analysis', *Sociological Methods Research*, 34(2), 147–72.

Cohen, M. and Nagel, E. (1934) *An Introduction to Logic and Scientific Method*, New York, NY: Harcourt, Brace & Company.

Coleman, S. and Sampaio, R.F. (2017) 'Sustaining a democratic innovation: A study of three e-participatory budgets in Belo Horizonte', *Information, Communication & Society*, 20(5), 754–69. doi:10.1080/1369118X.2016.1203971

Dahl, R.A. (1961) *Who Governs? Democracy and Power in an American City*, New Haven, CT: Yale University Press.

Dalton, R.J. (2004) *Democratic Challenges, Democratic Choices: The Erosion of Political Support in Advanced Industrial Democracies*, Oxford: Oxford University Press.

Davies, C., Whetherell, M. and Barnett, E. (2006) *Citizens at the Centre: Deliberative Participation in Healthcare Decisions*, Bristol: Policy Press.

Delwit, P. (2012) 'Still in Decline? Party Membership in Europe', in E. van Haute (ed) *Party Membership in Europe: Exploration into the Anthills of Party Politics*, Brussels: Editions de l'Université de Bruxelles, 25–42.

Dewey, J. (2012 [1927]) *The Public and its Problems: An Essay in Political Inquiry*, University Park, PA: Pennsylvania State University Press.

Dias, N. (ed) (2014) *Hope for Democracy: 25 Years of Participatory Democracy Worldwide*, São Brás de Alportel: In Loco. https://democracyspotdotnet.files.wordpress.com/2014/06/op25anos-en-20maio20141.pdf

Dias, N. (ed) (2018) *Hope for Democracy: 30 Years of Participatory Democracy Worldwide*, Faro: Oficina. www.oficina.org.pt/uploads/7/0/6/1/70619115/hope_for_democracy_-_digital.pdf

Dias, N. and Júlio, S. (2018) 'The Next Thirty Years of Participatory Budgeting in the World Start Today', in N. Dias (ed) *Hope for Democracy: 30 Years of Participatory Democracy Worldwide*, Faro: Oficina, 15–32.

Dias, N., Júlio, S., Martins, V., Sousa, V. and Biel, F. (2018) 'Participatory Budgeting in Portugal – Standing Between a Hesitant Political Will and the Impacts on Public Policies', in N. Dias (ed) *Hope for Democracy: 30 Years of Participatory Democracy Worldwide*, Faro: Oficina, 257–73.

Dias, N., Enríquez, S. and Júlio, S. (2019) *Participatory Budgeting World Atlas 2019*, Cascais/Faro: Oficina.

Dienel, P.C. (1989) 'Contributing to Social Decision Methodology: Citizen Reports on Technological Projects', in C. Vlek and G. Cvetkovich (eds) *Social Decision Methodology for Technological Projects*, Dordrecht: Kluwer Academic Publishers, 133–51.

Dowding, K. (2016) *The Philosophy and Methods of Political Science*, Basingstoke: Palgrave.

Dusa, A. (2019) *QCA with R: A Comprehensive Resource*, Cham: Springer International Publishing.

Elstub, S. and Escobar, O. (eds) (2019) *Handbook of Democratic Innovations and Governance*, Cheltenham: Edward Elgar Publishing.

Escobar, O., Garven, F., Harkins, C., Glazik, K., Cameron, S. and Stoddart, S. (2018) 'Participatory Budgeting in Scotland: The Interplay of Public Service Reform, Community Empowerment and Social Justice', in N. Dias (ed) *Hope for Democracy: 30 Years of Participatory Democracy Worldwide*, Faro: Oficina, 311–34.

Farrell, D.M., Suiter, J. and Harris, C. (2019) '"Systematizing" constitutional deliberation: The 2016–18 Citizens' Assembly in Ireland', *Irish Political Studies*, 34(1), 113–23. doi:10.1080/07907184.2018.1534832d

Fedozzi, L., Furtado, A. and Rangel, R. (2018) 'Participatory Budgeting in Brazil: Elements for a Brief Evaluation', in N. Dias (ed) *Hope for Democracy: 30 Years of Participatory Democracy Worldwide*, Faro: Oficina, 105–21.

Fishkin, J.S. (1996) 'The televised deliberative poll: An experiment in democracy', *The Annals of the American Academy of Political and Social Science*, 546, 133–7.

Fishkin, J.S. (2009) *When the People Speak: Deliberative Democracy and Public Consultation*, Oxford: Oxford University Press.

Fiss, P.C. (2011) 'Building better causal theories: A fuzzy set approach to typologies in organizational research', *Academy of Management Journal*, 54(2), 393–420.

Flyvbjerg, B. (2006) 'Five misunderstandings about case-study research', *Qualitative Inquiry*, 12(2), 219–45.

Font, J., Smith, G., Galais, C. and Alarcon, P. (2017) 'Cherry-picking participation: Explaining the fate of proposals from participatory processes', *European Journal of Political Research*, 57(3), 615–36.

Fordham, G. (2010) *The New Deal for Communities Programme: Achieving a Neighbourhood Focus for Regeneration – The New Deal for Communities National Evaluation: Final Report – Volume 1*, London: Department for Communities and Local Government.

Foroughi, B. (2017) 'Reading between the lines of participation: Tenant participation and participatory budgeting in Toronto community housing', *Journal of Public Deliberation*, 13(2), 11. doi:http://doi.org/10.16997/jdd.287

Francés, F., Carratalá, L. and Ganuza, E. (2018) '20 Years of Participatory Budgeting in Spain', in N. Dias (ed) *Hope for Democracy: 30 Years of Participatory Democracy Worldwide*, Faro: Oficina, 275–87.

Fung, A. (2003) 'Survey article: Recipes for public spheres: Eight institutional design choices and their consequences', *The Journal of Political Philosophy*, II(3), 338–67.

Fung, A. (2004) *Empowered Participation: Reinventing Urban Democracy*. Princeton, NJ: Princeton University Press.

Fung, A. and Wright, E.O. (eds) (2003) *Deepening Democracy: Institutional Innovations in Empowered Participatory Governance*, London: Verso.

Gallie, W. (1955) 'Essentially contested concepts', *Proceedings of the Aristotelian Society*, 56, 167–98.

Ganuza, E. and Baiocchi, G. (2012) 'The power of ambiguity: How participatory budgeting travels the globe', *Journal of Public Deliberation*, 8(2), Article 8.

Ganuza, E. and Francés, F. (2012) 'The deliberative turn in participation: The problem of inclusion and deliberative opportunities in participatory budgeting', *European Political Science Review*, 4(2), 283–302. doi:10.1017/S1755773911000270

Ganuza, E. and Baiocchi, G. (2019) 'The Long Journey of Participatory Budgeting', in S. Elstub and O. Escobar (eds) *Handbook of Democratic Innovations and Governance*, Cheltenham: Edward Elgar Publishing, 77–89.

Gastil, J., Richards Jr, R.C., Ryan, M. and Smith, G. (2017) 'Testing assumptions in deliberative democratic design: A preliminary assessment of the efficacy of the Participedia data archive as an analytic tool', *Journal of Public Deliberation*, 13(2), 1. doi:http://doi.org/10.16997/jdd.277

Geissel, B. and Hess, P. (2017) 'Explaining political efficacy in deliberative procedures – A novel methodological approach', *Journal of Public Deliberation*, 13(2), Article 4.

George, A. and Bennett, A. (2005) *Case Studies and Theory Development in the Social Sciences*, London: MIT Press.

Gilman, H.R. (2016) *Democracy Reinvented: Participatory Budgeting and Civic Innovation in America*, Washington, DC: Brookings Institution Press.

Goertz, G. (2006) 'Assessing the trivialness, relevance, and relative importance of necessary or sufficient conditions in social science', *Studies in Comparative International Development*, 41, 88–109. doi: 10.1007/BF02686312

Goldfrank, B. (2003) 'Making Participation Work in Porto Alegre', in G. Baiocchi (ed) *Radicals in Power: The Workers' Party (PT) and Experiments in Urban Democracy in Brazil*, London: Zed Books, 27–52.

Goldfrank, B. (2011) *Deepening Local Democracy in Latin America: Participation, Decentralization, and the Left*, Pennsylvania, PA: Pennsylvania State University Press.

Goldfrank, B. (2012) 'The World Bank and the globalization of participatory budgeting', *Journal of Public Deliberation*, 8(2), Article 7.

Gonçalves, S. (2014) 'The effects of participatory budgeting on municipal expenditures and infant mortality in Brazil', *World Development*, 53, 94–110.

Gret, M. and Sintomer, Y. (2005) *The Porto Alegre Experiment: Learning Lessons for Better Democracy*, London: Zed Books.

Grillos, T. (2017) 'Participatory budgeting and the poor: Tracing bias in a multi-staged process in Solo, Indonesia', *World Development*, 96(C), 343–58.

Gutmann, A. and Thompson, D. (1996) *Democracy and Disagreement*, London: Belknap.

Haesebrouck, T. (2015) 'Pitfalls in QCA's consistency measure', *Journal of Comparative Politics*, 8, 65–80.

Hall, J. and Röcke, A. (2013) 'Participatory Budgeting in Great Britain: Between a Neoliberal Agenda and Community Empowerment', in Y. Sintomer, R. Traub-Merz and J. Zhang (eds) (2013) *Participatory Budgeting in Asia and Europe: Key Challenges of Participation*, Basingstoke: Palgrave, 182–97.

Harrison, K. (2020) 'Can't, won't and what's the point? A theory of the UK public's muted response to austerity', *Representation*. doi:10.1080/00344893.2020.1728367

Hartz-Karp, J. and Weymouth, R. (2018) 'Australian Participatory Budgting', in N. Dias (ed) *Hope for Democracy: 30 Years of Participatory Democracy Worldwide*, Faro: Oficina, 403–22.

Herzberg, C. (2011) 'Bridging the Gap of Generalisation in Case Studies Analysis: What Can Be Expected from Weberian Ideal Types?', paper presented at the Colloquium 'Methodological Challenges in Participation Research', Córdoba, Spain, 4–5 November.

Herzberg, C. (2013) 'Participation and Modernisation. Participatory Budgeting in Germany: The Example of Berlin-Lichtenberg', in Y. Sintomer, R. Traub-Merz and J. Zhang (eds) (2013) *Participatory Budgeting in Asia and Europe: Key Challenges of Participation*, Basingstoke: Palgrave, 182–97.

Hibbing, J.R. and Theiss-Morse, E. (2002) *Stealth Democracy: American's Belief About How Government Should Work*, Port Chester, NY: Cambridge University Press.

Hino, A. (2009) 'Time-series QCA: Studying temporal change through Boolean analysis', *Sociological Theory and Methods*, 24(2), 247–65.

Hug, S. (2013) 'Qualitative comparative analysis: How inductive use and measurement error lead to problematic inference', *Political Analysis*, 21(2), 252–65.

Inglehart, R. (1997) *Modernization and Postmodernization: Cultural, Economic and Political Change in 43 Societies,* Princeton, NJ: Princeton University Press.

Jabola-Carolus, I. (2017) 'Growing grassroots democracy: Dynamic outcomes in building New York City's participatory budgeting program', *New Political Science*, 39(1), 109–25. doi:10.1080/07393148.2017.1278857

Jacquet, V. and van der Does, R. (2020) 'The consequences of deliberative minipublics: Systematic overview, conceptual gaps, and new directions', *Representation*. doi:10.1080/00344893.2020.1778513

Jaramillo, M. and Wright, G.D. (2015) 'Participatory democracy and effective policy: Is there a link? Evidence from rural Peru', *World Development*, 66, 280–92.

Keohane, R.O. (2009) 'Political science as a vocation', *PS: Political Science and Politics*, 42(2), 359–63.

King, G., Keohane, R.O. and Verba, S. (1994) *Designing Social Inquiry: Scientific Inference in Qualitative Research*, Princeton, NJ: Princeton University Press.

Krogslund, C., Choi, D. and Poertner, M. (2015) 'Fuzzy sets on shaky ground: Parameter sensitivity and confirmation bias in fsQCA', *Political Analysis*, *23*(1), 21–41. doi:10.1093/pan/mpu016

Lerner, J. and van Wagner, E. (2006) *Participatory Budgeting in Canada: Democratic Innovations in Strategic Spaces*, The Transnational Institute, New Politics Publications. www.tni.org/en/article/participatory-budgeting-in-canadaIt

Levitksy, S. and Ziblatt, D. (2018) *How Democracies Die*, New York, NY: Broadway Books.

Lieberson, S. (1994) 'More on the uneasy case for using Mill-type methods in small-N comparative studies', *Social Forces*, 72(4), 1225–37.

Lieberson, S. (2004) 'Comments on the use and utility of QCA', *Qualitative Methods* (Newsletter of the APSA Organized Section on Qualitative Methods), 2(2), 13–14.

Lijphart, A. (1971) 'Comparative politics and the comparative method', *American Political Science Review*, 65, 682–93.

Lijphart, A. (1997) 'Unequal participation: Democracy's unresolved dilemma, (Presidential Address, American Political Science Association)', *American Political Science Review*, 91(1), 1–14.

Lipsky, M. (1980) *Street-Level Bureaucracy: Dilemmas of the Individual in Public Services*, New York, NY: SAGE Publications Ltd.

Lucas, S.R. and Szatrowski, S. (2014) 'Qualitative comparative analysis in critical perspective', *Sociological Methodology*, 44(1), 1–79.

Lüchmann, W.R. and Borba, J. (2018) '20 Years of Participatory Budgeting in Brazil: The Lessons Learned', in N. Dias (ed) *Hope for Democracy: 30 Years of Participatory Democracy Worldwide*, Faro: Oficina, 89–103.

Mackie, J.L. (1988) *The Cement of the Universe: A Study in Causation*, Oxford: Clarendon Press.

Mahoney, J., Kimball, E. and Koivu, K. (2009) 'The logic of historical explanation in the social sciences', *Comparative Political Studies*, 42(1), 114–46.

Mair, P. (2013) *Ruling the Void: The Hollowing of Western Democracy*, London: Verso.

Mansbridge, J.J. (1983) *Beyond Adversary Democracy*, Chicago, IL: Chicago University Press.

Mansbridge, J.J., Bohman J., Chambers, S., Christiano, T., Fung, A., Parkinson, J., Thompson, D.F. and Warren, M.E. (2012) 'A Systemic Approach to Deliberative Democracy', in J. Parkinson and J.J. Mansbridge (eds) *Deliberative Systems: Deliberative Democracy at the Large Scale*, Cambridge: Cambridge University Press, 1–26.

Marquetti, A., Schonerwald da Silva, C.E. and Campbell, A. (2012) 'Participatory economic democracy in action: Participatory budgeting in Porto Alegre, 1989–2004', *Review of Radical Economics*, 44(1), 62–81.

Marshall, T.H. (1950) *T.H. Marshall, Citizenship and Social Class, and Other Essays*, Cambridge: Cambridge University Press.

McNulty, S. (2011) *Voice and Vote: Decentralization and Participation in Post-Fujimori Peru*, Stanford, CA: Stanford University Press.

McNulty, S. (2018) 'Mandating PB: Evaluating Fifteen years of Peru's National Participatory Budgeting Law', in N. Dias (ed) *Hope for Democracy: 30 Years of Participatory Democracy Worldwide*, Faro: Oficina, 147–59.

Mendel, J.M. and Ragin, C.C. (2011) 'fsQCA: Dialog between Jerry M. Mendel and Charles C. Ragin'. https://papers.ssrn.com/sol3/papers.cfm?abstract_id=2517966

Michels, R. (1911 [2001]) *Political Parties: A Sociological Study of the Oligarchical Tendencies of Modern Democracy*, Kitchener, ON: Batoche.

Mill, J.S. (1950) *John Stuart Mill's Philosophy of Scientific Method* (edited by E. Nagel), New York: Hafner.

Misangyi, V.F., Greckhamer, T., Furnari, S., Fiss, P., Crilly, D. and Aguilera, R.V. (2017) 'Embracing causal complexity: The emergence of a neo-configurational perspective', *Journal of Management*, 43, 255–82.

Montambeault, F. (2016) *The Politics of Local Participatory Democracy in Latin America: Institutions, Actors, and Interactions*, Stanford, CA: Stanford University Press.

Newton, K. (2006) 'Political support: Social capital, civil society and political and economic performance', *Political Studies*, 54(4), 846–64.

Niemeyer, S. (2011) 'The emancipatory effect of deliberation: Empirical lessons from mini-publics', *Politics & Society*, 39(1), 103–40.

No, W. (2018) 'History and Issues of Participatory Budgeting in South Korea', in N. Dias (ed) *Hope for Democracy: 30 Years of Participatory Democracy Worldwide*, Faro: Oficina, 211–21.

Norris, P. (2011) *Democratic Deficit: Critical Citizens Revisited*, Cambridge: Cambridge University Press.

Nuñez, T. (2018) 'Porto Alegre, From a Role Model to a Crisis', in N. Dias (ed) *Hope for Democracy: 30 Years of Participatory Democracy Worldwide*, Faro: Oficina, 517–35.

Nylen, W.R. (2003a) *Partiicpatory Democracy versus Elitist Democracy: Lessons from Brazil*, New York, NY: Palgrave.

Nylen, W.R. (2003b) 'An Enduring Legacy: Popular Participation in the Aftermath of the Participatory Budgets of Joao Monlevade and Betim', in G. Baiocchi (ed) *Radicals in Power: The Workers' Party (PT) and Experiments in Urban Democracy in Brazil*, London: Zed Books, 91–112.

Oana, I. and Schneider, C.Q. (2018) 'SetMethods: An add-on package for advanced QCA', *The R Journal*. https://journal.r-project.org/archive/2018/RJ-2018-031/index.html

Olsen, W.K. and Nomura, H. (2009) 'Poverty reduction: Fuzzy sets vs crisp sets compared', *Sociological Theory and Methods*, 24(2), 219–46.

O'Tuama, S. (2009) 'Rights, Recognition and Contingency: Opening a Discussion on the Right to Have Rights', in S. O'Tuama (ed) *Critical Turns in Critical Theory: New Directions in Social and Political Thought*, London: I.B. Tauris, 141–64.

Paine, J. (2016) 'Set-theoretic comparative methods: Less distinctive than claimed', *Comparative Political Studies*, 49(6), 703–41. doi: 10.1177/0010414014564851

Pateman, C. (1970) *Participation and Democratic Theory*, London: Cambridge.

Pateman, C. (2012) 'Participatory democracy revisited', *Perspectives in Politics*, 10(1), 7–19.

PB Unit (2008) *Participatory Budgeting in the UK: Toolkit*, Manchester: PB Unit

Peruzzotti, E. (2009) 'The Politics of Institutional Innovation: The Implementation of Participatory Budgeting in the City of Buenos Aires', in A. Selee and E. Peruzzotti (eds) *Participatory Innovation and Representative Democracy in Latin America*, Washington, DC: Woodrow Wilson Centre Press, 40–61.

Peters, B.G. (2013) *Strategies for Comparative Research in Political Science*, Basingstoke: Palgrave.

Phillips, A. (1995) *The Politics of Presence*, Oxford: Oxford University Press.

Pin, L. (2017) 'Does participatory budgeting lead to local empowerment? The case of Chicago, IL', *Alternate Routes: A Journal of Critical Social Research*, 28. www.alternateroutes.ca/index.php/ar/article/view/22420

Pogrebinschi, T. and Samuels, D. (2014) 'The impact of participatory democracy: Evidence from Brazil's national public policy conferences', *Comparative Politics*, 46. doi:10.5129/001041514810943045

Pogrebinshi, T. and Ryan, M. (2018) 'Moving beyond input legitimacy: When do democratic innovations affect policy making?', *European Journal of Political Research*, 57, 135–52. doi:10.1111/1475-6765.12219

Pont, R. (2004) 'Participatory Democracy and Local Power: The Experience of Porto Alegre', in I. Bruce (ed) *The Porto Alegre Alternative: Direct Democracy in Action*, London: Pluto Press, 111–9.

Porto de Oliveira, O. (2017) *International Policy Diffusion and Participatory Budgeting – Ambassadors of Participation, International Institutions and Transnational Networks*, Basingstoke: Palgrave Macmillan.

Pratchett, L., Durose, C., Lowndes, V., Smith, G., Stoker G. and Wales, C. (2009) *Empowering Communities to Influence Local Decision Making: A Systematic Review of the Evidence*, Report for the Department of Communities and Local Government, London: The Stationery Office.

Ragin, C.C. (1987) *The Comparative Method: Moving beyond Qualitative and Quantitative Strategies*, Berkeley, CA: University of California Press.

Ragin, C.C. (2000) *Fuzzy-Set Social Science*, Chicago, IL: University of Chicago Press.

Ragin, C.C. (2008) *Redesigning Social Inquiry: Fuzzy Sets and Beyond*, London: Chicago University Press.

Ragin, C.C. (2009) 'Qualitative Comparative Analysis Using Fuzzy Sets (fsQCA)', in B. Rihoux and C.C. Ragin (eds) *Configurative Comparative Methods: Qualitative Comparative Analysis (QCA) and Related Techniques*, London: SAGE Publications Ltd, 87–112.

Ragin, C.C. and Becker, H.S. (1992) *What Is a Case? Exploring the Foundations of Social Inquiry*, New York, NY: Cambridge University Press.

Ragin, C.C. and Strand, S.I. (2008) 'Using qualitative comparative analysis to study causal order: Comment on Caren and Panofsky', *Sociological Research Methods*, 36(4), 431–41.

Ribeiro, A.C.T. and de Grazia, G. (2003) *Experiéncas de Orçamento Participativo no Brasil: Período de 1997 á 2000*, Petrópolis: Editora Vozes.

Rihoux, B. and Ragin, C.C. (eds) (2007) *Configurative Comparative Methods: Qualitative Comparative Analysis (QCA) and Related Techniques*, London: SAGE Publications Ltd.

Rihoux, B. and Lobe, B. (2009) 'The Case for Qualitative Comparative Analysis (QCA): Adding Leverage for Thick Cross-Case Comparison', in D. Byrne and C.C. Ragin (eds) *The SAGE Handbook of Case-Based Methods*, London: SAGE Publications Ltd, 222–42.

Rihoux, B., Álamos-Concha, P., Bol, D., Marx, A. and Rezsöhazy, I. (2013) 'From niche to mainstream method? A comprehensive mapping of QCA applications in journal articles from 1984 to 2011', *Political Research Quarterly*, 66(1), 175–84.

Röcke, A. (2009) *Democratic innovation through ideas?: Participatory budgeting and frames of citizen participation in France, Germany and Great Britain*, PhD thesis, Department of Political and Social Sciences, Florence: European University Institute.

Röcke, A. (2014) *Framing Citizen Participation: Participatory Budgeting in France, Germany and the United Kingdom*, London: Palgrave Macmillan.

Rodgers, D. (2010) 'Contingent democratisation? The rise and fall of participatory budgeting in Buenos Aires', *Journal of Latin American Studies*, 42(1), 1–27.

Runciman, D. (2018) *How Democracy Ends*, London: Profile Books.

Ryan, M. (2014) 'Advancing Comparison of Democratic Innovations: A Medium-N Fuzzy-Set Qualitative Comparative Analysis of Participatory Budgeting', PhD thesis, Department of Politics and International Relations, Southampton: University of Southampton.

Ryan, M. (2016) 'Qualitative Comparative Analysis for Reviewing Evidence and Making Decisions', in G. Stoker and M. Evans (eds) *Evidence-Based Policy Making in the Social Sciences: Methods that Matter*, Bristol: Policy Press, 83–101.

Ryan, M. (2017) 'Using cases in political science: Reflections on Keith Dowding's *The Philosophy and Methods of Political Science*', *Political Studies Review*, 15(2), 194–200. doi:10.1177/1478929917693642

Ryan, M. (2018) 'The Comparative Method', in V. Lowndes, D. Marsh and G. Stoker (eds) *Theory and Methods in Political Science* (4th edn), Political Analysis, London: Palgrave Macmillan, 271–89.

Ryan, M. (2019) 'Comparative Approaches to the Study of Democratic Innovation', in S. Elstub and O. Escobar (eds) *Handbook of Democratic Innovations and Governance*, Cheltenham: Edward Elgar Publishing, 558–70.

Ryan, M. and Smith, G. (2012) 'Towards a comparative analysis of democratic innovations: Lessons from a small-N fsQCA of participatory budgeting', *Revista Internacional de Sociología*, 70(2), 89–120.

Ryan, M. and Smith, G. (2014) 'Defining Mini-Publics: Making Sense of Existing Conceptions', in K. Gronlund, B. Geisel and M. Setala (eds) *Deliberative Mini-Publics: Involving Citizens in the Democratic Process*, Colchester: ECPR Press, 9–26.

Ryan, M., Stoker, G., John, P., Moseley, A., James, O., Richardson, L. and Vannoni, M. (2018) 'How best to open up local democracy? A randomised experiment to encourage contested elections and greater representativeness in English parish councils', *Local Government Studies*, 44(6), 766–87. doi:10.1080/03003930.2018.1473769

Santos, B.S. (2005) 'Participatory Budgeting in Porto Alegre: Toward a Redistributive Democracy', in B.S. Santos (ed) *Democratizing Democracy: Beyond the Liberal Democratic Canon*, London: Verso, 307–76.

Sartori, G. (1970) 'Concept misinformation in comparative politics', *American Political Science Review*, 64(4), 1033–53.

Savolainen, J. (1994) 'The rationality of drawing big conclusions based on small samples: In defense of Mill's methods', *Social Forces*, 72(4), 1217–24.

Saward, M. (2003) 'Enacting democracy', *Political Studies*, 51, 161–79.

Saward, M. (2010) *The Representative Claim*, Oxford: Oxford University Press.

Schneider, C.Q. (2016) 'Real differences and overlooked similarities: Set-methods in comparative perspective', *Comparative Political Studies*, 49(6), 781–92. doi:10.1177/0010414015626454

Schneider, C.Q. and Rohlfing, I. (2013) 'Combining QCA and process tracing in set-theoretic multi-method research', *Sociological Methods & Research*, 42(4), 559–97.

Schneider, C.Q. and Wagemann, C. (2012) *Set-Theoretic Methods in the Social Sciences: A Guide for Qualitative Comparative Analysis (QCA) and Fuzzy- Sets*, Cambridge: Cambridge University Press.

Schumpeter, J.A. (1942 [1995]) *Capitalism, Socialism and Democracy*, London: Routledge.

Shah, A. (ed) (2007) *Participatory Budgeting*, Washington, DC: The World Bank.

Shulga, I. and Vagin, V. (2018) 'Developing Participatory Budgeting in Russia', in N. Dias (ed) *Hope for Democracy: 30 Years of Participatory Democracy Worldwide*, Faro: Oficina, 427–45.

Silva, M.K. (2003) 'Participation by Design: The Experience of Alvorada and Gravataí, Rio Grande do Sul, Brazil', in G. Baiocchi (ed) *Radicals in Power: The Workers' Party (PT) and Experiments in Urban Democracy in Brazil*, London: Zed Books, 113–30.

Sintomer, Y., Herzberg, C. and Röcke, A. (eds) (2005) *Participatory Budgets in a European Comparative Approach: Perspectives and Chances of the Cooperative State at the Municipal Level in Germany and Europe*. www.buergerhaushalt- europa.de/documents/Volumen_zwei_Endbericht_Buergerhaushalt_Euro pa5.pdf

Sintomer, Y., Herzberg, C. and Röcke, A. (2008) 'Participatory budgeting in Europe: Potentials and challenges', *International Journal of Urban and Regional Research*, 32(1), 164–78.

Sintomer, Y., Herzberg, C., Allegretti, G. and Röcke, A. (2010) *Learning from the South: Participatory Budgeting Worldwide – An Invitation to Global Cooperation*, Dialog Global Series No 25, Bonn: InWEnt gGmbH.

Sintomer, Y., Herzberg, C., Röcke, A. and Allegretti, G. (2012) 'Transnational models of citizen participation: The case of participatory budgeting', *Journal of Public Deliberation*, 8(2), Article 9.

Sintomer, Y., Traub-Merz, R. and Zhang, J. (eds) (2013) *Participatory Budgeting in Asia and Europe: Key Challenges of Participation*, Basingstoke: Palgrave.

Sintomer, Y., Röcke, A. and Herzberg, C. (2016) *Participatory Budgeting in Europe. Participatory Democracy and Public Governance*, Oxford: Routledge.

Smith, G. (2005) *Beyond the Ballot: 57 Democratic Innovations from Around the World*, London: Power Inquiry. www.makeitanissue.org.uk/Beyond%20the%20Ballot.pdf

Smith, G. (2009) *Democratic Innovations: Designing Institutions for Citizenship Participation*, Cambridge: Cambridge University Press.

Smith, G. (2019) 'Reflections on the Theory and Practice of Democratic Innovations', in S. Elstub and O. Escobar (eds) *Handbook of Democratic Innovations and Governance*, Cheltenham: Edward Elgar Publishing, 572–81.

Smith, G. and Wales, C. (2000) 'Citizen's juries and deliberative democracy', *Political Studies*, 48, 51–65.

Smithson, M. (1988) 'Fuzzy set theory and the social sciences: The scope for applications', *Fuzzy Sets and Systems*, 26, 1–21.

Smithson, M. and Verkuilen, J. (2006) *Fuzzy Set Theory: Applications in the Social Sciences*, London: SAGE Publications Ltd.

Songmin, A. (2013) 'Participatory Budgeting in Dong-gu, Ulsan: A Korean Case Study', in Y. Sintomer, R. Traub-Merz and J. Zhang (eds) *Participatory Budgeting in Asia and Europe: Key Challenges of Participation*, Basingstoke: Palgrave, 36–49.

Spada, P. (2010) 'The Effects of Participatory Democracy on Political Competition: The Case of Brazilian Participatory Budgeting', Draft Prepared for the General Conference of the American Political Science Association.

Spada, P. (2017) 'Dataset on Brazilian participatory budgeting: 1989 to 2012', Harvard Dataverse, V1. doi:10.7910/DVN/EDSNJS

Spada, P. and Allegretti, G. (2017) 'Integrating Multiple Channels of Engagement in Democratic Innovations: Opportunities and Challenges', in M. Adria and Y. Mao (eds) *Handbook of Research on Citizen Engagement and Public Participation in the Era of New Media*, IGI Global, 20–37. doi:10.4018/978-1-5225-1081-9.ch002

Spada, P. and Ryan, M. (2017) 'The failure to examine failures in democratic innovation', *PS: Political Science & Politics*, 50(3), 772–8. doi:10.1017/S1049096517000579

Steiner, J., Bächtiger, A., Spörndli, M. and Steenbergen, M. (2004) *Deliberative Politics in Action: Analysing Parliamentary Discourse*, Cambridge: Cambridge University Press.

Stoker, G. (2017) *Why Politics Matters: Making Democracy Work*, Basingstoke: Palgrave.

Su, C. (2018) 'Managed participation: City agencies and micropolitics in participatory budgeting', *Nonprofit and Voluntary Sector Quarterly*, 47(4_suppl), 76S–96S. doi:10.1177/0899764018757029

Swaner, R. (2017) 'Trust matters: Enhancing government legitimacy through participatory budgeting', *New Political Science*, 39(1), 95–108. doi:10.1080/07393148.2017.1278856

Talpin, J. (2011) *Schools of Democracy: How Ordinary Citizens (Sometimes) Become Competent in Participatory Budgeting Institutions*, Colchester: ECPR Press.

Thiem, A. and Dusa, A. (2013) *Qualitative Comparative Analysis with R: A User's Guide*, London: Springer.

Thiem, A. and Baumgartner, M. (2016) 'Back to square one: A reply to Munck, Paine, and Schneider', *Comparative Political Studies*, 49(6), 801–6. doi:10.1177/0010414015626455

Thiem, A., Baumgartner, M. and Bol, D. (2016) 'Still lost in translation! A correction of three misunderstandings between configurational comparativisits and regression analysts', *Comparative Political Studies*, 49(6), 742–74.

Thomann, E. (2020) 'Qualitative Comparative Analysis (QCA) for Comparative Policy Analysis', in G. Fontaine and B.G. Peters (eds) *Handbook of Research Methods and Applications in Comparative Policy Analysis*, Cheltenham: Edward Elgar, 254–96.

Thomann, E. and Maggetti, M. (2020) 'Designing research with qualitative comparative analysis (QCA): Approaches, challenges, and tools', *Sociological Methods & Research*, 49(2), 356–86. doi:10.1177/0049124117729700

Touchton, M. and Wampler, B. (2014) 'Improving social well-being through new democratic institutions', *Comparative Political Studies*, 47(10), 1442–69. doi:10.1177/0010414013512601

U-Decide (2009) 'Evaluating U-Decide!'. www.participatorybudgeting.org.uk/documents/2009%2007%2009%20Evaluation%20document%20APPROVED%20Tower%20Hamlets.pdf [Accessed 2015, link no longer active]

Walker, H.A. and Cohen, B.P. (1985) 'Scope statements: Imperatives for evaluating theory', *American Sociological Review*, 50(3), 288–301.

Wampler, B. (2007a) *Participatory Budgeting in Brazil: Contestation, Cooperation and Accountability*, Pennsylvania, PA: Penn State University Press.

Wampler, B. (2007b) 'A Guide to Participatory Budgeting', in A. Shah (ed) *Participatory Budgeting*, Washington, DC: The World Bank, 21–54.

Wampler, B. (2008) 'When does participatory democracy deepen the quality of democracy? Lessons from Brazil', *Comparative Politics*, 41(1), 61–81.

Wampler, B. and Avritzer, L. (2004). 'Participatory Publics: Civil Society and New Institutions in Democratic Brazil', *Comparative Politics*, 36(3), 291–312.

Wampler, B., Mcnulty, S. and Touchton, M. (2018) *Participatory Budgeting: Spreading across the Globe*, Report for Transparency & Accountability Initiative. www.transparency-initiative.org/wp-content/uploads/2018/03/spreading-pb-across-the-globe_jan-2018.pdf

Warren, M.E. (2009) 'Governance-driven democratisation', *Critical Policy Studies*, 3(1), 3–13.

Warren, M.E. and Pearse, H. (eds) (2008) *Designing Deliberative Democracy: The British Columbia Citizens' Assembly*, Cambridge: Cambridge University Press.

Weber, M. (2004 [1919]) *The Vocation Lectures: 'Science as a Vocation'; 'Politics as a Vocation'*, D. Owen and T.B. Strong (eds), translated by R. Livingstone, Indianapolis, IN/Cambridge: Hackett Publishing.

Weber, R., Crum, T. and Salinas, E. (2015) 'The civics of community development: Participatory budgeting in Chicago', *Community Development*, 46(3), 261–78. doi:10.1080/15575330.2015.1028081

Wickham-Crowley, T.P. (1991) 'A Qualitative Comparative Approach to Latin American Revolutions', *International Journal of Comparative Sociology*, 32(1), 82–109.

Young, I.M. (2000) *Inclusion and Democracy*, Oxford: Oxford University Press.

Zadeh, L.A. (1965) 'Fuzzy sets', *Information and Control*, 8, 338–53.

# Index

N



O



P



Q



R



S



T